RELIGION & *Sexuality*

"*Religion & Sexuality* is a masterful accomplishment and fulfills a vital need in the church today. C. K. Robertson and his colleagues tackle tough, complex, and highly charged issues with reason, faith, and grace. You won't agree with everything in this book, but you will certainly think about it and, I hope, talk about it, pray about it, and be transformed by it."

Peter Wallace, *Executive Producer and Host of* Day 1,
and Author of Out of the Quiet

"*Religion & Sexuality* is a welcome addition to thoughtful conversation about sexuality, gender, religion, and ethics. Written by accomplished scholars representing a variety of disciplines and religious perspectives, this collection offers fresh and realistic examinations of sexual issues old and new. With prose ranging from playful, to provocative, to purposeful, this book will be a catalyst for fruitful discussion among pastors, students, and scholars."

John S. Grabowski, *Associate Professor and Director of*
Moral Theology/Ethics, *The Catholic University of America, Washington, D.C.,*
and Author of Sex and Virtue: An Introduction to Sexual Ethics

"This is a collection of intellectually stimulating and at times provocative essays emerging from a wide spectrum of voices. The reader will encounter fresh thinking as well as new interpretations of older approaches. *Religion & Sexuality* is a fine contribution to the conversation and worthy of wide readership."

The Right Reverend J. Neil Alexander, *Episcopal Bishop of Atlanta,*
and Author of This Far by Grace: A Bishop's Journey
Through Questions of Homosexuality

RELIGION

&

Sexuality

PETER LANG
New York • Washington, D.C./Baltimore • Bern
Frankfurt am Main • Berlin • Brussels • Vienna • Oxford

RELIGION

&

Sexuality
PASSIONATE DEBATES

C. K. ROBERTSON, EDITOR

PETER LANG
New York • Washington, D.C./Baltimore • Bern
Frankfurt am Main • Berlin • Brussels • Vienna • Oxford

Library of Congress Cataloging-in-Publication Data

Religion & sexuality: passionate debates / edited by C. K. Robertson.
p. cm.
Includes bibliographical references and index.
1. Sex—Religious aspects—Christianity.
I. Robertson, C. K. (Charles Kevin).
II. Title: Religion and sexuality.
BT708.R445   261.8'357—dc22   2005023167
ISBN 0-8204-7424-X

Bibliographic information published by **Die Deutsche Bibliothek**.
Die Deutsche Bibliothek lists this publication in the "Deutsche
Nationalbibliografie"; detailed bibliographic data is available
on the Internet at http://dnb.ddb.de/.

Cover photo by Justin Kasulka
Cover design by Sophie Boorsch Appel

The paper in this book meets the guidelines for permanence and durability
of the Committee on Production Guidelines for Book Longevity
of the Council of Library Resources.

✧ Table of Contents

✧ Acknowledgments

As the editor of *Religion and Sexuality: Passionate Debates,* I have found myself once again amazed at my good fortune in working alongside such gifted and fascinating contributors. All have impressed me deeply with their intelligent and honest studies of complex and potentially explosive topics. Having served as the editor of two previous volumes published by Peter Lang, *Religion as Entertainment* (2002) and *Religion and Alcohol: Sobering Thoughts* (2004), I can say that the joys of editing have far outweighed any struggles I have faced along the way.

I am also highly indebted to Heidi Burns, my senior editor at Peter Lang Publishing, as well as to Bernadette Shade, my chief support in the New York office. Thanks also to Nanette Towsley for her on-site editing.

In the midst of enormous changes in recent years, changes both geographical and vocational, what has remained constant throughout has been the support and encouragement of many people, mentors and lifelong friends who have inspired me. I especially wish to thank Gary and Laurie Reichard, Kevin Jamison, Michael Maichak, the Rev. Michael Rusk, Dr. Charles Gravenstine, Floyd and Berry Trogdon, Bishop Michael Turnbull, and Prof. James D. G. Dunn.

Special thanks also go to my former parishioners at St. Stephen's Episcopal Church in Milledgeville, Georgia, as well as my former colleagues and students at Georgia College & State University. I also am grateful for the support I have received from my friend and bishop, the Rt. Rev. Kirk Steven Smith, Ph.D., and from my wonderful teammates in The Episcopal Diocese of Arizona.

Of course, I am most deeply thankful for the support and love I continually receive from my wife Debbie, and from my children, David, Jonathan, and Abigail.

C. K. Robertson, Editor

Imagination and Innuendo:
An Introduction
C. K. Robertson

Sex is like _____.

Pick your simile. There are more than enough from which to choose. My personal favorite is "Sex is like a rollercoaster." You stand in line for what feels like an eternity with countless others experiencing the adventure while you simply wait and watch. Finally, when it is your turn, you find yourself strapped in, trapped, unable to reverse your path. Anticipation builds as you rise slowly, inexorably to new heights. At the moment you reach the seemingly unreachable crest, time stands still ... only to be replaced by instantaneous freefall into the unknown. You barely have a moment to remind yourself that others have lived through this before all rational thought disappears, giving way instead to primal sensation, absolute exhilaration, and wide-eyed terror all at the same time. Suddenly you are spinning through space, your perceptions altered, your world turning inside out and upside-down. You cry out in wild abandon, raise your hands to heaven, and wonder if you could possibly feel more alive than you do in this moment. Then, with a harsh jolt, the moment is gone and you come screeching to a halt, the dénouement in some ways as disappointing as the anticipation was great. Unclenching sweaty palms and letting loose a silly grin, you repeat the words said by countless others before you, "Let's do that again!"

This book carries a serious title, *Religion and Sexuality: Passionate Debates*. Essentially, however, it is about that familiar ride, with different scholars considering the rollercoaster experience of the sacred and the sensual in very different—and intentionally provocative—ways. Neither a "how-to" guide for the shy and lonely, nor a puritanical treatise on the "evils of sex," this book is overflowing with both imagination and innuendo. The essays that comprise this compendium explore the various ways in which human sexuality and religion have interacted in different times and in different traditions, from the ascetic to the accepting, from the missionary position to compromising positions. Oral, anal, and genital sex; autoerotic, homoerotic, and heteroerotic passion; equality and complementarity; monogamy and polygamy … all manners of difficulty of definition in regards to sexual forms, roles, and relationships all receive attention herein, albeit in radically divergent ways by scholars whose experiences and thinking are quite often poles apart from one another. Indeed, the wide assortment of essays and essayists is intended to reflect the wide range of religious opinions on sex.

In the initial chapters of the book, two biblical scholars consider questions of boundary definitions in light of present-day interpretations of Hebrew and Christian scriptural texts. First, Douglas C. Mohrmann, Co-Director of the Center for the Study of Antiquities, asks whether there is a place in today's moral reasoning for controversial scriptural passages such as the Holiness Code in the Book of Leviticus or Paul's allusions to homosexuality in Romans 1. Then, B. J. Oropeza of Azusa Pacific University utilizes New Testament texts to discuss the so-called gray areas of oral sex, anal sex, and masturbation.

Issues of gender roles are highlighted in the two studies that follow. In chapter 3, Georgia Newman, a Flannery O'Connor scholar, explores the roles and rights of women in religious institutional life and leadership. A different approach to male-female sexual relations is examined in chapter 4, as Latter-day Saints scholar David D. Peck details the historical and ongoing controversy of Mormon polygamy.

The next three chapters offer reflections on the unique struggles facing ordained ministers. In chapter 5, film specialist Douglas MacLeod discusses the treatment of clerical sexuality in movies. Following this, in chapter 6, psychologist John W. Gamble reviews the sexual temptations facing real-life clergy and the results of breaching clerical/pastoral boundaries. In chapter 7, history professor and Benedictine oblate Deborah Vess turns the spotlight on Roman Catholic priests and mandatory clerical celibacy.

Given the debate on the national and international level on the question of same-sex relationships (and accompanying "non-traditional" forms of sexual expression), it seems appropriate to devote not one, but two detailed chapters to this topic. First, in chapter 8, American religion specialist Lesley Northrup offers an historical overview of homosexuality in U.S. religious life, while in chapter 9, professor and psychotherapist Philip Culbertson offers a fascinating and honest account of life in drag in relation to the not-always-healthy relationships between famous "golden sons" and their mothers, including the Freuds and Wildes and, interestingly, Jesus and Mary! The book concludes with a brief glance at the power of sexuality to threaten religious-minded individuals and institutions.

It has often been said that an individual's brain, not her or his genitalia, is the key sexual organ. It may be added that many, if not most, individuals find themselves confused about sexual issues and experiences at some point in their human journey. It is little wonder, then, that the collective mind of society in every age finds it most difficult to grasp, much less communicate, a coherent and unified understanding of human sexuality. If Albert Einstein is correct in saying that knowledge is far less important than imagination, then it is easy to see how the mere increase in knowledge of sexual acts and sexual expression has not necessarily made our collective consciousness more comfortable with the powerful realities of sexuality.

The essays contained in this volume bear witness to the multifaceted and often contradictory approaches to sex in western society. Reading through the chapters that follow, you may find yourself, as I have, nodding in agreement with many of the statements made by various contributors. Similarly, you may also find yourself, as I have, vehemently at odds with certain conclusions that are reached or assumptions that are made. Again, the goal of this collection is not to present a uniformity of thought, but rather to offer a taste of the full continuum of contemporary religious thought regarding human sexuality. By intentionally including a wide range of theological and socio-political positions—and the positions expressed within these pages do indeed extend from the very conservative to the extremely progressive—it is hoped that the comfort that usually results from hearing or reading only those things with which we already concur may give way to a sense of unease with our own certainty concerning issues that are as personal as they are profound. With this in mind, this book may serve equally well as a text for college students, a starting point for researchers, a discussion-starter for study groups, or a provocative survey for the individual reader.

Returning to the opening analogy, the true rollercoaster ride may not be the sexual act itself, but rather the ongoing struggle to define and live with sex in light of deep-seated religious and philosophical belief structures. There is nothing comfortable about such a struggle. Indeed, what may be most nerve-racking about this rollercoaster is that there is no clear end to the ride in sight and no guarantee that either our religious institutions or the culture at large might not be derailed along the way.

1 Is Anyone Listening? The Waning Voice of the Bible in Sexual Ethics

Douglas C. Mohrmann

As late as the 1950s, substantial books on Christian ethics could be written without a discussion of gender and sexuality. All the traditional, historical topics could be found: faith, character, virtue, reason and knowledge, revelation, government, love of neighbor, sin and judgment.[1] Such issues were the very heart of the definition of Christianity and of ethical considerations that were Christian. This was soon to change, however, with the rise of the Civil Rights movement.[2] Despite the fact that in the United States suffrage had been guaranteed for non-white males in 1870 by the Fifteenth Amendment to the Constitution and for women in 1920 by the Nineteenth Amendment, it was not until the 1950s and 1960s that racism and sexism would rise to prominence generally in social, political, and ethical discourse.[3] Much work has been accomplished in the establishment of equal rights since then, yet most observers recognize that much is yet to be done. Indeed, for many authors of the late twentieth century and early twenty-first century these issues continue to be defining issues for Christian ethics. The constitutional amendments represented just an early stage of cultural transformation in the United States. In order for the issues of racism and sexism to permeate the American consciousness, they need to be discussed and debated in every area of life: commerce, education, housing, broadcasting, and (certainly!) religion. The United States is, therefore, still struggling to embrace the implications of non-discriminatory policies on these secondary levels. This struggle is evidenced by the 2003–04 legal battle over the admission procedures at the University of Michigan. Education is obviously still coming to grips with the details of its "ownership" of the Civil Rights movement.

What could be said about such debates in the field of religion? The present article cannot do justice to that important question—for either racism or sexism. The project at hand will only deal with sexism and

Christianity, and of that only a small part. What may be of value is a discussion of the process in which we research, deliberate, and converse. While it is clear that sexuality has become a major component of western society's identity, the Church (both in the U.S. and outside) has struggled to define itself in this age of civil rights and of sexual revolution. Divisions in the Church have arisen because of questions over the place of the Bible in contemporary morality and of the intent of the Bible.

However, now, a half century into the debates, many Christians feel that agreement within the Church on any level is impossible. Consensus on matters of Christian sexuality may be the "holy grail" of the twenty-first century. Indeed, for all the progress made, it appears that the Church is still in for a long and protracted debate. Major unresolved matters include the "sacramental equality" for women and homosexuals.[4] In the minds of some, the definition of Christianity is at stake at these very points. Perhaps an argument could be reasonably made that to define Christian sexuality is to define Christianity fundamentally for our present age. Clearly some would feel such a definition would be reductionistic, yet others would take this to be of primary importance. These debates then will continue to shape Christianity in whole or in part; they are unavoidable for the present at least. For example, Christian voices were very active in the political elections in 2004 when eleven states accepted proposals that "define" marriage as between heterosexuals exclusively. More proposals and counterproposals will undoubtedly ensue. Will Christians eventually agree to disagree upon these matters, allowing them to keep open lines of communication and coordinated worship? Should they? Within the Congregational, Presbyterian, and Episcopalian churches, the wounds are fresh and deep from the debates on homosexuality. Perhaps healing will overcome the bitter discourse, if not by ecclesiastical agreement, then by the fatigue of fighting.[5] William H. Willimon, former dean of Duke University's cathedral, made the following comment regarding the 2000 United Methodist annual conference, "I left the General Conference [of the United Methodist Church] last year tired of both sides in the debate on homosexuality, wondering who told them that this was the most important issue in our church, an issue worth fighting over, dividing over."[6] Nevertheless, giving in to fatigue is a myopic option. The culture at large will continue assessing matters of sexism, so the question that really remains is what role will the Church and the Bible play in this ongoing cultural transformation.

The Bible Among Other Symbols of Cultural Authority

The Barna Research Group regularly checks the pulse of American religious sentiments. A series of their reports indicate the question just raised resists an easy answer. Four areas of these religious sentiments that relate to sexuality deserve specific comment: trends in church attendance, diversity of religious practices related to the Church and the Bible, the Bible in competition with other cultural authorities, and outcomes of an evangelical worldview.

It is well documented that mainline Protestant denominations have generally suffered declining attendance in the past four decades.[7] Barna has also discovered since 2001 a number of trends among younger people that indicate that they are more likely to remain outside the church, to ignore the Bible, to practice or condone unmarried sexual relations, and to be more tolerant of homosexual unions. For example, the "Baby Busters" group currently in their twenties and thirties, is a group which engages less than previous generations such as the "Baby Boomers" in attending churches or religious education classes, in reading the Bible, and in serving other people. One consequence that Barna sees from these trends is that "Busters" are less likely to "maintain views related to moral behavior that are consistent with the Bible."[8] Among the steadily growing population of single adults in the United States, now at 40% of all adults, church attendance is lower and skepticism of biblical teachings is rising. This is true despite 80% of singles reporting that they are Christian.[9] From a survey in 2004 Barna reports, "Since 1991, the adult population in the United States has grown by 15%. During that same period, the number of adults who do not attend church has doubled, rising from 39 million to 75 million—a 92% increase."[10] That comprises more than a third of the adult population. The median average age of the "unchurched" is 38, while the median age of U.S. adults is 43, meaning that the younger generation is over-represented among adults who do not attend church. Not surprisingly this group is less likely to consult the Bible on a regular basis. Surely, if these trends hold as the "Busters" mature and move into positions of leadership, then it should be expected that the cultural voice of the Church and the Bible will be represented less.

One expects that "unchurched" people are unswayed by the teachings of the Church or Bible. What is surprising is that even among those who attend churches regularly, the Bible is becoming less a factor in moral choices. Only 26% of Catholics and 34% of mainline Protestants believe the Bible is totally accurate, with only 22% of Episcopal adults registering a great confidence in the Bible's accuracy.[11] Furthermore, even though more than nine of ten American adults own a Bible, 44% believe that it, the Book of Mormon, and the Qu'ran are "all different expressions of the same spiritual truths."[12] The erosion of the Bible's primacy may be connected to the sentiment of 46% of Protestants and 62% of Catholics that truth is discernible *only* through reasoning and personal experience.

A shift from the Bible to experience is reflected in the simple data of Americans who still pray weekly (82%) when compared with those read the Bible weekly (38%).[13] The Barna Group began its research in 1984. Thus, in view of these recent finds, they were able to conclude the following about the role of the Church and the Bible in American culture:

> Over the past 20 years we have seen the nation's theological views slowly become less aligned with the Bible. Americans still revere the Bible and like to think of themselves as Bible-believing people, but the evidence suggests otherwise. Christians have increasingly been adopting spiritual views that come from Islam, Wicca, secular humanism, the eastern religions and other sources.[14]

Observers of culture will recognize that this phenomenon is accompanied by the growth of relativism in moral choices. But again, the difference in moral relativism between the "unchurched" and the "churched" is not as great as one would perhaps have guessed: 87% vs. 76%, respectively.[15] Moral absolutism is affirmed by only 22% of Americans, with the lowest assurance among those between 18 and 35 years old (14%).

The conclusion is apparent: The Bible is not the leading criterion for moral decisions in American life. Barna's research indicates that the Bible forms the basis of moral choices for only 13% of American adults, lagging behind other factors such as "whatever feels right or comfortable" (30%) and guidelines taught by parents (15%); it narrowly edged past self-interest in the choice's outcome (10%). These statistics hardly put the Bible in a good light, but the results were even less encouraging for teenagers who claimed the basis of their choices were feelings (38%), that which produces a positive, personal outcome (16%), principles taught by parents (10%), what makes others happy (10%), what family or friends expect (10%), the Bible (7%), and other factors (9%).

Like a mosaic, the pieces of these reports show the Bible and the Church's stature shrinking in American culture. Another recent study, sponsored by the Pew Foundation, demonstrated exactly this: namely, the impact of religious convictions on politics has steadily declined since the 1950s.[16] The challenges for the Church are manifold: stiffer competition from other worldviews, postmodern critiques of traditional authorities, and discrediting sex scandals in the Church, among others.

These statistics form the context for interpreting the changing opinions on sexuality in America. Nearly half of the population who claim to be "born-again" find heterosexual, unmarried, co-habitation acceptable; 28% do not object morally to pornography; and 20% see homosexual relations as acceptable.[17] Overall national sentiments vary from these only by 7–11%. Interestingly, one finds in two groups, evangelicals and atheists/agnostics, each of which makes up 8% of the population, the widest variation in both habits of consistent reading of the Bible and their moral choices.

To the Barna Research Group, this suggested that to subscribe deliberately to a biblical worldview would have a significant impact on these issues of sexual practices. Their work in December 2003 confirmed this, discovering among atheists/agnostics acceptance of co-habitation was 87%; pornography was 70%, and homosexual sex was 72%.[18] Among evangelicals, on the other end of the spectrum, acceptance of co-habitation was 2%, pornography was 0.5%, and same-gender sex was 2%.[19]

Struggle over the Intent of the Bible

One factor that has not surfaced in these studies, however, has been the Church's own ambivalence on some of the finer questions of sexual morality. Having already alluded to contentious issues of sexuality in today's churches, our attention now turns to detailed consideration of what the Bible says about one particular issue of sexual morality. An obvious choice is the case of homosexuality and the Bible, since it has been at the center of debate in recent years.

If those who read the Bible most regularly and use it as a basis for their moral choices tend to oppose homosexual relationships, then one might infer that the Bible *clearly* stands against homosexuality. This inference certainly is made by many evangelicals, but it is hardly a foregone conclusion in certain ecclesiastical discussions today. Several scholars, such as Robin Scroggs and Victor Paul Furnish, have contended with this very assumption. Is this scholarly ambivalence a reflection of a lack of clarity in the biblical texts? This question will occupy the remainder of the present study with a view to demonstrating how the debate on the Bible and sexuality can move forward. The following discussion primarily engages four authors who have made important contributions to studying the Bible's intent on homosexuality: Richard Hays, Daniel Helminiak, Robin Scroggs, and William Webb.[20]

Leviticus 18 and 20

Leviticus 18, above others in the Hebrew Bible, is a key text for determining the biblical view of homosexuality. A surface reading of 18:22, along with its parallel in 20:13, appears to denounce homosexual relationships for ancient Israel:

> You [a man] will not lie with a man, as in the lying with a woman; this is an abomination (Lev. 18:22).

> When a man lies with a man, as in the lying with a woman, the two of them have committed an abomination; they will surely be put to death; their blood is on themselves (Lev. 20:13).

One simple observation, however, indicates that a surface reading is insufficient. Namely, it is obvious that this prohibition is aimed at men in homoerotic relations and that it makes no mention of women with women. No text of the Hebrew Bible, in fact, addresses lesbianism, which reveals both the androcentrism of the ancient near east and the Hebrew Bible's indifference to lesbianism. The triad of prohibitions in 18:21–23, which are against offering child sacrifices to Molech, male-male sex, and bestiality, all deal with practices which were notorious from other cultures (Canaan and Egypt, 18:2-4) and which blunted procreation.[21] Lesbianism would not inhibit procreation and would probably fall outside of the interests of this textual tradition. It might be possible to infer a prohibition against lesbianism as the corollary of 18:22, just as the later Essenes inferred reciprocity from Lev 18:7 (mother-son incest implies father-daughter incest) in the Damascus Document 5:9–11. Nonetheless, it takes a stretching of the text to see a blanket condemnation of homosexuality here.

Helminiak argues that one should not read even a blanket condemnation of male homoeroticism in Lev. 18. He admits that Leviticus forbids the penetration of one male by another, but this is too narrow, he believes, to address either all male homogenital acts or male-male attraction in general.[22] His rightful stress on the precision of one's reading is typical of pro-gay scholarship, and this precision should be welcomed by all serious readers of the biblical texts. Furthermore, he notes that Lev. 18 and 20 belong to the so-called "Holiness Code" (H), where many rules for the maintenance of Israel's holiness were persevered (chapters 17–25). His analysis of these purity codes stands upon the shoulders of William Countryman's work, *Dirt, Greed & Sex*, which itself stands upon the older work of anthropologist Mary Douglas (*Purity and Danger*).[23] Douglas's focus has been chiefly on the food laws (Lev. 11), and there she determined that the Israelite dietary taboos were analogous to other cultural systems of taboos (e.g., to those among certain African tribes where her work began). She has observed that systems of taboo reinforced the social practices of a particular local group through implied, comprehensive codes of morality, particularly in the areas of food and sex. Such codes protect and preserve the locality's distinctions from other cultural competitors. Countryman and Helminiak have taken warrant from her work to argue that these sexual laws of Lev. 18 are merely expressions of Israel's localized customs. As customs change so do taboos; thus the ancient convictions of Israel's about purity and property need have no moral bearing on contemporary societies. Helminiak likens the taboo against male homoeroticism in Lev. 18 to elements in contemporary social systems of good taste or bad taste, such as burping or passing gas in public, even picking one's nose.[24] Whatever repulsion one feels for "snot," it does not follow that such implied codes of social dirt or pollution would be disgusting in every society and are thus inherently evil. Since taboos are not very different from superstitions, then the aversion to male homoeroticism may be abandoned now where the same taboos no longer obtain. Finally, Helminiak believes that "abomination" (Hebrew: *tō'ēbah*) in our text is evidently "just another word for 'unclean.'" [25] If that is true, then the grave punishments—exile (for Israel) or capital punishment (for individuals)—may be viewed in the same cultural light: particular to Israel and irrelevant for the Church today.

Robin Scroggs, however, finds in the awkwardness of the phrase, "as in the lying with a woman" (*mishkᵉvi 'ishah*), an ambiguity that reasonably allows a reading of this text as a sentiment against male homosexual behavior generally.[26] The Hebrew language, he argues, lacked a general term for homosexuality, so this might be a substitute for it. Scroggs wonders if the lack of a technical term indicates that male homosexuality was not a major concern in light of Israel's culture that was dominated by an interest in reproduction.[27] Richard Hays also finds, in a more recent work, the arguments on purity less convincing than Helminiak might have hoped for.[28] Hays sees in the univocal witness of Jewish literature, which often cites Lev. 18 and 20, a potent and early testimony that the text "categorically proscribed" the substitution of heterosexual by male homosexual relations. Eventually, Scroggs and Hays part company on their interpretation of the relevant NT texts, but neither sees room for reading the Hebrew Bible as against certain narrowly defined homosexual practices among men.[29] William Webb, like Hays, is not very much impressed by the approach to Leviticus 18 that emphasizes purity taboos. For one, he believes that the purity laws that were matched with capital punishments must be separated from those taboos that could be ameliorated by ritual washings or periods of "time-out" from participation in the temple cult.[30] This would differentiate sex between men and sex with a menstruating woman (*b^{e}niddah*) (Lev. 18:19; cf. 15:24 and 20:18). Both regulations signal impurity, but they certainly mark different degrees of danger to the social group.[31] Moreover, Webb finds in the law's close proximity with the statute on bestiality an expressed desire to exclude nonheterosexual behavior from Israel, and Webb interprets the oddly placed non-sexual law (a child sacrificed to Molech) that follows all the rulings on heterosexual relations as initiating such a transition.[32]

Much in this way, the arguments about Leviticus have been presently framed; each side takes aim at the unstated premises of Lev 18 and then tries to interpret the text in light of the underlying, implied intention. What is encouraging about this process is not that agreement is imminent, but that there is conscientious historical research being conducted on both sides of the debate. Even if the exegetical differences do not immediately bode well for the hermeneutics (i.e., application of the texts to the modern context), the arguments are all a valuable part of moving the science of reading Lev. 18 and 20 forward. Helminiak (and Countryman) have striven rightly for as precise an understanding of the reference as possible. They are also justified in seeing purity taboos as part of this text's strategy. Nonetheless, Helminiak's interpretation of social dirt, and especially by his making an analogy of Lev. 18 to "burping," indicates a foundational misunderstanding of Countryman and Douglas.[33] A better analogy would be pedophilia. No one would argue that burping in public deserves banishment or death, as Lev. 20 calls for in cases of serious sexual malfeasance, but by contrast one may have heard such arguments made for those who prey upon children for sexual gratification.[34] Similarly, the best arguments for the application of Lev. 18 and 20 will also recognize the social and religious breadth of the things that are abhorred in the Hebrew Bible (*t'b* / *tō'ēbah*); see e.g., whole people groups (Deuteronomy 23:8); truth and correction (Amos 5:10); God's anointed (Isa 49:7); dishonest business dealings (Deut. 25:16); social justice (Micah 3:9); etc. From this brief listing, it should be clear that an "abomination," whether cultic or civil (or both), is problematic not in its own right but because of the jeopardy it places certain entities in relationship to others. Discussions of Lev. 18 should naturally mention its social strategies (Israel vis-à-vis Canaan), but they also must calculate the potential for stating theological strategies, i.e., being out of right relationship with God (Lev. 18:1–5 and 24–30). The question going forward then is this: Does Lev. 18 simply reflect one possible social norm (and may thus be discarded today), or are there signals of God's special design for humanity also present?

Many readers may wonder why Genesis 19 or Judges 19 is not foremost in a discussion of the biblical view of homosexuality. Here again, a surface reading may allow a modern reader to "hear" a message against homosexuality. Only three brief points need be made here. First, the weight of these two passages rests upon violations of hospitality codes rather than sexual codes.[35] Second, they depict violent homosexual acts, and many who would advocate for homosexual rights in the Church would likewise decry the injustice of these actions. Third, because homosexuality clearly is not the main concern of these texts, the most mileage any anti-homosexual interpretation could get from these passages is by an argument of "guilt by association," noting incidentally that homosexuality is portrayed again in a negative context. This inference is hardly decisive, but it may contribute to a case of circumstantial evidence.

In addition to these texts, some relevant arguments have arisen around the stories of David and Jonathan/Saul (1 Samuel 18–20; 2 Samuel 1:26).[36] Although this author sees no clear evidence of homoerotic attraction between these characters, even if it was present, this evidence would only demonstrate a tolerance of the behavior for a certain period of biblical history.

Romans 1

The oft-discussed counterpart to Leviticus 18 in the New Testament is the Roman 1:26–27. There are other minor texts that will be mentioned in passing, but the chief work must be done in Romans 1. For this text, the discussion will begin with the study by Scroggs.

Scroggs addresses the issue of interpreting Romans 1 with a subtle sophistication that continues to be echoed in more recent studies. There are three main elements to his treatment. First, he reads Romans 1 as a theological text rather than as a moral text. Any moral stances Paul takes served as mere illustrations of his theology, according to Scroggs. His own words illustrate this, "Here, as we shall see, Paul has a major *theological* goal in mind; ethical concerns or admonitions lie far from his purpose."[37] Second, Paul was not innovative in the production of these illustrations, instead he pulled them from a stock-in-trade list of vices which were characteristic of Hellenistic Judaism. Scroggs discovers in Wisdom of Solomon 14 a parallel that establishes his point.[38] For instance, the literature of Hellenistic Judaism, in Scroggs's reconstruction, reacted against homosexuality vociferously in order to curb the danger of Jewish assimilation into the wider Hellenistic cultural forces. Scroggs concludes at the end of his study that Paul was not articulating a view of homosexual behavior generally in Romans 1, but rather he was operating with the specific model of homosexuality in antiquity, namely pederasty. Scroggs had argued in his book before his attention turned to Rom 1 that the pattern of homosexuality in antiquity was pederasty.

A careful reading of Scroggs must pick out his contributions from his unhelpful, distracting points. An example of each may suffice presently. Scroggs heads into a cul-de-sac during his guided tour of Paul's text when he finds Paul as a mere copyist of Jewish moral tradition. By this argument Scroggs paints Paul as a traditionalist who, perhaps for sheer convenience, cited some moral codes, some of which he may not fully agree to. His understanding of the use of tradition is, however, upside down. For one, Paul's introduction of female-female relations (1:26)— even by Scroggs's admission[39]—is without any obvious external motivation. It alone indicates that Paul was no slave to his alleged sources. Scroggs cannot reasonably claim that Romans 1 is "completely informed by Hellenistic Jewish propaganda against Gentiles."[40] For another, our observation of any author's choice to borrow an idea or a text from another source, should not lead us to assume that that borrowing was done mechanistically, thoughtlessly, unreflectively.

Scroggs's conclusion that Romans 1 is dealing with pederasty, in the final analysis, is completely an argument from silence, a silence he fills with his previous conclusions about homosexuality in Greco-Roman culture.[41]

On a more helpful note, Scroggs has assisted subsequent readers of Romans 1 by pointing out that *arsenes en arsesin* (1:27; "men with men") and *arsenokoites* (1 Corinthians 6:9; "sodomites" in the NRSV) are dependent upon LXX Leviticus 18 and 20.[42] His study brings to light the inter-biblical relationship between these texts. As we will see, different authors have found different values from this observation. His treatment of 1 Corinthians 6 has been likewise beneficial. In that text he points out that *arsenokoites* and *malakoi* probably refer particularly to relations between a man and a male prostitute.[43] This text does not deal with homosexuality generally. Even if he is not successful in pointing out the pederasty in Romans 1, his treatment of 1 Corinthians 6:9–11 is persuasive (cf. also 1 Timothy 1:10).

Richard Hays represents an example of a reader who acknowledges Scroggs's contributions but uses them for different ends. Because Romans 1 is in a theological context and because it, along with 1 Corinthians 6 and 1 Timothy 1, probably allude to Leviticus 18 and 20, then by Hays's reckoning it is likely that Paul was capitalizing on a wider Jewish disdain for homosexual acts. Hays describes Paul's argument in the following way:

> The ensuing discussion (Romans 1:19–32) explains, documents, and elaborates this human unrighteousness. ... The genius of Paul's analysis, of course, lies in his refusal to posit a catalog of sins as the cause of human alienation from God. Instead, he delves to the root: all other depravities follow from the radical rebellion of the creature against the Creator.[44]

Hays finds in the list of individual vices evidence for God's wrath which is ironically turning humanity, through its own choices (*metalassein*), from freedom to enslavement. Thus, Hays agrees with Scroggs that Paul's intent is theological in this section. Nevertheless, he describes Paul's intent as the casting of a moral vision, or as the creating of a symbolic world, where God's wrath is realized to be present and active in the various forms of human sinfulness, including his allowing homosexual behavior to be engaged in and applauded.[45] Paul thereby describes the root of humanity's many sins as a rejection of God (1:21), but Hays, in contrast to Scroggs, does not infer from this that Paul's ethical standards are cleanly divisible from his beliefs about God or humanity. To make such a point, Scroggs would need to show that Paul regularly divided his ethical from his theological concerns and that they were essentially unrelated areas of Paul's thoughts. Little hope should be reserved for the success of that enterprise. If Paul was depicting homosexual acts as a secondary cause of disaffection with God, that is still an important cause to acknowledge. Hays's use of "symbolic world" points up their linkage, especially as links between Creator and created order (1:25), and Hays would want us to see the 'natural' imagery of Paul's argument (1:26–27, *phusikos*), as motivated by an allusion to the creation story where the vision includes a man coupled with a woman (Gen 1–2).[46]

Paul's argument from "nature" has attracted much scholarly attention. Hays is convinced that Paul has chosen to condemn homosexual actions because it reflects not only his inherited Hellenistic Jewish bias, but also because it typifies in Romans 1 a diversion from what he understood to be a divinely created order, an order that among many other areas of human life seems to be in disarray.

Both Hays and Helminiak cite the Stoic writers in their treatment of "natural" versus "unnatural" affections. While Hays saw the biblical creation story as ultimately determinative for Paul's symbolic world, Helminiak finds the weight of Paul's argument to be located on a more particular, temporal plane. Helminiak's treatment places the language of purity/impurity (1:24—*akatharsia*) alongside the language of natural/unnatural (1:26–27). Together they depict, in his view, Paul's social structures that were by definition culturally biased and therefore specifically anchored to his temporal frame of reference. Paul could hardly have been making a pan-temporal, pan-situational description here. In fact, Helminiak believes that Paul treats homogenital actions as morally neutral.[47] When Paul labels lesbianism as "against nature" (*para phusin*) he intends "atypical," rather than "inherently evil." Helminiak justifiably objects to this leap of logic, for the very phrase is later used in the context of God's actions (11:24). Nonetheless, even if he avoids this problem, he creates another by failing to see in the later text Paul's use of the phrase to describe the inherently (or "naturally") different qualities of the two olive branches. Context stipulates the semantic value of the differences, and for Romans 1 he does not adequately address the theological or moral context of "unnatural." [48] Still, his overall analysis challenges readers of Paul to remember that a sense of the "natural" world is often bound to philosophical, social, scientific, and technological perspectives; compare 1 Cor. 11:14. [49] A deliberate approach to Paul's natural arguments needs to assess where Paul's symbolic world is impossible to translate into the present, where difficult, where unnecessary. Obviously, this is a challenging task to accomplish with consistency of method and with charity in disagreement.

Gray Temple's spirited discussion of the Bible's intent regarding homosexuality cries out in frustration about this vexation of consistency of method: "Will no Evangelical acknowledge to the rest of us the difficulties a devout Bible reader must struggle with?" and "Who wrote in your Bible authorizing women to wear slacks?"[50] Any honest reader of the Bible faces similar questions, and every teacher of the New Testament at one point has been questioned (or cornered!) by a student about this very struggle to appropriate consistently biblical teachings to the modern setting. William Webb's work, *Slaves, Women, & Homosexuals*, is one recent attempt to accomplish some hermeneutical consistency, and whether or not one agrees with the details of his proposals, his vision is pointed in the right direction. As his title reminds us, the movement of western culture towards total equality has caused many Christians to return to their sacred texts to wonder if there might be guidance for seeking ethnic, gender, and sexual ethics.

In summary, Webb believes that Paul's vision for humanity would justify the present movement towards egalitarian status for minority ethnic groups and women. Yet, he denies this for homosexuality. Why? His reasons are multiple but a sampling will help clarify his method:

1. "In contrast to the submission lists, e.g., Titus 2:4–5, 9–10; Ephesians 5:21–6:9; etc. (and their explicit purpose statements), we do not have any biblical texts where the purpose of prohibiting homosexual activity is linked to making the Jewish or Christian movement more attractive to its surrounding culture." (109)

2. Inasmuch as the Bible sees homosexual behavior as a pagan practice, the "countercultural dimension of these pronouncements serves as a strong indicator that the prohibitions should be viewed as transcultural." (161)

3. Homosexuality, as a one among a list of vices, in Romans 1 is surrounded by transcultural moral issues. (192–97)

Webb does not give each of these findings equal weight; in fact the configuration above moves from the stronger to the weaker arguments. Essentially, Webb agrees with Hays, that the few passages in the Bible that mention homoeroticism, in their variety of contexts and manifestations, uniformly associate it with divine disapproval.[51] Webb assesses the biblical texts on slavery, women, and homosexual behavior for their movement with or against the grain of their cultural contexts as a basis for his hermeneutic. He believes that this approach, especially if it reveals an underlying rationale for the biblical ethic, is fruitful for moving the Church's methods of hermeneutics to greater consistency. He details eighteen possible criteria, ranging from persuasive criteria to inclusive criteria. Indeed, this is a grasping at specificity and explicitness of hermeneutics holds much promise.

Conclusion

Several points may be taken away from the voices surveyed above. First, the declining role which the Church and Bible appear to be having in American political and civil decisions is undeniable and regrettable. The Church is coming perilously close to abdicating its prophetic function amongst the younger generations. More erosion in the cultural value of the Bible should be expected. Therefore, this is no time to let fatigue overcome those who lead the mainline denominations in discussions of Christian social ethics. Second, it is suggested that the marginalization of the Bible's role in ethical decision has arisen in part from the Church's own ambivalence with the intent of the Scriptures. A lack of determined hermeneutical clarity has predictably triggered uncharitable disputations and has delayed determination of the role of women and homosexuals in the Church's membership. An image of an un-Christ-like twentieth and twenty-first century Church emerges.[52] Finally, among the ranks of biblical scholars important discoveries of historical background, lexicography, and theological context have moved the science of studying these pressing ethical issues beyond a fundamentalist reading of Scripture. While this author has found problems in discussions by pro-gay scholars of both the purity regulations of Leviticus 18 and the moral/theological argument of Romans 1, the work of Countryman, Boswell, Helminiak, Temple, just to name a few, have been found to be fruitful and persuasive at many other points. Consistency in hermeneutics will lag behind the exegetical efforts, perhaps, but Hays's and Webb's work in exposing, articulating, and exemplifying means of applying the Bible are valuable too. New proposals and discussion will doubtlessly benefit all Christian readers.

Notes

[1] George F. Thomas, *Christian Ethics and Moral Philosophy* (New York: Charles Scribner's Sons, 1955); Waldo Beach and H. Richard Niebuhr, *Christian Ethics: Sources of the Living Tradition* (New York: The Ronald Press Co., 1955); Albert T. Rasmussen, *Christian Social Ethics* (Englewood Cliffs: Prentice Hall, 1957). Emil Brunner, *The Divine Imperative*, trans. By Olive Wyon (Philadelphia: Westminster Press, 1947), 373–83 is an earlier exception (published in Germany in the 1930s) which deals with women's issues under the rubric of "Individual problems connected to marriage." Quite ahead of his times, he said (373–74) everyone "will be forced to regard the modern movement for the freedom of woman as one of the most significant facts of recent history. ... In any case it obliges us to reformulate the significance of sex-individuality."

[2] Georgia Harkness, *Christian Ethics* (New York: Abingdon Press, 1957), dedicated a chapter to "Christianity and the Race Problem," but ironically treats women/gender issues briefly (125–27). A quick survey shows major portions of books on ethics are now dedicated to racism and sexism; see E. Clinton Gardner, *Biblical Faith and Social Ethics* (New York: Harper & Brothers, 1960), 207–47, 342–78; Philip E. Hughes, *Christian Ethics in Secular Society* (Grand Rapids: Baker Book House, 1983), 149–82; John Mahoney, *The Making of Moral Theology: A Study of Roman Catholic Tradition* (Oxford: Clarendon Press, 1987), 259–348; Roger G. Betsworth, *Social Ethics: An Examination of American Moral Traditions* (Louisville: Westminster John Knox Press, 1990), 138–77.

[3] For more development of such trends, see J. Philip Wogaman, *Christian Ethics: A Historical Introduction* (Louisville: Westminster John Knox Press, 1993).

[4] The language of "sacramental equality" is borrowed from Gray Temple, *Gay Unions* (New York: Church Publishing, 2004).

[5] Quoted by Paul McKay in "Noted Author, Clergyman Defends Duke Decision" (Feb. 16, 2001), *United Methodist Review* 2.

[6] Ibid.

[7] See Douglas C. Mohrmann, "Megachurch, Virtual Church," in C. K. Robertson, ed., *Religion as Entertainment* (New York: Peter Lang, 2002), 28.

[8] "Spiritual Progress Hard to Find in 2003." *The Barna Update* (Dec. 22, 2003), *www. barna.org/FlexPage.aspx?Page=BarnaUpdate&BarnaUpdateID=155,* confirms an earlier study, "Practical Outcomes Replace Biblical Principles as the Moral Standard," *The Barna Update,* (Sept. 10, 2001), which concluded, "the Baby Bust generation were more inclined than any other group to support behaviors that conflict with Christian morals."

[9] "A Revealing Look at Three Unique Single Adult Populations", *The Barna Update* (March 11, 2002), *www.barna.org/FlexPage.aspx?Page=BarnaUpdate&BarnaUp dateID=108.*

[10] "Number of Unchurched Adults Has Nearly Doubled Since 1991," *The Barna Update* (May 4, 2004), *www.barna.org/FlexPage.aspx?Page=BarnaUpdate&Barna UpdateID=163.*

[11] "Religious Beliefs Vary Widely by Denomination," *The Barna Update* (June 25, 2001), www.barna.org/FlexPage.aspx?Page=BarnaUpdate&BarnaUpdateID=92.

[12] "Americans Draw Theological Beliefs from Diverse Points of View," *The Barna Update* (Oct. 8, 2002), *www.barna.org/FlexPage.aspx?Page=BarnaUpdate&Barna UpdateID=122.*

[13] "Protestants, Catholics and Mormons Reflect Diverse Levels of Religious Activity," *The Barna Update* (July 9, 2001), *www.barna.org/FlexPage.aspx?Page=Barna Update&BarnaUpdateID=93.*

[14] "Americans Draw Theological Beliefs."

[15] "Americans Are Most Likely to Base Truth on Feelings," *The Barna Update* (Feb. 12, 2002), *www.barna.org/FlexPage.aspx?Page=BarnaUpdate&BarnaUpdateID= 106.*

[16] News Release. July 24, 2003, 4:00 p.m. by The Pew Research Center for The People and The Press, 38.

[17] "Morality Continues to Decay," *The Barna Update* (Nov. 3, 2003), *www.barna.org/ FlexPage.aspx?Page=BarnaUpdate&BarnaUpdateID=152.*

[18] "Born Again Adults Remain Firm in Opposition to Abortion and Gay Marriage," *The Barna Update,* July 23, 2001, *www.barna.org/FlexPage.aspx?Page=BarnaUpdate &BarnaUpdateID=94* and "Morality Continues to Decay," *The Barna Update* (Nov. 3, 2003), *www.barna.org/FlexPage.aspx?Page=BarnaUpdate&BarnaUpdateID=15 2.*

[19] "A Biblical Worldview Has a Radical Effect on a Person's Life," *The Barna Update* (Dec. 1, 2003), *www.barna.org/FlexPage.aspx?Page=BarnaUpdate&BarnaUpdate ID=154.*

[20] William J. Webb, *Slaves, Women, & Homosexuals: Exploring the Hermeneutics of Cultural Analysis,* (Downers Grove: InterVarsity Press, 2001), 286–90 offers a

useful bibliographic listing of important scholarship on homosexuality and the Bible.

[21] Douglas C. Mohrmann, "Making Sense of Sex: A Study of Leviticus 18," *Journal for the Study of the Old Testament*, 29.1 (2004), 57–79.

[22] Daniel Helminiak, *What the Bible Really Says about Homosexuality* (New Mexico: Alamo Square Press, 2000), 66–67. Consequently, mutual masturbation and other non-anal sex was not hereby outlawed (also see page 60). Cf. also Jerome T. Walsh, "Leviticus 18:22 and 20:13: Who Is Doing What to Whom?" *Journal of Biblical Literature* 120/2 (2001), 201–09, who argues that Lev. 18:22 differs from 20:13 by intending only for the free male Israelite citizen to refuse anal penetration. Lev. 20, by contrast, which is written later in his estimation, threatens the penetrator and the one being penetrated. Walsh, however, ignores the implication for the "sojourner" (*ger*) in 18:26 in this context, so social class is not a factor in this law as he alleges.

[23] L. William Countryman, *Dirt, Greed, and Sex: Sexual Ethics in the New Testament and Their Implications for Today* (Philadelphia: Fortress Press, 1988) and Mary Douglas, *Purity and Danger: An Analysis of the Concepts of Purity and Taboo* (London: Routledge, 1966).

[24] Helminiak, *What the Bible Really Says,* 61–64, 66.

[25] Ibid., 56.

[26] Robin Scroggs, *The New Testament and Homosexuality* (Philadelphia: Fortress Press, 1983), 72.

[27] Ibid., pp.77–79. Scroggs supports this assertion with his observations of the few extant discussions of homosexuality in the Mishnah and Talmud. Even in these few, one often finds talk of homosexuality as a Gentile issue that does not directly relate to rabbinic Judaism. Scroggs concludes that Palestinian Judaism was consistently disposed against male homosexual behavior.

[28] Richard Hays, *The Moral Vision of the New Testament: A Contemporary Introduction to New Testament Ethics* (New York: HarperCollins, 1996), 381–82. Hays argues that the neat divisions between civil and ritual purity cannot be invoked here because of the application of "abomination" in 18:26 to all the laws of verses 6–23. The motivation for the laws is, therefore, not clear in Hays's estimation.

[29] Scroggs even sees Genesis 19 and Judges 19 as evidence against homosexuality, but he is careful to note the violent contexts in each case. See his *New Testament and Homosexuality*, 73–75). His conclusions on texts from Palestinian Judaism, pp. 83–84, indicate that he will be focusing on pederasty in the New Testament texts.

[30] Webb, *Slaves,* 166–76.

[31] Mohrmann, "Making Sense," 68–73.

[32] Webb, *Slaves*, 197–98.

[33] Even Countryman's treatment of purity, pollution, and taboo are outdated, since he relies on Douglas's earliest work, a work that received criticism by fellow anthropologists for its lack of connectedness to Israel's legal system overall as well as their cosmology. For a more current presentation of Mary Douglas's research, see her *Leviticus as Literature* (Oxford: Oxford University Press, 1999).

34 This trivializing of the purity systems could threaten to overshadow the insights of Douglas. For another poor example, see Temple, *Gay Unions*, pp. 62–64.

35 One may see this most efficiently by looking at the inner-biblical exegesis of the Sodom story in cf. Ezek. 16:48–49; Isa 1:10–17; 3:9; Jer 23:14; Zeph 2:8–11; Wis 19:13. Jude 7 might understand this differently, but it is unclear about what it sees in the story of Sodom that it would find as an "unnatural" quality to their lust. Is Jude commenting on the unnatural intensity (selfishness) or unnatural homoeroticism?

36 Helminiak, *What the Bible Really Says*, 123–27.

37 Scroggs, *New Testament*, 109.

38 Ibid., 112.

39 Ibid., 115.

40 Ibid., 110. Scroggs attempts to make this point several times in his chapter, "The Early Church: Echoes of a Tradition." He ignores the semantic value of an author's choice to include a tradition or not. Unless Scroggs can demonstrate that an author had quoted a tradition without his/her approval, it would be fairer reading to conclude that the author assumes its validity and does not feel the need to prove it. Thus Scroggs's inferences about the traditional nature of Paul's texts should lead him in the exact opposite direction.

41 To his credit he appends two brief treatments of non-pederastic homosexuality (male and female) to his work; see 130–44. However, he dismisses the exceptions too quickly and this has ramifications for his reading of Romans 1. Paul's attempt to show the unrighteousness of male-male and female-female relations may be his own attempt at being comprehensive, without the convenience of a technical term like "homosexuality." Thus, the possibility of non-pederastic homosexuality in Romans 1:16–27 must be allowed.

42 Ibid., 86.

43 Ibid., 106–09. His argument builds on that of John Boswell's in *Christianity, Social Tolerance, and Homosexuality* (Chicago: University of Chicago Press, 1980) 338–53.

44 Hays, *Moral Vision*, 384.

45 Ibid, 385–86.

46 Ibid., 387.

47 Helminiak, *Bible*, 77.

48 Ibid., 77–104. The number of non-sequiturs in his argument are many. He strains beyond credibility to divide social convention from ethical conviction in Paul's argument. In certain texts this may work, but the highly theological context of Romans 1 renders his exegesis untenable.

49 Cf. Temple, *Gay Unions*, 69–76 for a well informed discussion. He emphasizes the Greek philosophical traditions behind Paul rather than the Hellenistic Jewish traditions. His conclusions about Paul's uses of traditions are susceptible to the same faults of Scroggs's analysis, which was discussed above.

50 Ibid., 81.

[51] Hays, *Moral Vision,* 389. Their conclusions, obviously, betray their views against reading a positive homosexual model in the stories of David and Jonathan or Ruth and Naomi.

[52] Again, a lesson from Temple's book is to be learned, both when he asks that his explanation of the biblical texts not be met with a thoughtless "snort of derision" (137) and when he himself succumbs to the temptation to demonize his opponents with the manipulative title *homophobia* (116). Both are shameful power plays that derail constructive Christian dialogue.

Bibliography

Beach, Waldo and H. Richard Niebuhr. *Christian Ethics: Sources of the Living Tradition.* New York: The Ronald Press Co., 1955.

Betsworth, Roger G. *Social Ethics: An Examination of American Moral Traditions.* Louisville: Westminster John Knox Press, 1990.

Boswell, John. *Christianity, Social Tolerance, and Homosexuality.* Chicago: University of Chicago Press, 1980.

Brunner Emil. *The Divine Imperative.* Trans. Olive Wyon. Philadelphia: Westminster Press, 1947.

Countryman, L. William. *Dirt, Greed, and Sex: Sexual Ethics in the New Testament and Their Implications for Today.* Philadelphia: Fortress Press, 1988.

Douglas, Mary. *Leviticus as Literature.* Oxford: Oxford University Press, 1999.

———. *Purity and Danger: An Analysis of the Concepts of Purity and Taboo.* London: Routledge, 1966.

Gardner, E. Clinton. *Biblical Faith and Social Ethics.* New York: Harper & Brothers, 1960.

Harkness, Georgia. *Christian Ethics.* New York: Abingdon Press, 1957.

Hays, Richard. *The Moral Vision of the New Testament: A Contemporary Introduction to New Testament Ethics.* New York: HarperCollins, 1996.

Helminiak, Daniel. *What the Bible* Really *Says about Homosexuality.* New Mexico: Alamo Square Press, 2000.

Hughes, Philip E. *Christian Ethics in Secular Society.* Grand Rapids: Baker Book House, 1983.

Mahoney, John. *The Making of Moral Theology: A Study of Roman Catholic Tradition.* Oxford: Clarendon Press, 1987.

McKay, Paul. "Noted Author, Clergyman Defends Duke Decision." *United Methodist Review* 2 (Feb. 16, 2001).

Mohrmann, Douglas C. "Making Sense of Sex: A Study of Leviticus 18." *Journal for the Study of the Old Testament,* 29.1 (2004).

———. "Megachurch, Virtual Church." In C. K. Robertson. Editor. *Religion as Entertainment.* New York: Peter Lang, 2002.

Rasmussen, Albert T. *Christian Social Ethics.* Englewood Cliffs: Prentice Hall, 1957.

Robertson, C. K., ed. *Religion as Entertainment*. New York: Peter Lang, 2002.

Scroggs, Robin. *The New Testament and Homosexuality*. Philadelphia: Fortress Press, 1983.

Temple, Gray. *Gay Unions*. New York: Church Publishing, 2004.

Thomas, George F. *Christian Ethics and Moral Philosophy*. New York: Charles Scribner & Sons, 1955.

Walsh, Jerome T. "Leviticus 18:22 and 20:13: Who Is Doing What to Whom?" *Journal of Biblical Literature* 120/2 (2001), 201–9.

Webb, William J. *Slaves, Women, & Homosexuals: Exploring the Hermeneutics of Cultural Analysis*. Downers Grove: InterVarsity Press, 2001.

Wogaman, J. Philip. *Christian Ethics: A Historical Introduction*. Louisville: Westminster John Knox Press, 1993.

2 What Is Sex?
Christians and Erotic Boundaries
B. J. Oropeza

Once when surfing online dating sites, I came across the profile of a very attractive blonde woman from Southern California who described herself as "Christian." In her pictures she sprawled provocatively on an uncovered bed wearing pink panties. She confesses in her profile that, although she hates to brag, men have told her repeatedly that she is the best partner in oral sex that they have ever experienced. To be sure, this woman could justify her sexual encounters by claiming she has violated no specific Christian ethic. She is not entirely nude; she is only sucking her finger in the picture, and after all, the Bible nowhere says, "Thou shalt not commit oral sex before marriage."

The previous generation's sexual revolution left its mark not only in secular western society but also in the portals of the church. Recent statistics suggest that, although Americans are less approving of extramarital affairs and teen sex than they were in the 1970s, premarital sex is becoming more acceptable.[1] This is not merely an adolescent problem, nor a purely secular one, for premarital sex tempts an ever-increasing amount of Christians between the ages of twenty and forty-something or more who find themselves unattached because of school, career, divorce, widowhood, lack of social skills, bad looks, or just not being fortunate enough to find the right person.[2] While it is true that remaining a virgin until marriage does seem to lessen the odds of a later divorce,[3] most adult singles, some Christians included, do not want to wait until the wedding before having sex. It is hardly astonishing that Catholics, Episcopalians, and Presbyterians as a whole are more open to the idea of premarital sex than Baptists and Pentecostals.[4] What turns out more surprising is that there are growing numbers of single Evangelicals who have engaged in premarital sex. In one study, while the total amount of high school Evangelicals who have premarital sex was less than half the rate of other high school students, around 27% claimed to have had sexual intercourse by the age of 17 or 18, with this rate accelerating to between 55% and 60% for Evangelicals between the ages of 18 and 24.[5] More studies are needed to verify these claims. However, it may not be an exaggeration to say that less than half of churchgoing singles are virgins.

The tendency in contemporary western society for single people to delay marriage until well into adulthood only agitates sexuality problems in the church. Today's single Christians experience the difficult paradox of a sex-obsessed culture telling them not to get married until their late twenties, thirties, or even forties, while at the same time their churches expect them to remain celibate all those years. Western culture drives almost everyone to be self-conscious about looking younger, dressing sexier, getting a smaller waist yet larger breasts, or growing bigger muscles and a larger penis. As scholar Stephen Barton perceptively points out, our society invests an economic interest in sexual desire: "It is as if the only language we understand is the language of unfulfilled desire, where sexuality is the master symbol and the products of consumer capitalism the means of fulfillment."[6]

Is the struggle Christians have with sex truly that serious? Seeing is believing. Simply visit any number of dating services on the Internet that possess a category related to sexual practice and find the perplexing phenomenon of profilers who claim to be "Christian" in the category of religion and yet "Adventurous" in the category of sex. Join almost any progressive Christian small group and hear the stories of sexual temptations for yourself. The paradox is that many believers—mainline Protestant, Roman Catholic, and even conservative Evangelicals—have all heard that sexual intercourse outside of marriage is wrong, but when the opportunity arises for them to engage in it with an attractive partner, many do so. They know the Bible condemns sex outside marriage, but this has not necessarily stopped many of them.

What do the Christian Scriptures actually say about sex? When texts refer to "sexual misconduct" are they referring to adultery, premarital sexual intercourse, certain sexual acts, or something else? What about oral sex, anal sex, or mutual masturbation? More to the point, which sexual activities, if any, do Christians in our contemporary western world consider to be prohibited by Scripture?

What Kind of Sex Is It?
Looking at *Porneia* in the Biblical Scriptures
(1 Thessalonians 4:3–8; 1 Corinthians 6–7)

The Bible often uses the word *fornication* or *sexual immorality* to describe sexual misconduct. The Greek text uses *porneia*, which biblical scholar Bruce Malina defines as "unlawful sexual conduct" *when prohibited by the oral or written Torah (Law of Moses)*. Malina concludes that since there is no law against premarital sex, *porneia* does not refer to this activity.[7] Joseph Jensen, on the other hand, points out that virginity was so highly valued among the Israelites that non-virginity on a wedding night provided grounds for a woman's defamation (Deut. 22:13–21; cf. Jud. 9:2; Sir. 42:9–11; Lev. 19:29 LXX; 21:7–14 LXX).[8] Kathy Gaca emphasizes that *porneia* in the Septuagint is related to religious rebellion and non-endogamous marriages, referring to "acts of sexual intercourse and reproduction that deviate from the norm of worshipping God alone."[9] Monotheism is therefore required to comprehend the sexual rule. In actuality, early Jewish literature used variations of *porneia* to describe harlotry and adultery (Gen. 38:24 LXX; Num. 25:1 LXX; Sir. 23:16ff; 41:17; Test. Jos. 3:8; Jos. Ant. 5.7ff), homosexual activities (Jub. 16:5; 20:5; Test. Ben. 9:1; Sib. Or. 3.764), incest (T. Reub. 1:6; T. Jud. 13:6; CD 4:17–20), and marriage to pagans (Jub. 25:1; cf. 30:7ff). Sexual deviance in the Bible finds its origin in the Mosaic sexual holiness codes of Leviticus 18–21 and Deuteronomy 22, where a number of sexual practices such as incest, bestiality, and homoeroticism are considered illegitimate. Sex offenders were to be punished either by God or Israel (Gen. 19; Lev. 20:10; Num. 25; Deut. 22:20–24; Judges 19–20; Job 24:15–24; Prov. 7; Wisd. 3:16–19).

Gaca maintains that in the New Testament Paul stresses religious endogamy when he tells Christians they are free to marry but only to someone "in the Lord" (1 Cor. 7:39; cf. 2 Cor. 6:14), and that the apostle Paul views *porneia* "for the most part" as "outside of the institution of marriage in the Lord."[10] In this view, a Christian commits *porneia* primarily by marrying someone who is a non-Christian or who leads them away from worshipping the one true God. The New Testament, however, uses *porneia* and its derivatives for a range of sexually illegitimate activities including incest (1 Cor. 5:1–5), cultic prostitution (1 Cor. 6:13, 18, 10:8; Rev. 2:14, 20–21), and extramarital sex (1 Cor. 7:1–2; Matt. 5:32; 19:9; cf. 1 Tim. 3:2; Heb. 13:4). In the Fourth Gospel, Jesus' opponents considered him a bastard, born from *porneia,* insinuating that his mother had a sexual relationship out of wedlock (John 8:41). In Hebrews, Esau is labeled as sexually immoral (*pornos*) because he essentially prostituted himself by selling his birthright (Heb. 12:16).[11] More typically *porneia* appears as one vice among many others in various lists related to the practices of the pagan Greco-Romans. The Christians are warned not to engage in these sins; to do so jeopardizes their inheritance in the kingdom of God (1 Cor. 5:9–11; 6:9–11; 10:5–12; 2 Cor. 12:21; Gal. 5:19–21; Col. 3:5; Eph. 5:3–5; 1 Tim. 1:9–10; Mark 7:21; Matt. 15:19; Rev. 9:21; 21:8; 22:15; Did. 3:3; Barn 19:4).[12] Those who commit *porneia* and other illegitimate sex acts incur God's judgment that may happen as a consequence of their own sins, the wrath of Satan, divine calamity, or eternal punishment at the end of time (1 Cor. 5:1–5; Rom. 1:24–32; 10:8; Heb. 13:4; Rev. 2:20–23; 21:8).[13]

Thus the early Christian writers of the New Testament, similar to their Jewish contemporaries, identify *porneia* as including various kinds of sexual misbehaviors. Since the earliest Christians originally came from early Judaism, they probably considered the same or similar sex acts as illegitimate. Both presupposed to some extent the Old Testament sexual holiness codes: Leviticus 18 seems to be the assumed backdrop behind the early apostolic decree for Gentile believers to abstain from *porneia* in Acts 15:28–29.[14]

The apostle Paul elaborates on *porneia* in both 1 Corinthians 6–7 and 1 Thessalonians 4. In 1 Corinthians 6:9–20 he warns against sexual immorality, which in this context refers to sexual intercourse with non-believers, more specifically, prostitutes. The Corinthian believers apparently thought much like their fellow Greek pagans: Having sexual intercourse with a prostitute was as natural as eating or drinking (cf. 1 Cor. 6:13a).[15] In the now famous words of the Athenian orator Demosthenes, "The *hetaerae* [prostitutes] we have for our pleasure, the concubines for the daily care of our bodies, and our wives so that we can have legitimate children" (*Against Neaera* 59.122).[16] Paul warns the Corinthians to flee from *porneia* and that the believer who has sex with a prostitute/non-believer sins against his own body (1 Cor. 6:13b, 18; cf. Rom. 1:24).[17] His view of "body" in this context may have a double entendre: it means both the individual body of the believer and the social body of Christ in which all believers are members through God's spirit. The believer's body is also considered the temple in which the Holy Spirit dwells (1 Cor. 6:15; 3:16–17; 10:16–17; 12:12–14, 27; cf. Eph. 1:22–23; 5:28–32). *Porneia* therefore defiles not only the believer's holy temple—that which is owned and purchased by Christ's atoning death and will be raised from the dead in the future—but it also dishonors the entire fellowship of believers who are members of the corporate body of Christ (1 Cor. 6:14–16, 19–20). Paul considers non-believers and prostitutes as members of the fallen world (*cosmos*), a location and age controlled by Satan and passing away (1 Cor. 5:1–5, 13; 7:31; 2 Cor. 4:4). Hence when a believer from the body of Christ becomes "one body" by having sex with a prostitute, this represents on a macro-scale the unthinkable sexual union between Christ and the corrupt world belonging to Satan (1 Cor. 6:15–16).[18] With this understanding Paul warns the Corinthians to "flee *porneia*" (1 Cor. 6:18a).

He begins a new topic in 1 Corinthians 7:1 in response to a letter the Corinthians had sent him earlier: "now concerning the things about which you wrote" (cf. 5:1, 9; 8:1; 12:1). Apparently some believers in the region promoted abstinence from having sex with their wives (1 Cor. 7:1b).[19] Paul responds to this misconceived virtue by telling married couples to satisfy each other sexually in order to avoid *porneia,* which here would mean all extramarital sex with or without prostitutes (1 Cor. 7:1–5).[20] He then turns his attention to the single/unmarried believers and suggests they remain single, but he permits them to get married if they are burning with sexual desire (1 Cor. 7:7–9, 34, 36–37), no doubt implying that premarital sex would be morally wrong. For Paul, the only legitimate sex is marital sex, and the only options for the early Christians were marriage or celibacy. There was no third alternative to participate in premarital sex. Single believers were expected to remain chaste virgins (1 Cor. 7:7–9, 7:25ff; 7:34; Tit. 2:5 cf. 2 Cor. 11:2; Eph. 5:25–27).

In 1 Thessalonians 4:3–8 Paul exhorts every believer to abstain from *porneia* and to possess his own "vessel" (*skeous*) in holiness and honor; not in the passion of "lust" (*epithumia*); they are not to take advantage of or cheat their brothers (fellow believers) in this regard. If the term "vessel" refers to a wife (cf. 1 Pet. 3:7), this passage is directed at the single men—they are to get married. The verb "acquire/take" (*ktaomai*) finds support in early Jewish texts in relation to *getting* a wife (Ruth 4:10; Sir. 36:24).[21] But there are several problems with this perspective. First, the same verb also can be translated as "possess/gain mastery over," and Paul uses *vessel* elsewhere in reference to the body, not a wife (2 Cor. 4:7). Second, Jewish sources affirming the vessel=wife view might not have been readily understood by the Gentile readers of 1 Thessalonians. A third problem is this—Paul does not tip off the readers beforehand that he wishes to address only the single males in the congregation. We might expect him to distinguish between married and singles as he did in 1 Corinthians 7:8–11. Finally if the vessel refers to a wife, this interpretation creates tensions with 1 Corinthians 7:9: "better to marry than to burn with passion." How does Paul assert that the Thessalonians should get married but not have passionate sexual desire for their wives (1 Thes. 4:5) if this, in essence, is the *very reason* why he affirms the Corinthian believers should get married?

George Carras has argued rather persuasively that, given the Gentile background of the Thessalonian believers, the vessel is a euphemism for the penis (cf. 1 Sam. 21:4–5 LXX).[22] The ubiquitous phallic symbols in the ancient cults of Thessalonica complement the notion that the Thessalonians were quite familiar with such vessels.[23] An alternative possibility is that the word *vessel* refers to both penis and body in this passage; the penis could be understood as a synecdoche for the entire body. Perhaps Paul deliberately chooses the ambiguous term vessel intending to be more inclusive, having both the body and penis in view.[24] In any case, the word applies to everyone, or at least every male who has a penis, whether married or single. Paul also wants the women to be sexually pure (1 Cor. 7:34ff; Rom. 1:24–27), but in this particular context the message seems directed primarily to men. It is the will of God that every male, married or single, holds his penis in "holiness and honor" by refraining from *porneia*. The believer's sexual practices should not resemble those of the Gentiles who "do not know God" (1 Thes. 4:3–5).

What does Paul mean, then, by exhorting the Thessalonians not to transgress or take advantage of their brothers in this matter (1 Thes. 4:6)?[25] If the person wronged is a "brother," Paul means a fellow believer, which is the way he normally addresses Christians throughout the letter (1 Thes. 4:1, 9, 13 cf. 1:4; 2:1, 9, 17; 5:1, 12, 25–26). Here *porneia* does not focus on believers having sex with prostitutes or non-believers, as was the case in 1 Corinthians 6:12–20, but believers fornicating with fellow believers! This perspective makes sense bearing in mind the Thessalonian situation. The Christians in that area became idle and did not work due to their belief that the second coming of Christ would take place any minute (1 Thes. 4:11–18; 2 Thes. 2:1–3; 3:6–11). Outsiders persecuted them as well (1 Thes. 1:6–7; 2:13–16; 2 Thes. 1:6 cf. Acts 17:5–10). Given these circumstances, some unemployed Gentile Christians probably entertained themselves by having sex with other congregation members. Their promiscuity arose from *within* the congregation rather than with non-believers outside of it.

Inasmuch as 1 Thessalonians 4:6 is related to a male transgressing and taking advantage of another male, it has been argued that Paul is forbidding homoerotic relationships in the congregation.[26] Elsewhere he warns the believers against homosexual activities and considers them as a vice practiced by unconverted Gentiles (1 Cor. 6:9–11; Rom. 1:24–27; cf. 1 Tim. 1:10).[27] If so, the meaning in 1 Thessalonians 4:6 still seems more inclusive than just Christians practicing homoerotic sex. In the patriarchal Greco-Roman world of Paul, if a man's wife had sexual relationships with another person, this act was seen as wronging the man of his property and rightful possession (e.g., Exod. 20:14–15).[28] While adultery definitely fits the idea of stealing someone else's property (in this case a believing neighbor's wife), Paul's intention is still broader. If the man who was wronged was the head of his household, his household included wife, concubines, daughters, sons, female and male slaves, and possibly sisters and brothers (Col. 3:18–4:1; Eph. 5:22–6:9; cf. 1 Cor. 7:36–38). His property was violated if the offender had sex with any one of the members of his household. If a daughter lost her virginity outside of marriage, both her father and her future husband would be violated of their "possession." The deflowered woman was no longer a new commodity, but a used, damaged product (cf. Pliny *Ep.* 1.14; Philo *Spec.*

Leg. 3.79–82; Deut. 22:13–21).[29] Paul argues that when a believer has sex with anyone from another believer's household, this is *porneia.*

Paul's outlook on *porneia* is thus very similar to other Jews of his time. He considered premarital sex to be illegitimate sex. He calls believers to abstain from all extramarital sex if married and all premarital sex if single, regardless of whether the person they had sex with was a believer or not. Jennifer Glancy is not far from the mark by relating Paul's definition of *porneia* to prostitution narrowly, and "sexual irregularity" more broadly; this includes all "sexual activity outside of marriage," since marriage and celibacy were the only legitimate options.[30] Yet fornication, if understood only as non-marital sex, would not be a broad enough concept to define *porneia* because the Greek word also refers to a monogamous or marital sexual relationship that is illegitimate, such as when Paul condemns a Corinthian Christian for committing incest with his stepmother (1 Cor. 5:1–5). *Porneia* in marriage may also relate to incest in Tobit when Tobias takes Sarah to wife according to Levirate customs and not for *porneia* (Tob. 8:7). Tobias's pious attitude here probably stems from a Jewish tradition that taking a relative's widow for sexual license instead of procreation is like committing incest (cf. b. Yeb. 39b; Gen. 38:8–9).[31] Consequently illegitimate sexual activity or sexual immorality captures *porneia*'s meaning better, but these terms are rather vague. The precise nuance of *porneia* depends more on the context in which it appears than on one standard definition. The New Testament considers all sexual intercourse outside of marriage as *porneia* and vice; this includes premarital sex.

Impurity/uncleanness (*akartharsia*) is another term related to *porneia* (1 Thes. 4:7), which sometimes refers to sexual excess seen as the nemesis of holiness and practiced by the unregenerate Gentiles (1 Thes. 4:3,4,7,8; Rom. 1:24ff). Believers are delivered from this sin through the process of sanctification after they convert to Christ (Rom. 6:19–23; Eph. 4:17–23). Paul adds this word to his vice lists and sometimes couples it with *porneia* or other terms of sexual deviance (Gal. 5:19f; 2 Cor. 12:21f; Col. 3:5; Eph. 5:3–5). Another word for erotic misconduct in the New Testament is *aselgia,* which is translated as licentiousness, lasciviousness, debauchery, wantonness, or sexual excess. It too is found in a number of vice lists (2 Cor. 12:21f; Rom. 13:13–14; Eph. 4:19; 5:3–

5; 1 Pet. 4:3f; cf. Hermas Sim. 9.15:3; Herm. Vis. 3.7.2; T. Jud. 23:1; Wisd. 14:26). In classic Greek it basically denoted excess in pleasure or passion and a lack of self-control.[32] Lot was distressed by the licentiousness of Sodom and Gomorrah (2 Pet. 2:7ff; Jude 4, 7 cf. Gen. 19), and Balaam instigated the Moabite women to lead Israelite men astray through this vice (Philo, *De Vit. Mos.* 1.305; cf. Num. 25). *Aselgia* thus appears to be the opposite of the virtue of the Spirit translated as "self-control" in Galatians 5:22.

New Testament terms such as *impurity* and *licentiousness* seem very broad and vague; they may at times appear almost synonymous with *porneia,* and yet when coupled with *porneia* in the same vice lists they are different in meaning. Early Christian writers, Paul in particular, may have added the various words to the same vice lists to emphasize a point: Non-marital sexual acts in all their various nuances were off-limits for Christians. It is almost as though Paul used several terms for sexual vice in order to counter possible claims by Gentile Christians who might consider their sexual deviances to be exceptions to the rule.

Oral Sex and Other Erotic Delights:
Is It Abstinence or Premarital Sex?

Problems surrounding the question on whether oral sex is "having sex" received public attention after former President Bill Clinton claimed he did not have sex with Monica Lewinsky. When it was discovered that the couple engaged in oral sex, media coverage prompted a *Newsweek* article to give advice to parents on how to discuss oral sex with their pre-adolescent children, just in case they asked.[33] Parents, teachers, and social workers discourage teenagers from premarital sex due to sexual transmitted diseases and teen pregnancies, but they frequently overlook the problem of defining exactly what premarital sex is. A gathering of recent statistics put forward the revelation that many teens begin experimenting with oral sex in junior high school, and about half or more high school students have either performed fellatio (oral-penile sex) or cunnilingus (oral-vaginal sex).[34] The percentage of young single adults who practice oral sex is even higher than this.[35] Many singles, especially young females, see oral sex as a win-win situation: They can sexually satisfy their boyfriends, remain virgins, and not have to worry about getting pregnant. They also hold to a misconception that oral sex does not transmit sexual diseases. One study shows that adult males seek out fellatio with prostitutes more than any other type of sex, and this is not necessarily related to its unavailability with more conventional partners.[36] Among heterosexual singles, oral sex is practiced far more frequently than anal sex, and studies have uncovered that young adults normally consider anal sex to be having "sex," while they do not consider oral sex to be having "sex."[37] Alternatively, an Internet survey revealed that a greater number of homosexuals and bisexuals label activities such as oral and anal sex to be "sex."[38] The heterosexual singles are the ones who hold the double standard between oral and anal sex, and they happen to practice oral sex far more frequently than anal.

If single Christians are to refrain from sexual intercourse outside marriage, would the same abstinence apply to anal and oral sex? Paul's argument in 1 Corinthians 6:9–20 seems applicable. Abstinence from *porneia* in this passage relates to sex with prostitutes, but this does not necessarily mean penile-vaginal sex. In the world of the ancient Corinthians, sex with prostitutes involved a diversity of sexual pleasures. Graffiti from the ruins of Pompeii, ancient pornographic art, and related evidence from Greco-Roman sources serve as explicit reminders of the sexual variety available to first-century clients.[39] It would be naïve for us to think that these prostitutes did not perform fellatio as one of their many specialties. What makes this topic relevant for our discussion is that Paul does not address sex with prostitutes as wrong because it exploited women, children, or the less privileged classes; as we examined earlier, it was wrong because it involved *a union* between two dissimilar bodies. No doubt Paul has sexual penetration in mind by this union.[40] Sexual penetration makes two bodies become one through sex, and it occurs at least three ways, all of which have been practiced by prostitutes with their clients for ages: Penile-vaginal sex, oral sex, and anal sex.[41] Hence, Paul's use of *porneia* does not necessarily assume penile-vaginal sex as the only physical means of penetration by which this vice is accomplished. The upshot of this is that the New Testament considers *porneia* off-limits for Christians, and penile-vaginal, oral, and anal forms of penetration are instrumental ways in which *porneia* happens.

We also do well to suspect that other sexual vices such as licentiousness (*aselgia*), impurity (*akatharsia*), lust (*epithumia*), and related words would include some premarital sexual activities besides coitus. The multiplication of sex words in the biblical vice lists seems to be added in order to amplify the forbiddance of sexual deviance and many of its anticipated nuances. One example of this is the warning against sexually vulgar language and joking associated with *porneia* in Ephesians 5:3–5 (cf. 4:29).[42] Today's phone sex and "sexy dirty talking" would seem to fit well with this description. Indeed, inasmuch as the sex vices mentioned in Paul's list in Galatians 5:19–21 (*porneia, aselgia,* and *akatharsia*) cannot predict the entire extent of wrongful sex, he then adds the phrase, "and things such as these," anticipating other sexual deviances and "works of flesh" that otherwise might have been missed! A more thorough examination of this issue, however, is beyond the scope of this study. One thing is clear: The burden of proof rests on those who would deny that sexual vice in biblical scripture implies not only coitus but acts such as oral sex, anal sex, and similar things if done outside the setting of marriage.

If vices related to extramarital or premarital sex include other activities besides sexual intercourse, this raises new questions. How far is too far in a relationship between non-married heterosexuals? Where do single Christians draw the line? If we define extramarital and premarital "sex" as *sexual penetration*, this may include oral sex, but it does not clarify non-penetrating sexual activities. The four tiers I have developed below might be useful in clarifying some grey areas:

Tier 1	Penile-vaginal penetration
Tier 2	Other sexual acts involving penetration: oral, anal
Tier 3	Non-penetrating sexual acts: caressing genitals, frottage, sexual talk, etc.
Tier 4	Activities related to public displays of affection: kissing, hugging, holding hands, etc.

Figure 1: Tiers of Sexual Activities

Tier one involves penile-vaginal copulation. Normally speaking, this is the only sexual act that can cause pregnancy. Tier two relates other forms of sexual penetration. This includes oral and anal sex. Along with tier one, these acts can transmit disease, are considered rape if forced upon another person, and comprise the vast majority of images found in hard-core pornography. It is less clear whether heavy petting (or mutual masturbation) and the use of sex toys fits best in this tier or number three. Fingers and other objects provide a form of penetration. There are also variations of oral sex involving things such as kissing, licking, and blowing in which the question of penetration remains uncertain.

Tier three includes non-penetrating sexual acts such as non-penetrative caressing of genitals (light petting), frottage (rubbing against each other until orgasm), or other activities in which the genitals get touched or caressed. It generally includes acts that have much less potential to cause sexually transmitted diseases (STDs) than the previous tiers and are often defined as sexual foreplay rather than sexual intercourse. Some of these acts nonetheless lead to orgasm. Like tiers one and two, they are normally done in private (unless they occur on the Internet or the silver screen), because they would not be considered appropriate for public behavior. Exceptions must be made, however, in relation to sexual communications such as dirty talking and sex jokes; they are often shared between more intimate social circles. Ambiguous practices in this category include sexual nudity and exposure of genitals (such as masturbating in front of a partner). These particular activities, outside of a marriage, do not appear to escape the notion of sexual lust if their goal is to deliberately tempt or sexually arouse someone.

Tier four involves other activities that might be considered sexually affectionate but normally can be done in public. This would include everything from holding hands and foot massages to long embraces with deep French kissing. Activities in this tier may or may not lead to sexual arousal. In terms of marital faithfulness, spouses commit adultery if they engage in tiers one or two with someone other than their spouse. Tier three would seem to constitute "marital unfaithfulness." Tier four is more questionable. Many forms of affection in western culture, such as seeing a spouse kissed by another person, may or may not be offensive. Context, motive, and circumstance become important in such cases.

The tiers are useful for clarifying degrees of sex and arousal, but they cannot anticipate and accurately categorize every sexual activity. One unusually vague subject is sexual innuendo (e.g., sucking on a banana or finger), which may be done for purposes of sexual arousal but is publicly acceptable in western culture. Suggestive sexual gestures and language probably fit somewhere within tiers three or four but not in every case. Much depends on the intent and level of clarity of the gesture or language. Another area of ambiguity is related to visual lust. It is not clear when sexy dressing turns into lust or partial nudity. Although lusting after a naked body for illegitimate sexual purposes violates biblical precepts (e.g., Matt. 5:28; see the section below), we do not know what constitutes the boundary between right and wrongful looking in less obvious cases. Does perusing a magazine inundated with beautiful men or women skimpily clad in sexy lingerie or swimwear entice a person to lust? What about watching a movie that has sex and nudity or admiring Botticelli's nude painting, *The Birth of Venus*? Does looking under a woman's miniskirt as she walks up a flight of stairs constitute lust? The proper boundary lines and level of objectification in every case are different. These and similar examples may or may not lead to arousal, voyeurism, pornography, rape; much depends on the eye of the beholder. Clear universal boundaries on visual lust are difficult to draw because everybody's intention and level of enticement are different.

All the same we can arrive at some general conclusions when comparing the sex tiers with our study of the scriptures. Outside of marriage tier one would definitely fall under the category of *porneia,* and since penetration is both an issue with tiers one and two, non-marital oral and anal sex would seem to be included under this definition. It is at tier three or with the heavy petting at tier two that the subject of abstinence and non-abstinence becomes blurry. However, other New Testament words for sexual illegitimacy such as lust, licentiousness, sexual uncleanness, and vulgar language may be applicable for this tier, even if the biblical writers did not have the exact practices I have listed in mind. Certain sex acts may not be defined as *porneia* but are still considered vices that bring people into conflict with biblical scripture, and these activities might harm the believers and/or their partners. A conclusion about the first three tiers can be established even with unclear parameters at the edges of each: *The New Testament seems to consider non-marital sexual acts between two (or more) persons as vice, whether these acts are accomplished by penile-vaginal sex, penile-anal sex, oral sex, or possibly other sexual activities also.*

What level of biblical permission is allowed in the lower tiers? It may be argued that most if not all activities under tier three seem to be biblically impermissible. Consider asking a non-married couple successfully to stop at tier three and go no further; it is like asking a levee filled beyond its capacity not to break. Sooner or later human nature will relentlessly drive the couple from tier three to a deeper sexual intimacy until orgasm vis-à-vis penetration is reached. Still there is the question about tier four. Here the biblical texts may enlighten by virtue of principle: "All things are permissible to me but not all things are beneficial; all things are permissible but I will not be enslaved by anything" (1 Cor. 6:13; cf. 10:23). In relation to sex, Paul advises the Corinthians that some things do not benefit the body of believers and some sexual activities enslave the practitioners.

Paul also warns that a Christian could cause a weaker Christian to fall into sin by virtue of the stronger believer's freedom to engage in eating things that would cause the weaker to stumble (Rom. 14:19–23; 1 Cor. 8:7–13). Perhaps the same principle can apply for single relationships. Even if we could handle some activities in tiers three or four without falling into tiers two and one, we must always be sensitive to the possibility that our dating partners may not be as sexually self-controlled. A woman may feel fine about deep French kissing while such affection may be her date's stumbling block. A man may feel it is okay to caress his date's breasts, but this may be her sexual weak point. It may take months or only minutes, but what starts off as fairly innocent can very easily turn into full-blown sex! Here communication, honest self-evaluation, and advice from an intelligent counselor or minister will help the dating couple determine which boundaries are mutually best for them. While individual Christians will draw their boundary lines differently, they should be more concerned about the benefit to the other person than about the benefit to themselves. This is in fact a variation of the greatest commandment to love your neighbor as yourself and do to others what you would want them to do to you (Rom. 13:8–10; Gal.

5:13–14; Matt. 7:12; 22:36–40). Love involves wanting what is best for our lover, and what is biblically best is to stay sexually pure (1 Cor. 7). Nevertheless looking at sexual activities in terms of what the single believer can or cannot do misses the point. Paul is clear: Sexual purity should not turn into legalism. His suggestions are for the purpose of encouraging single Christians to serve God with unrestrained and undivided allegiance (1 Cor. 7:35). All things should be done to the glory of God, including acts of affection (cf. 1 Cor. 10:24, 31; Col. 3:17; Phil. 2:4).

Sex Alone? Masturbation and Lust

One puzzling sexual topic for Christians is whether private masturbation is a sexual vice or virtue.[43] While certain Christian traditions discourage masturbation, there is nothing in the biblical records that speak for or against it. The Mosaic Law affirms that after a seminal emission, a bath is required for cleansing the discharge. This precept might include masturbation, but it is more accurately targeting all seminal release, including nocturnal emissions and regular sexual intercourse (Lev. 15:16–18). Such a discharge probably would not be considered immoral any more than would skin diseases/leprosy or a woman's menstruation, even though these things were also considered ritually unclean (Lev. 14; 15:19–24). The Genesis story about Onan spilling his semen on the ground is not related to masturbation but refusing to carry on the blood lineage of his deceased brother. According to the ancient Hebrew custom of Levirate law, a surviving brother was to marry the dead brother's wife and produce offspring for that brother (Gen. 38:6–10; Deut. 25:5–10). While Mark 9:22–28 speaks hyperbolically about cutting off one's limbs in order to escape eternal judgment, it would be reading too much into this passage to claim that Jesus included masturbation as an activity worthy of cutting off one's hand.[44]

A more pointed concern relates masturbation to lust or covetousness (*epithumia*) because many who masturbate use some form of visual arousal while masturbating. It has been argued that when people stimulate themselves, they fantasize about a person, often a popular celebrity or someone they know personally. Others look at pornography while they masturbate, and others become compulsive sex addicts.[45] Lust is seen as the chief of vices in some Jewish literature (T. Jud. 16:1; 4 Macc. 2:2–6; cf. 2 Pet. 2:10) and a violation of one of the Ten Commandments (Exod. 20:17 LXX; Deut 5:21 LXX; Rom. 7:7; 13:9).[46] The concept of lust was related to the sexual sin of the angelic watchers who, according to Jewish tradition, desired the women of earth and committed fornication with them (e.g., 1 En. 10:1–11; cf. Gen. 6:1–2). Paul himself may have struggled with sexual lust (Rom. 7:7–25).[47] Simon Blackburn defines lust broadly: "the desire that infuses the body, for sexual activity and its pleasure for their own sake."[48] A New Testament definition would probably come closer to Gaca's view: when lust is associated with sin, it is desiring something against God.[49] Jesus warns that lusting after a woman in one's heart parallels committing adultery with her (Matthew 5:28; cf. Job 31:1, 9; 1QS 1.6). Not all desire is negative, but sexually desiring a person when either the viewer or the object is married fits the description in Matthew 5:28. And if having non-marital sex with someone is wrong (regardless of whether they are married or single), then fantasizing about having sex with that person would still seem to fit the warning in this passage. A vivid example of illegitimate lust is found in 2 Samuel 11 when David first saw Bathsheba bathing (presumably nude) before committing adultery with her.

Hence, some argue that masturbation is a stepping-stone to vices such as pornography and voyeurism. Granted, pornography exploits and dehumanizes women and children, making them objects of lust whether they pose in a nude centerfold, dance naked, or perform sex acts on a digital screen.[50] Porn and voyeurism make humans whom God loves impersonal and objectified, and this runs contrary to the idea of loving one's neighbor as oneself and regarding every individual as having dignity and being specially made in God's image (Matt. 22:37–40; Gen. 1:26–27).[51]

The major problem when associating visual lust with masturbation is that not every masturbator needs or uses porn, voyeurism, or sexual fantasy when masturbating. A case could be made that masturbation can actually be healthy, having physiological and psychological benefits if not done compulsively. In this light, masturbation would be more a virtue than a vice.[52] Moreover, masturbation is certainly a more acceptable alternative than engaging in illegitimate sex, whether porn, prostitution, premarital, or extramarital sex. A man on a business trip, for instance, might be better off masturbating than having sex with a hooker or viewing Internet porn if he knows he is prone to do these things when left alone. While it is true that some believers can at least temporarily overcome masturbation through prayer and fasting, Christian youth workers will testify that a number of well-meaning believers, especially male teenagers and young adults, pray and cry that God would take away their desire to masturbate only to find themselves doing it again. Maybe God considers it more important to develop a healthy human sex drive than nullify every Christian's desire to masturbate.[53] Ultimately, masturbation seems to be an issue of *adiaphora*, a non-essential matter of the faith that is neither forbidden nor commanded in the Christian scriptures. Similar to drinking alcoholic beverages, it could lead to vice and addiction or remain clear of such things depending on the individual, his/her reason for doing it, and the manner in which he/she does it. Paradoxically masturbation is both a pleasurable and lonely experience, functioning as the ape of marital sex.

Glorify God in Your Bodies: A Sexual Ethic for Christians

Although this study helps clarify sexual boundaries, a person wanting a change in sexual behavior needs something more than simply being told what not to do. In fact, this approach may even tempt some to experiment with forbidden fruits or dabble and stretch abstinent forbidden zones, seeking to get away with as much pleasure as possible. For married couples, pleasurable and frequent sex works as a preventative against sexual temptation. For some believers seclusion from society or a vow to lifelong celibacy or both have been solutions. Many single Christians, however, only desire temporary celibacy until marriage. If we derive an ethic for sexual purity based on 1 Corinthians 6–7, it will involve the concept of embodiment. When Paul warns the Corinthian congregation against *porneia*, he commands: "glorify God in your bodies" (1 Cor. 6:20; cf. 7:34). To the hyper-spiritual Corinthians, the physical body seemed to be a thing of indifference (1 Cor. 6:13–14; 7:1b; 15:12), but Paul makes it the ground for a constructive sexual imperative. For Paul the body (*soma*) is not the same thing as the flesh (*sarx*). Although the definitions may overlap on occasion, there are important distinctions: It is the body rather than the flesh that is redeemable and will be unified again with the created order God intended. Paul anticipates an incorruptible body made alive and empowered by God's spirit in the resurrection (1 Cor. 6:13b–14; 1 Cor. 15:12–57). The same is not true about the flesh; the flesh is associated with the sinful nature and old perishing self of the fallen *cosmos* that is hostile toward the Spirit (Rom. 8:5–7; Gal. 5:16–21). A truly positive approach to sexuality should be body affirming while at the same time opposed to the sinful nature.

The human also connects and communicates with others via the body, and it is in the imagery of the body of Christ that believers share solidarity with both Christ and one another. To be joined to Christ or "in Christ," involves communion with his body, and baptism in Christ reinforced a sense of belonging to him (1 Cor. 10:16–17; 12:13; 2 Cor. 5:17; Rom. 12:5; Gal. 3:27–28).[54] The believer's body is no longer a self possession, but at conversion he or she gets transferred to a new owner, Christ. Christ becomes the husband of the believer who is considered the bride of Christ. He is the rightful owner of the body (1 Cor. 6:16–17, 19b–20a; 2 Cor. 11:2f; Rom. 7:1–4; cf. Hos. 3:1–3; Isa. 54:5). In addition, the Pauline world understands that Christ is the head of the household of believers (Eph. 1:22–23; 2:19–21; 3:13; 4:4, 15–16; 5:23–32); he has the right to give a member of his household in marriage to someone else.[55] Glorifying God in our bodies includes acknowledging Christ as the owner of our bodies; it follows from this that having sex with some other body, unless given in marriage to that person, becomes unfaithfulness to Christ. Loving Jesus in this sense means staying sexually pure for his honor and glory.

Because body language relates to all believers in the body of Christ, which is his church (1 Cor. 12:13–14, 27–28; Eph. 1:22–23), Paul's sexual ethics seems to be part of a larger social ethic, an aspect that modern sexual ethicists often miss by stressing individualism, personal choice, and authenticity. Stephen Barton elaborates: "Perhaps our quest for personal freedom and individual choice in sexual and other matters has brought us to the point where we do not know any longer who we really are and what our 'freedom' is for."[56] Christians find their identity and establish their values through a community of believers. Conversely when a believer sins, the entire community is affected. Genuine social body life means that members love, encourage, and care for one another, rejoicing when one member is honored and suffering when one member suffers (1 Cor. 12:24–25). In this sense glorifying God in one's body means genuine fellowship with a body of believers.

Adultery and premarital sex are often selfish and individualistic, disregarding true commitment to a relationship and losing a strong focus on the relational quality of the sexual experience. Sexual pleasure for its own sake strips sex of its truly relational meaning. As Judith and Jack Balswick affirm, "It's like having a penis and vagina get together without the persons attached," where the individuals take far more than they give.[57] Perhaps a valid social dynamic to sex is what sets apart Paul's view from the Greco-Roman philosophers who also stood against sexual excesses. According to Lisa Cahill, Paul was concerned about sexual damage done to the community, whereas the philosophers were more concerned with the "perfection of the individual."[58] Because sexual intercourse binds two people together physically, emotionally, and spiritually, where two become one through the act itself, then it follows that when one partner breaks up the relationship, this will inevitably create emotional distress and scars. Some people never completely recover from such breakups. One thing is definitely false: the idea that no one gets hurt by premarital or extramarital sexual relationships. This is why total commitment in a relationship, something only marriage brings, is vitally important. If I cannot totally commit all of myself to another person, then I have no business expecting that other person to totally commit all of herself and her body to me.[59] Saving our bodies for the right person, the one we intend to spend the rest of our lives with, is itself a virtue. It is through embodiment that sexual intercourse becomes the seal of final commitment to a newly married couple. John Grabowski rightly affirms, "To engage in sexual activity is to imply an unconditional and faithful gift of self within the covenant of marriage."[60]

To summarize, glorifying God involves acknowledging Christ's ownership of the human body and actively participating in the social body of Christ. In fact, Paul provides two more significant remedies against sexual sin. First, "walk after the Spirit" in order to resist the lusts of the sinful nature including *porneia* and other wrongful sexual activities (Gal. 5:16–26; Rom. 8:5–6); and 2). Second, "love your neighbor as yourself" fulfills relational obligations (Gal. 5:14; 6:1–10; Rom. 13:9; Matt. 7:12; 22:36–40).

To walk or be led by the Spirit is associated with putting away the former unconverted self and living a new life by exercising the "fruit of the Spirit": godly virtues, such as love, joy, peace, and self-control. It would also involve praying in the Spirit (Gal. 5:21–22; Rom. 7:6–7, 8:12–16, 26–27; Tim. 2:22; Col. 3:5–17; Eph. 4:22–24; 6:11–18; cf. Jude 18–21). What is more, there is freedom from sex addiction through conversion, forgiveness, and the power of the Spirit. Although some of the Corinthian believers were formerly involved in sexual vice, Paul affirms that they have been justified, cleansed, and sanctified from these activities by the name of Jesus and the working of the Spirit (1 Cor. 6:11).

Loving our neighbor as ourselves in a relationship with the opposite sex means we should treat the person with the same love and respect with which we wish to be treated. Because true love wants what is best for the other person, and authentic Christianity involves sexual purity, we should want to encourage each other to sexual faithfulness (if married) and abstinence (if single). It is unhelpful to argue the differences between our world and the New Testament's as warrant for the legitimacy of non-marital sexual activities today. Paul's arguments against *porneia* have little to do with the ancient world having or not having proper contraception, abortion options, the variable of "safe sex" and catching sexually transmitted diseases, or societal problems related to children born out of wedlock.[61] The biblical answer why *porneia* was wrong involves defrauding another person, essentially, not loving my neighbor as myself. A married person commits *porneia* by cheating on the spouse, and a single Christian violates this principle by taking what does not rightfully belong to him/her in premarital sex; the body belongs to Christ. Furthermore, the single Christian who engages in premarital sex may eventually belong to a future husband or wife who has now been cheated of marrying a virgin. To selfishly take this away from another member of Christ swindles a fellow believer and swindles Christ, the owner of that believer. Premarital and extramarital sex violates the reciprocating principle of love. To love my neighbor as myself means that I will not rob my neighbor's sexual purity and the blessings pertaining to it.

What if a Christian couple is engaged? Some wrongly reason that it is better for serious relationships to have sex and think it is comparable to the "test drive beforehand," in order to determine the couple's sexual compatibility before marriage. This attitude arises sometimes from a misguided premise that genital size and sexual technique are the means to the goal of achieving personal sexual pleasure. Here again the bodily relational and social value of sex gets eclipsed by individualistic self authentication. If our purpose for premarital sex is to find out our sexual compatibility with someone, this may sound reasonable, but it leads to several problems. First, apart from standard dangers such as unwanted pregnancies, the potential of getting sexually transmitted diseases, or guilty feelings related to committing sin, there is also the danger of severe emotional trauma should the relationship end. The more intimate a relationship, the more difficult the trauma. Second, it provides no guarantee that the person who was so great in bed before marriage will remain so afterwards. A number of men and women can attest to their disappointment with their new spouse who lost much of his/her sexual consideration once they married. Third, those who have premarital sexual relations tend to have their judgment clouded by the intense emotional sense of oneness caused by having sex with their partner; consequently, they are often susceptible to ignoring red flags or incompatibilities in other areas of the relationship.

Finally, studies have shown that couples who live together before marriage have a higher divorce rate than those who do not.[62] One reason for this phenomenon might relate to the greater value placed on a couple who waits until marriage before having sex. Wendy Shalit suggests that if a person takes marriage seriously enough to be concerned about it lasting for ever, a person avoiding premarital sex is making a statement that there is a very significant thing to look forward to after marriage, and if it has that much value, perhaps it will last forever.[63]

All the negatives aside, there still remain legitimate reasons for finding out before marriage about one's sexual compatibility with a partner. It seems inadvisable to go into a marriage sexually ignorant or with two completely different sets of sexual expectations, especially if the persons getting married have been married before. A widow, for example, may prefer her future husband to have a small penis because she experienced painful coitus with the oversized genital of her first husband. Having premarital sex with the second man is not the best answer, however. If Christian sexual relations have a strong socially based dimension, the Christian community should be involved with instructing and mentoring engaged and serious couples. Sexual compatibility may be discovered by open and honest communication with each other and with a trusted counselor, therapist, or minister *before* engagement or marriage. Good sex after marriage usually involves an attitude more than physical endowments. It comes more from a mutually unselfish desire to please the other person, a couple's commitment to work out sexual differences and preferences once married, and from the ongoing support of the couple's spiritual community.

Glorify God in Your Eroticism:
Marital Pleasures and Mutual Self-Donation
(Song of Solomon; 1 Corinthians 7:1–5)

In the Hebrew Scriptures, penile-vaginal intercourse is assumed by many of the texts to be related to monogamous sex, because conception often occurs as a result (e.g., Gen. 4:1, 17; Ruth 4:13; Isa. 8:3). However, sexual lovemaking was not merely for procreation but also for pleasure (Gen. 18:12; 26:8; Prov. 5:18–19; Cant. 1–8; Sir. 26:16–18). The later Jewish traditions adapt this perspective also by encouraging the married man to sexually satisfy his wife, have sex frequently (even nightly), and engage in sex, even if the wife was barren, pregnant, or nursing.[64]

Although the biblical scriptures do not directly address the subject of oral sex within a marital context, several passages might imply this. A suggestive text is Ruth 3:4–14 which mentions Ruth uncovering and sleeping at the place of Boaz's "feet." Scholars have noted that the feet in this passage may be a euphemism for the penis or urinary opening (cf. Judg. 3:24; 1 Sam. 24:3f; Isa. 7:20; Ezek. 16:25; Deut. 28:57; possibly Ex. 4:25; Isa. 6:2), but it is also possible that it refers to Boaz's uncovered legs. In either case the text remains sexually risqué and ambiguous.[65] It is not entirely clear if Ruth actually had oral sex/sexual intercourse with Boaz during the encounter.

Biblical poetic and prophetic/apocalyptic literature lean toward oral-genital implications when they associate sex with food and drink.[66] If such a relationship involved illegitimate sex, as in adultery or prostitution, the sex/food/drink combinations are negative (Prov. 5:15–17, 20; 7:18; 9:17–18; 30:20; Sir. 26:12; Rev. 17:4 cf. Ezek. 16; 23). To this negative list might be added Greco-Roman cultic practices, which seem to mention fellatio in the Qumran version of Isaiah 65:3.[67] Nevertheless when the biblical texts use food/drink/sex imagery in the context of a legitimate relationship, the activity is sanctioned (Cant. 2:3–5, 16; 4:10–5:6; 6:2–3; 7:1–9; 8:2–3; Prov. 5:18–19). In Song of Solomon 2:3, it is possible that the "fruit" (*peri*) of the male lover is a euphemism for the penis or semen, which the woman finds sweet in taste.[68] If this interpretation is correct, the inevitable conclusion would seem to be that the female enjoys giving her lover fellatio or swallowing his semen, which may be a way of implying her absolute love and total acceptance of him.[69] Likewise cunnilingus may be implied when the male lover feeds/browses on the *lotus*, a euphemism for the vagina (Cant. 2:16b; 6:3b). It is difficult to mistake the implication related to oral sex in Song of Solomon 4:12–5:1: the female's well-lubricated "garden" represents the vulva where the male lover eats and drinks.[70] Both fellatio and cunnilingus would therefore seem to be supported biblically in marital relationships. However, if only one form of oral sex is supported in the Song of Solomon and not the other, the other form would still seem to be implied because the couple seeks mutual love: "My beloved is mine and I am his" (Cant. 2:16a; 6:3a; 7:10).

Anal sex seems more biblically allusive in a marital context than oral sex. Some counselors caution couples against this practice for health reasons, most notably its ability to damage rectal tissue.[71] But this does not necessarily mean it is immoral in such a context. There also seems to be nothing biblically immoral about using sex toys, sex games, sexual caressing, and many other sexual foreplay activities in a marriage between two people. Common sense, respect, discernment, and open communication go a long way in establishing healthy erotic preferences.

In the Christian scriptures, a healthy view of the marital bedroom begins by taking the concept of loving one's neighbor as oneself a step further: Sexual love making involves mutual pleasure. 1 Corinthians 7:3–5 affirms that both the husband and wife are to give sexual satisfaction to one another. Nowhere does this text discuss procreation; here sex is intended for pleasure rather than having babies. As a well-learned Jew, Paul probably read in the Song of Solomon something similar about reciprocal benefits in lovemaking (e.g., Cant. 2:16). Elsewhere Paul affirms mutual benefit and mutual submission in marriage (Eph. 5:21–22; Gal. 5:13; Phil. 2:3–4).[72] Moreover, if love does not insist on its own way (1 Cor. 13:3–5), there will be times when both the husband and wife must relinquish and submit to the other in the relationship including their sex life. The type of sexual love 1 Corinthians 7:3–5 fosters might be captured by what John Grabowski calls "mutual self-donation."[73] Our perspective provides a biblical basis in the affirmation that Christian couples are free to engage in creative sexual pleasures as long as their goal is to love one another and seek mutual rather than selfish ends. The erotic marital bed should promote faithfulness, oneness, and human dignity as male and female created in God's image.[74] Mutual self-donation strives for pleasuring the other partner and trusts the other partner will reciprocate; it also allows for shared voluntary submission when sexual disagreements arise. Both partners are willing givers, even servants, to the other's sexual desires.

Lastly, marital sex in Christian context should be *celebrative* self-donation. God-given sex offers a dimension of recreation—it embraces celebration. Because a significant facet of marital sex involves pleasure, there is nothing wrong with improving one's sexual techniques. Marital sex does not need to pit the notions of *sobriety/sex for love's sake* against the concepts of *sexual technique/sex for recreational sake*. As long as love and total commitment is the ground for sexual activity, Christian couples can have sex for the sheer fun of it too! If the fruit of the Spirit in Galatians first entails love, its second virtue is joy. A voluntary sex partner that shows reluctance does not seem to be operating this virtue in a proper manner. Being full of joy and God's Spirit helps enable the couple to long for sexual union, be passionate when making love, and enthusiastic about pleasing the other person. Mutual love-making transcends an attitude that merely affirms, "I must try to please my spouse sexually because I have to love him/her as myself." Instead it eagerly asks the other partner, "How can I best please you when it comes to sex?" If the wife communicates that she wants her husband to cuddle with her in a very long afterglow, this means the husband will not roll over and sleep but will learn to fulfill his wife's desire completely. If the husband craves a healthy sexual fetish, this means the wife will try to do her best at satisfying her husband's fetish. Celebrative self-donation continually seeks to augment sexual pleasure.

Sex is more than coitus, and sexual vice is more than fornication. We are called to honor God with our bodies, and Christian sexual ethics should nurture this belief. Loving God in this sense means loving our body, which includes spiritual and social communion as well as mutual-celebrative characteristics.

Notes

[1] See the research statistics in Judith Treas, "How Cohorts, Education, and Ideology Shaped a New Sexual Revolution on American Attitudes toward Nonmarital Sex, 1972–1998," *Sociological Perspectives* 45.3 (2002), 267–83.

[2] This chapter targets younger singles in this study partly because I currently attend a Christian group ambiguously considered Generation X and because younger singles as whole tend to be more promiscuous than older ones.

[3] See the study done in Joan R. Kahn, "Premarital Sex and the Risk of Divorce," *Journal of Marriage and the Family* 53 (1991), 845–55.

[4] See the studies of Scott H. Beck, Bettie S. Cole, and Judith A. Hammond, "Religious Heritage and Premarital Sex: Evidence from a National Sample of Young Adults," *Journal for the Scientific Study of Religion* 30.2 (1991), 173–180; John K. Cochran, Leonard Beeghley, "The Influence of Religion on Attitudes toward Nonmarital Sexuality: A Preliminary Assessment of Reference Group Theory," *Journal for the Scientific Study of Religion* 30.1 (1991), 45–62.

[5] Tom W. Smith, *American Sexual Behavior: Trends, Socio-Demographic Differences, and Risk Behavior* (Chicago: National Opinion Research Center, University of Chicago, Dec. 1998), 46. See also "1994 Churched Youth Survey," Barna Research Group, cited in Terry Wier (with Mark Carruth), *Holy Sex: God's Purpose and Plan for Our Sexuality* (New Kensington, Penn.: Whitaker House, 1999), 155–57, 172.

[6] Stephen C. Barton, "'Glorify God in Your Body' (1 Corinthians 6:20): Thinking Theologically about Sexuality" in *Religion and Sexuality,* ed. Michael A. Hayes, Wendy Porter, and David Tombs; Studies in Theology and Sexuality 2; Roehampton Institute London Papers 4 (Sheffield: Sheffield Academic Press, 1998), 370.

[7] Bruce J. Malina, "Does *Porneia* mean Fornication?" *Novum Testamentum* 14.1 (1972), 17.

[8] Joseph Jensen, "Does *Porneia* Mean Fornication? A Critique of Bruce Malina," *Novum Testamentum* 20.3 (1978), 165–66. LXX refers to the Septuagint, the Greek translation of the Hebrew Scriptures, the version of the Old Testament often used by Paul and other New Testament leaders.

[9] Kathy L. Gaca, *The Making of Fornication: Eros, Ethics, and Political Reform in Greek Philosophy and Early Christianity* (Berkeley: University of California Press, 2003) 19–20, 124.

[10] Gaca, 151.

[11] Cf. Harold W. Attridge, *The Epistle to the Hebrews: A Commentary on the Epistle to the Hebrews* (Hermeneia; Philadelphia: Fortress, 1989), 369. The idea of Esau as a fornicator derives from Jewish traditions that refer to him as a sensual man and denounce his marriage with the two foreign Hittite women (Philo *Virt.* 208–10; Jub. 25:1–8; Gen. Rab. 65–67 cf. Gen. 26:32).

[12] Gaca notes that while the early Christians included *porneia* in their vice lists; the Hellenistic philosophers do not (Gaca, 13–14).

[13] Gaca suggests too much in maintaining that Paul sentences the death penalty for the man who committed *porneia* in 1 Corinthians 5 (Gaca, 139–140). If Paul commanded a Corinthian militia that executed those who were a threat to his churches, we would expect him to use this power to quickly rid himself of his opponents in Galatians 1–6 and 2 Corinthians 9–13! Paul believes instead that vengeance is the Lord's: God will punish the wicked (cf. Rom. 12:14–21).

[14] Cf. Richard Hays, *Moral Vision of the New Testament: A Contemporary Introduction to New Testament Ethics* (San Francisco: HarperCollins, 1996), 383. Here the word seems primarily associated with Gentile banqueting or cultic activities.

[15] The biblical verse is probably a Corinthian slogan rather than Paul's own belief, as has been affirmed in several writings, including John C. Hurd, *The Origin of 1 Corinthians* (London: SPCK, 1965), 67. Also cf. C. K. Robertson, *Conflict in Corinth* (New York: Peter Lang, 2001).

[16] Translation from H. Reisser, "πορνευω," in *The New International Dictionary of New Testament Theology*, ed. Colin Brown (Grand Rapids: Regency Reference Library/Zondervan, 1986), 1:498.

[17] His argument resembles the Stoic philosopher Muson, who believed that the man who had sex with a prostitute (*hetaerae*) was sinning against his own person, defiling the god in himself by unclean acts. Cf. Friedrich Hauck and Siegfried Schulz, "πορνη, πορνο∼, πορνεια, πορνευω, ἐκπορνευω," in *Theological Dictionary of the New Testament*, ed. Gerhard Kittel and Gerhard Friedrich (Grand Rapids: Eerdmans, 1968), 6:582–83.

[18] Dale Martin's study graphically elaborates this point in *The Corinthian Body* (New Haven: Yale University Press, 1995), 176–78.

[19] This too appears to be another Corinthian slogan rather than Paul's thought (cf. note 13). Paul encourages marital sex (1 Cor. 7:2–5; cf. 1 Tim. 4:1–5).

[20] In 1 Corinthians 7:1–2 single Christians do not seem to be in view (they are not addressed until 7:7ff). In 7:1–2 to "touch [*haptô*] a woman" and "have [*echô*] a wife...husband" mean "have sex" with your spouse, not "get married," which normally requires the verb *lambano* or perhaps *ktaomai*. Gordon Fee cites Gen. 20:6LXX; Ruth 2:9LXX; Plato *Leg.* 8.840a; Jos. *Ant.* 1.163 as examples of sex using *haptô* and Exod. 2:1LXX; Deut. 28:30LXX; Isa. 13:16LXX; Mark 6:18; John 4:18 as examples of monogamous sex using *echô*. He cites Test. Lev. 9:9–10 and Tobit 4:12 for *lamhano* in relation to getting married (Fee, *The First Epistle to the Corinthians*; NICNT (Grand Rapids: Eerdmans, 1987), 275–79).

[21] For more examples, see O. Larry Yarbrough, *Not Like the Gentiles: Marriage Rules in the Letters of Paul* (SBL Dissertation Series 80; Atlanta: Scholars Press, 1985), 65–87.

[22] George P. Carras, "Jewish Ethics and Gentile Converts: Remarks on 1 Thes 4,3–8," in *The Thessalonian Correspondence* (Bibliotheca Ephemeridum Theologicarum Lovaniensium; Ed. Raymond F. Collins; Uitgeverij Peeters Leuvan: Leuvan University Press, 1990), 306–315.

[23] Cf. Karl Donfried, "The Cults of Thessalonica and The Thessalonian Correspondence," *New Testament Studies* 31 (1985), 336–56.

[24] This is not the only time he would give polyvalent meaning to a word: the "*spiritual rock ... was Christ*" in 1 Corinthians 10:3–4 appears to have metaphorical, historical, and rhetorical meanings; cf. B. J. Oropeza, *Paul and Apostasy: Eschatology, Perseverance, and Falling Away in the Corinthian Congregation;* WUNT 2.115 (Tübingen: Mohr-Siebeck, 2000), 104–13. Could Paul have in mind the penis, body *and* wife by the term vessel? While this is possible, the tension between 1 Thes. 4:5 and 1 Cor. 7:9 needs some resolution.

[25] The "matter" (*pragma*) refers to the sexual issue under discussion in 1 Thessalonians 4:3–5. Because sexual uncleanness is mentioned in 4:7, the subject remains the same in 4:6; Paul does take up a new subject related to business dealings in 4:6. For a compelling critique of the business dealings interpretation, see Charles A. Wanamaker, *The Epistles to the Thessalonians: A Commentary on the Greek Text* (NIGTC; Carlisle: Paternoster/Grand Rapids: Eerdmans, 1990), 154–55.

[26] Cf. O. L. Yarbrough, 75–76.

[27] Arguments that reduce Paul's homoerotic passages to pederasty, male prostitution, or mere cultic idolatrous activities are not convincing. Looking at passages related to homosexuality in the Bible, Carol Smith's perceptive article shows that "the method of biblical interpretation that someone chooses usually reflects the prior agenda of the interpreter" (Smith, "'It's in the Book': Using the Bible in Discussions of Human Sexuality," in *Religion and Sexuality*; Studies in Theology and Sexuality 2; Ed. M. A. Hayes, W. Porter, D. Tombs (Sheffield: Sheffield Academic Press, 1998) 126. Paul's Gentile readers would not have made clear distinctions between valid

and invalid homoerotic practices based on Paul's writings. As was the case with most Jews of his day, Paul most likely considered all homosexual activity as sin, especially if he used the sex codes of the Septuagint version of Leviticus 18–20 as the backdrop behind these passages. For instance, the wording in Lev. 18:22 LXX (male having sex with male) seems to be the best explanation for how Paul derived the term *arsenokoitai* in 1 Cor. 6:9 and 1 Tim. 1:10. And if he condemned a monogamous incestuous relationship in 1 Corinthians 5, which he based on the same sex code of Leviticus 18–20, we must seriously consider why he would not have done the same thing had the problem been a monogamous homosexual relationship. This tends to point us in the direction of admitting Paul's negative stand against homosexuality and asking instead questions related to whether or not Paul was right for holding the view he did. I think such an approach would be more fruitful for the homosexual debate than trying to get Paul to not say something he almost surely does. For some updated discussions related to the biblical passages on homosexuality, see Gaca, 2003:124–26; Dan O. Via and Robert A. Gagnon, *Homosexuality and the Bible: Two Views* (Minneapolis: Fortress, 2003); Robert A. J. Gagnon, *The Bible and Homosexual Practice: Text and Hermeneutics* (Nashville: Abingdon, 2001); Richard B. Hays, *Moral Vision,* 379–406; Raymond F. Collins, *Sexual Ethics and the New Testament: Behavior and Belief* (New York: Crossroad, 2000), 86–99, 128–46; William J. Webb, *Slaves, Women & Homosexuals: Exploring the Hermeneutics of Cultural Analysis* (Downers Grove: InterVarsity Press, 2001). Also, cf. Lesley Northrup's and Philip Culbertson's respective chapters in this book.

[28] Cf. L. William Countryman, *Dirt, Greed & Sex: Sexual Ethics in the New Testament and their Implications for Today* (London: SCM Press, 1989), 109, 147–67, 175–81, 190–220; Brian S. Rosner, *Paul, Scripture, and Ethics: A Study of 1 Corinthians 5–7* (Grand Rapids: Baker, 1994), 159–60. F. F. Bruce notes that the word *pleonektein* ("take advantage of") in this verse suggests the idea of "greed for property." Pauline sources occasionally combine the word with *porneia* or impurity elsewhere (1 Cor. 5:10–11; Eph. 4:19; 5:3–5). Although Bruce thinks the brother was wronged because his wife was violated (adultery), he also rightly suggests that the violated person could be "another member of the brother's household"; see Bruce, *1 & 2 Thessalonians*; Word Biblical Commentary (Waco: Word, 1982), 84.

[29] Also, in classic Roman history the father had *patria potestas* or absolute control over his family members; cf. J. A. Crook, "Patria Potestas," *Classical Quarterly* 17 (1967), 113–22. Countryman recognizes that the daughter was her father's property and could be devalued if she lost her virginity, but he overlooks this implication in 1 Thessalonians 4:6 (Countryman, 158, cf. 105).

[30] Jennifer A. Glancy, "Obstacles to Slaves' Participation in the Corinthian Church," *Journal of Biblical Literature* 117 (1998), 493, 497, 501. Her work addresses the perplexing silence of the New Testament on the issue of slaves who were not at liberty to say no to their masters' lustful desire to have sex with them. Perhaps this situation functions more as rape than *porneia.* It does not fit the category of willful sexual activities, which is normally what is assumed by marital and premarital sex. The slave is not guilty of sexual immorality if she cannot say no to her master. It is

not known, however, what Paul would have thought. Jensen suggests that unless this relevant issue was entirely ignored, the early Christians must have understood that Christian masters were not to have sex with their own slaves; they would consider such an act as *porneia* (Jensen, 183–84).

[31] The same tradition also mentions an alternative Jewish tradition was to take her "whatever" the motive.

[32] Holt N. Parker, "Love's Body Anatomized: The Ancient Erotic Handbooks and the Rhetoric of Sexuality," in *Pornography and Representation in Greece and Rome,* ed. Amy Richlin (Oxford: Oxford University Press, 1992), 98.

[33] Barbara Kantrowitz, "The Home Front: Mom, What's Oral Sex?" *Newsweek* 132.12 (1998), 44.

[34] Lisa Remez, "Oral Sex Among Adolescents: Is It Sex or Is It Abstinence?" *Family Planning Perspectives* 32.6 (2000), 298–304; Mitchell J. Prinstein, Christina S. Meade, Geoffrey L. Cohen, "Adolescent Oral Sex, Peer Popularity, and Perceptions of Best Friends' Sexual Behavior," *Journal of Pediatric Psychology* 28.4 (2003), 243–49.

[35] Cf. Stephanie A. Sanders, June M. Reinisch, "Would You Say You 'Had Sex' If…" *Journal of the American Medical Association* 281.3 (1999), 275–77; Malissa A. Bailey, "College Students' Perceptions of and Intentions to Engage in Sexually Abstinent versus Not Abstinent Behaviors," Master of Science Thesis; North Carolina State University, 1998.

[36] Martin A. Monto, "Prostitution and Fellatio," *Journal of Sex Research* 38.2 (2001), 140–45.

[37] In one study 60% of the college students surveyed did not believe oral sex was "sex," while only 20% did not believe anal sex with "sex"; see Laura M. Bogart, Heather Cecil, David A. Wagstaff, Steven D. Pinkerton, Paul R. Abramson, "Is It 'Sex'? College Students' Interpretations of Sexual Behavior Terminology," *The Journal of Sex Research* 37.2 (2000), 108–16. Similar results are found in Remez (301) and Malissa A. Bailey (2–7, 36–40).

[38] Remez, 301.

[39] Cf. Ove Brusendorff and Poul Henningsen, *A History of Eroticism* (New York: Lyle Stuart, 1963); Amy Richlin, ed. *Pornography and Representation in Greece and Rome* (Oxford: Oxford University Press, 1992); Albert Bell, *A Guide to the New Testament World* (Scottdale, Penn.: Herald Press, 1994), 235; Antonio Varona, *Eroticism in Pompeii* (Los Angeles: J. Paul Getty Museum, 2001); Judith P. Hallett and Marilyn B. Skinner, ed. *Roman Sexualities* (Princeton: Princeton University Press, 1997); John R. Clarke, *Looking at Lovemaking: Constructions of Sexuality in Roman Art, 100 B.C. – A.D. 250* (Berkeley: University of California Press, 2001).

[40] Cf. D. Martin, 177–78.

[41] To what extent would Paul have known about these various types of sexual penetration? Did he ever visit a brothel or read/heard the testimonies of others who did? If he was indeed a learned man, frequent traveler, and missionary to pagan Gentiles, the latter would at least seem likely. Moreover, sexually explicit talk and

graphic imagery related to prostitution was not void in ancient Jewish traditions (e.g., Ezek. 16:22, 27, 36, 46ff, 23:8, 19–21, 29; cf. Rev. 17:4, 16; Prov. 30:20).

[42] Cf. Raymond Collins, 151.

[43] For a generally negative conclusion, see John S. Grabowski, *Sex and Virtue: An Introduction to Sexual Ethics* (Washington: Catholic University Press, 2003), 114–116; for a generally positive conclusion, see Steve Gerali, *The Struggle* (Colorado Springs: NavPress, 2003).

[44] Raymond Collins attempts to interpret Mark 9:42–48 with the Talmud's denouncement of masturbation (67–68). The connection is not convincing. If Jesus were speaking against masturbation, we might expect something reminiscent to what is found in the Hebrew Scriptures or the literature of Second Temple Judaism, which is more contemporary with Mark's gospel. Collins does not even qualify masturbation when he claims it a vice that excludes a person from inheriting God's kingdom (189). If it were this wicked, we should expect to find it more clearly condemned *somewhere* in the Scriptures.

[45] The growing epidemic of porn addicts who view the Internet is one testimony to sexual addiction. Recent studies show that more than 20 million Internet users visit sex sites regularly, and more than 200,000 people are now plagued by the relatively new disorder of cybersex addiction; cf. Al Cooper, ed. *Cybersex: The Dark Side of the Force;* A Special Issue of the Journal *Sexual Addiction & Compulsivity* (2000) 25.

[46] Sometimes *pleonexia* takes on a similar meaning that relates to sexual lust (Eph. 5:3; Col. 3:5).

[47] Robert Gundry relates Romans 7 to Paul's pre-Christian *bar mitzvah*, which is one possible way of reading the "I" in Romans 7:7–25; see Gundry, "The Moral Frustration of Paul Before His Conversion: Sexual Lust in Romans 7:7–25," in *Pauline Studies;* Festschrift for F. F. Bruce; ed. D. A. Hagner and M. Harris (Exeter: Paternoster Press, 1980), 228–45. Whether Paul's lust came before or after his conversion (or both) does not nullify his struggled in Romans 7:7, unless the "I" here is purely rhetorical or representative of Adam. In either case Paul would have to completely *exclude* himself from the "I" if we wish to say that he did not personally struggle with *epithumia*.

[48] Simon Blackburn, *Lust: The Seven Deadly Sins* (New York/Oxford: Oxford University Press, 2004), 19.

[49] Cf. Gaca, 155–57.

[50] Some also argue rather persuasively that pornography has an indirect connection with sexual aggression and sex crimes such as rape; cf. Donna Rice Hughes and John D. McMickle, "Pornography Incites Violent Sexual Crime," in *Pornography: Opposing Viewpoints,* ed. Carol Wekesser (San Diego: Greenhaven Press, 1997), 36–39. Judith K. Balswick and Jack O. Balswick write: "viewing pornography may not *cause* sexual aggression toward women, but it is a significant factor in attitudes of sexual aggression and behavior," *Authentic Human Sexuality: An Integrated Christian Approach* (Downers Grove: InterVarsity Press, 1999), 241.

[51] Some enlightening articles on pornography include Read Mercer Schuchardt, "Hugh Hefner's Hollow Victory," *Christianity Today* (Dec. 2003), 50–54; Rosaline Bush,

"Pornography Harms Society," in *Pornography: Opposing Viewpoints*, ed. Carol Wekesser (San Diego: Greenhaven Press, 1997), 17–27.

[52] William E. Phipps, "Masturbation: Vice or Virtue?" *Journal of Religion and Health* 16 (July 1977), 183–95; Gerali, 84–85.

[53] Cf. Steve Gerali on this point, 112–121; 129–41.

[54] Cf. Oropeza, *Paul and Apostasy*, 85–90, 97–99.

[55] If the patriarchal world considered the husband as owner and possessor of the bride's body, Paul expands this to mutual ownership in human marriages—the husband's body also belongs to the wife (1 Cor. 7:1–5). In any case Christ is still seen as the spiritual owner of the believer.

[56] Barton, "Glorify God," 378–379.

[57] Cf. Balswick and Balswick, 119; cf. 121.

[58] Lisa Sowle Cahill, "Sexual Ethics: A Feminist Biblical Perspective," *Interpretation* 49; 1995: 11–12.

[59] I have Henry Cloud and John Townsend's *Boundaries in Dating* to thank for this insightful point (2000:246).

[60] Grabowski, 117; cf. Stanley J. Grenz, *Sexual Ethics: An Evangelical Perspective* (Louisville: Westminster John Knox, 1990), 204.

[61] On ancient forms of birth control, see John M. Riddle, *Contraception and Abortion from the Ancient World to the Renaissance* (Cambridge: Harvard University Press, 1992); see also Vern L. Bullough, *Sexual Variance in Society and History* (New York: John Wiley & Sons, 1976), 79, 99, 148–49.

[62] See statistic samplings in Balswick and Balswick 134–137.

[63] Wendy Shalit, *A Return to Modesty: Discovering the Lost Virtue* (New York: Free Press, 1999).

[64] See Bullough (76–79, 87–89) for sources.

[65] Cf. Kirsten Nielsen, *Ruth: A Commentary* (Louisville: Westminster John Knox, 1997), 49, 52, 55; and note also the parallels between Ruth 3 and Lot drinking and having sex with his daughters (Gen. 19:30–38), the "threshing floor" as a place for having sex (Hos. 9:1), and the corner or extremity of the garment in relation to sex (Ezek. 16:8). If Ruth did have sex with Boaz before marriage, would this couple still be considered virtuous? We should remember that the period of Judges in which they lived was generally a time of lawlessness (Judges 17:6; 21:25); even Israel's heroes committed shocking acts, such as sacrificing a daughter as a burnt offering (Jephthah; Judges 12:30–40) and sleeping with a prostitute (Samson; Judges 16:1).

[66] On the imagery of food in the Song of Solomon, see Athalya Brenner, "The Food of Love: Gendered Food and Food Imagery in the Song of Songs," *Semeia* 86.1 (1999), 197–212.

[67] Marvin H. Pope posits the "hand" as a popular ancient euphemism for the penis. This verse speaks of sucking the "hands" (penis) and "stones" (testicles?); cf. Pope, *Song of Songs* (Anchor Bible 7c; Garden City, NY: Doubleday, 1977), 224–25.

[68] For support of this view and ancient comparative sources, see Joseph C. Dillow, *Solomon on Sex* (Nashville: Thomas Nelson, 1977), 31, 41, and the Sumerian sacred marriage parallels in Pope, *Song of Songs,* 372–73.

[69] The semen's pleasant flavor might arise from the popular but unproven belief that eating fruits make the body's semen taste sweet.

[70] See Pope, *Song of Songs,* 368, 406–07, 499, who also argues that "vulva" is the correct way to interpret Song of Solomon 7:2/7:3a "Your vulva a rounded crater," and 7:8/7:9d "The scent of your vulva like apples" (617–18, 636–37). Cf. *New Brown, Driver, Briggs, Gesenius Hebrew-English Lexicon* (Peabody: Hendrickson, 1979) 1057§8270; Dillow, 82–85.

[71] Cf. Wier (326–27). Regarding oral sex Wier also cautions that good dental hygiene will help prevent yeast infections when performing cunnilingus, and he advises wives not to swallow semen when performing fellatio, suggesting that some researchers "believe" that sperm "has the potential to cause normal body cells to turn cancerous" (326). But he offers no evidence for this claim, which would be important to demonstrate given that others suggest seminal-oral benefits (e.g., C.A. Koelman, A.B.C. Coumans, H.W. Nijman, et al., "Correlation between Oral Sex and a Low Incidence of Preeclampsia: A Role for Soluble HLA in Seminal Fluid?" *Journal of Reproductive Immunology* 46.2 (2000), 155.

[72] Too often the church has stressed the wife's submission to the husband and has overlooked the husband's implicit submission to the wife (Eph. 5:21). The Pauline writer points to the example of Christ as the head in Ephesians 5:22–23. In the gospels, however, Christ teaches that Christian leadership must take on the role of submission, unlike Greco-Roman hierarchical structures (Mark 10:42–45; John 13). In light of this perspective if the husband insists on being the head, he is to act like the servant!

[73] Grabowski, 46–47.

[74] A threesome or an orgy would therefore seem to violate this principle, as would sadistic sexual activities.

Bibliography

Attridge, Harold W. *The Epistle to the Hebrews: A Commentary on the Epistle to the Hebrews.* Hermeneia; Philadelphia: Fortress, 1989.

Bailey, Derrick Sherwin. *Sexual Relation in Christian Thought.* New York: Harper & Brothers, 1959.

Bailey, Malissa A. "College Students' Perceptions of and Intentions to Engage in Sexually Abstinent versus Not Abstinent Behaviors." M.S. thesis, North Carolina State University, 1998.

Balswick, Judith K., and Jack O. Balswick. *Authentic Human Sexuality: An Integrated Christian Approach.* Downers Grove, Ill.: InterVarsity Press, 1999.

Bartchy, Scott S. "Who Should Be Called Father? Paul of Tarsus between the Jewish Tradition and Patria Potestas." *Biblical Theology Bulletin* 33.4 (2003): 135–47.

Barton, Stephen C. "'Glorify God in Your Body' (1 Corinthians 6.20): Thinking Theologically about Sexuality." Pages 366–79 in *Religion and Sexuality.* Studies in Theology and Sexuality 2; Roehampton Institute, London Papers 4. Edited by

Michael A. Hayes, Wendy Porter and David Tombs. Sheffield: Sheffield Academic Press, 1998.

Beck, Scott H., Bettie S. Cole, and Judith A. Hammond. "Religious Heritage and Premarital Sex: Evidence from a National Sample of Young Adults." *Journal for the Scientific Study of Religion* 30.2 (1991): 173–80.

Bell, Albert. *A Guide to the New Testament World.* Scottdale, Penn.: Herald Press, 1994.

Blackburn, Simon. *Lust: The Seven Deadly Sins.* Oxford: Oxford University Press, 2004.

Bogart, Laura M., Heather Cecil, David A. Wagstaff, Steven D. Pinkerton, and Paul R. Abramson, "Is It 'Sex'? College Students' Interpretations of Sexual Behavior Terminology." *The Journal of Sex Research* 37.2 (2000): 108–16.

Brenner, Athalya. "The Food of Love: Gendered food and Food Imagery in the Song of Songs." *Semeia* 86.1 (1999): 197–212.

Brown, David Mark. *Tainted Love: God, Sex and Relationships for the Not-So-Pure-at-Heart.* Downers Grove, Ill.: InterVarsity Press, 2002.

Bruce, F. F. *1 & 2 Thessalonians.* Word Biblical Commentary. Waco: Word, 1982.

Brusendorff, Ove, and Poul Henningsen. *A History of Eroticism.* New York: Lyle Stuart, 1963.

Bullough, Vern L. *Sexual Variance in Society and History.* New York/ London/ Sydney/ Toronto: John Wiley & Sons, 1976.

Bush, Rosaline. "Pornography Harms Society." in *Pornography: Opposing Viewpoints.* Edited by Carol Wekesser. San Diego: Greenhaven Press, 1997.

Cahill, Lisa Sowle. "Sexual Ethics: A Feminist Biblical Perspective," *Interpretation* 49; (1995): 5–16.

Carras, George P. "Jewish Ethics and Gentile Converts: Remarks on 1 Thes 4,3–8." Pages 306–15 in *The Thessalonian Correspondence.* Bibliotheca Ephemeridum Theologicarum Lovaniensium 87. Edited by Raymond F. Collins. Uitgeverij Peeters Leuvan: Leuven University Press, 1990.

Clarke, John R. *Looking at Lovemaking: Constructions of Sexuality in Roman Art, 100 B.C.–A.D. 250.* Berkeley: University of California Press, 2001.

Cloud, Henry, and John Townsend. *Boundaries in Dating: Making Dating Work.* Grand Rapids: Zondervan, 2000.

Cochran, John K., and Leonard Beeghley. "The Influence of Religion on Attitudes toward Nonmarital Sexuality: A Preliminary Assessment of Reference Group Theory." *Journal for the Scientific Study of Religion* 30.1 (1991): 45–62.

Collins, Raymond F. *Sexual Ethics and the New Testament: Behavior and Belief.* New York: Herder & Herder/Crossroad Publishing Company, 2000.

Cooper, Al, ed. *Cybersex: The Dark Side of the Force.* A Special Issue of the journal *Sexual Addiction & Compulsivity.* Philadelphia: Bruner-Routledge, 2000.

Countryman, L. William. *Dirt, Greed & Sex: Sexual Ethics in the New Testament and Their Implications for Today.* London: SCM Press, 1989.

Crook, J. A. "Patria Potestas," *Classical Quarterly* 17 (1967): 113–122.

Davies, Jon, and Gerard Loughlin, editors. *Sex These Days: Essays on Theology, Sexuality and Society.* Studies in Theology and Sexuality 1. Sheffield: Sheffield Academic Press, 1997.

Dillow, Joseph C. Dillow, *Solomon on Sex.* Nashville: Thomas Nelson, 1977.

Donfried, Karl. "The Cults of Thessalonica and the Thessalonian Correspondence," *New Testament Studies* 31 (1985): 336–56.

Dover, K. J. "Classical Greek Attitudes to Sexual Behaviour." Pages 143–57 in *Women in the Ancient World: The Arethusa Papers.* Edited by John Peradotto and J. P. Sullivan. Albany: State University of New York Press, 1984.

Dumais, Marcel. "Couple et sexualité dans le Nouvean Testament." *Église et theologie* 8 (1977): 47–72.

Fee, Gordon. *The First Epistle to the Corinthians.* NICNT. Grand Rapids: Eerdmans, 1987.

Ferguson, John. *Moral Values in the Ancient World.* Morals and Law in Ancient Greece. New York: Arno Press, 1979.

Flacelière, Robert. *Love in Ancient Greece.* Westport, Conn.: Greenwood Press, 1973.

Foucault, Michel. *The History of Sexuality.* New York: Vintage Books, 1980–88; 3 Volumes.

Fuchs, Eric. *Sexual Desire and Love: Origins and History of the Christian Ethic of Sexuality and Marriage.* Translated by Marsha Daigle. Cambridge: James Clarke & Co. New York: The Seabury Press, 1983.

Furnish, Victor Paul. *The Moral Teaching of Paul: Selected Issues.* 2nd rev. edition. Nashville: Abingdon, 1985.

Gaca, Kathy L. *The Making of Fornication: Eros, Ethics, and Political Reform in Greek Philosophy and Early Christianity.* Berkeley: University of California Press, 2003.

Gagnon, Robert A. J. *The Bible and Homosexual Practice: Text and Hermeneutics.* Nashville: Abingdon, 2001.

Gallagher, Charles A., George A. Maloney, Marry F. Rousseau, and Paul F. Wilczak. *Embodied in Love: The Sacramental Spirituality of Sexual Intimacy.* New York: Crossroad, 1983.

Gerali, Steve. *The Struggle.* Colorado Springs: NavPress, 2003.

Glancy, Jennifer A. "Obstacles to Slaves' Participation in the Corinthian Church," *Journal of Biblical Literature* 117.3 (1998): 481–501.

Grabowski, John S. *Sex and Virtue: An Introduction to Sexual Ethics.* Washington: Catholic University of America Press, 2003.

Grenz, Stanley J. *Sexual Ethics: An Evangelical Perspective.* Louisville, Kent.: Westminster John Knox, 1990.

Grimal, Pierre. *Love in Ancient Rome.* Arthur Train, translator. New York: Crown, 1967.

Gudel, Joseph P. "Homosexuality: Fact and Fiction." *Christian Research Journal* 15.1 (1992), 20–23, 30–33.

Gudorf, Christine E. *Body, Sex, and Pleasure: Reconstructing Christian Sexual Ethics.* Cleveland: Pilgrim, 1994.

Gundry, Robert. "The Moral Frustration of Paul Before His Conversion: Sexual Lust in Romans 7:7–25." Pages 228–45 in *Pauline Studies.* Festschrift for F. F. Bruce. Donald A. Hagner and Murray J. Harries, editors. Exeter, Devon: Paternoster Press, 1980.

Hallet, Judith P., and Marilyn B. Skinner, ed. *Roman Sexualities.* Princeton: Princeton University Press, 1997.

Hauck, Friedrich, and Siegfried Schulz. "povrnh, povrno~, porneiva, porneuvw, ejkporneuvw." Volume 6, Pages 579–95 in *Theological Dictionary of the New Testament.* Edited by Gerhard Kittel and Gerhard Friedrich. Grand Rapids: Eerdmans, 1968.

Hays, Richard B. *The Moral Vision of the New Testament: A Contemporary Introduction to New Testament Ethics.* San Francisco: HarperCollins, 1996.

Hughes, Donna Rice, and John D. McMickle. "Pornography Incites Violent Sexual Crime." In *Pornography: Opposing Viewpoints.* Edited by Carol Wekesser. San Diego: Greenhaven Press, 1997.

Hurd, John C. *The Origin of 1 Corinthians.* London: SPCK, 1965.

Jensen, Joseph. "Does *Porneia* Mean Fornication? A Critique of Bruce Malina." *Novum Testamentum* 20.3 (1978): 161–84.

Kahn, Joan R. "Premarital Sex and the Risk of Divorce." *Journal of Marriage and the Family* 53 (1991): 845–55.

Koelman, C. A., A. B. C. Coumans, H. W. Nijman, I. N. Doxiadis, G. A. Dekker, and F. H. J. Claas "Correlation between oral sex and a low incidence of preeclampsia: a role for soluble HLA in seminal fluid?" *Journal of Reproductive Immunology* 46.2 (2000):155.

Kuriansky, Judith. *The Complete Idiot's Guide to Dating.* New York: Alpha Books/Macmillan/ Simon & Schuster, 1998.

Lebacqz, Karen. "Appropriate Vulnerability: A Sexual Ethic for Singles." *Christian Century* 104.15 (2001): 435–38.

McGinn, Thomas A. J. *Prostitution, Sexuality, and the Law in Ancient Rome.* New York/Oxford: Oxford University Press, 1998.

Malina, Bruce J. "Does *Porneia* mean Fornication?" *Novum Testamentum* 14.1 (1972): 10–17.

Martin, Dale. *The Corinthian Body.* New Haven: Yale University Press, 1995.

Monto, Martin A. "Prostitution and Fellatio." *Journal of Sex Research* 38.2 (2001): 140–45.

Nelson, James B. "The Liberal Approach to Sexual Ethics." Pages 354–58 in *From Christ to the World: Introductory Readings in Christian Ethics.* Edited by Wayne G. Boulton, Thomas D. Kennedy, and Allen Verhey. Grand Rapids: Eerdmans, 1994.

———. *Between Two Gardens: Reflections on Sexuality and Religious Experience.* New York: Pilgrim Press, 1983.

Nielsen, Kirsten. *Ruth: A Commentary.* Louisville: Westminster John Knox, 1997.

Oropeza, B. J. "Intimacy in Dating." No Pages. August, 2001. Online: http://www.victoryoutreach.org/beliefs/relations02.asp.

———. *Paul and Apostasy: Eschatology, Perseverance, and Falling Away in the Corinthian Congregation.* Tübingen: J. C. B. Mohr (Paul Siebeck), Wissenschaftliche Untersuchungen zum Neuen Testament; 2. Reihe. 115. Herausgegeben von Martin Hengel und Otfried Hofius. Tübingen, Germany: J. C. B. Mohr (Paul Siebeck), 2000.

Parker, Holt N. "Love's Body Anatomized: The Ancient Erotic Handbooks and the Rhetoric of Sexuality." In *Pornography and Representation in Greece and Rome.* Edited by Amy Richlin. Oxford: Oxford University Press, 1992.

Phipps, William E. "Masturbation: Vice or Virtue?" *Journal of Religion and Health* 16 (July 1977): 183–95.

Pope, Marvin H. *Song of Songs.* Anchor Bible 7c. Garden City, NY: Doubleday, 1977.

Prinstein, Mitchell J., Christina S. Meade, and Geoffrey L. Cohen. "Adolescent Oral Sex, Peer Popularity, and Perceptions of Best Friends' Sexual Behavior." *Journal of Pediatric Psychology* 28.4 (2003): 243–49.

Punzo, Vincent C. "Morality and Human Sexuality." Pages 220–24 in *Ethics in Practice: An Anthology.* Second Edition. Blackwell Philosophy Anthologies. Edited by High LaFollette. Malden, Mass./Oxford: Blackwell, 2002.

Rediger, G. Lloyd. *Beyond the Scandals: A Guide To Healthy Sexuality for Clergy.* Minneapolis: Fortress, 2003.

Reisser, H. "πορνευω." Vol. 1, pages 497–501 in *The New International Dictionary of New Testament Theology.* Edited by Colin Brown. Grand Rapids: Regency Reference Library/Zondervan, 1986.

Remez, Lisa. "Oral Sex Among Adolescents: Is It Sex or Is It Abstinence?" *Family Planning Perspectives* 32.6 (2000): 298–304.

Richlin, Amy, ed. *Pornography and Representation in Greece and Rome.* Oxford: Oxford University Press, 1992.

Riddle, John M. *Contraception and Abortion from the ancient World to the Renaissance* Cambridge: Harvard University Press, 1992.

Robertson, C. K. *Conflict in Corinth.* New York: Peter Lang, 2001.

Rosenau, Douglas E. *A Celebration of Sex.* Nashville: Thomas Nelson, 1994.

Rosner, Brian S. *Paul, Scripture, and Ethics: A Study of 1 Corinthians 5–7.* Grand Rapids: Baker, 1994.

Rouselle, Aline. *Porneia: On Desire and the Body in Antiquity.* Felicia Pheasant, translator. Oxford: Basil Blackwell, 1988.

Sanders, Stephanie A., and June M. Reinisch, "Would You Say You 'Had Sex' If…" *Journal of the American Medical Association* 281.3 (1999): 275–77.

Schuchardt, Read Mercer. "Hugh Hefner's Hollow Victory." *Christianity Today* (Dec. 2003): 50–54.

Shalit, Wendy. *A Return to Modesty: Discovering the Lost Virtue.* New York: Free Press, 1999.

Smith, Carol. "'It's in the Book': Using the Bible in Discussions of Human Sexuality." Pages 125–34 in *Religion and Sexuality.* Studies in Theology and Sexuality 2; Roehampton Institute, London Papers 4. Edited by Michael A. Hayes, Wendy Porter and David Tombs. Sheffield: Sheffield Academic Press, 1998.

Smith, Tom W. *American Sexual Behavior: Trends, Socio-Demographic Differences, and Risk Behavior.* Chicago: National Opinion Research Center, University of Chicago, Dec. 1998.

Stafford, Tim. "Getting Serious About Lust in an Age of Smirks." *Journal of Biblical Counseling* 13.3 (Spr. 1995): 4–6.

Tannahill, Reay. *Sex in History.* New York: Stein and Day, 1980.

Treas, Judith. "How Cohorts, Education, and Ideology Shaped a New Sexual Revolution on American Attitudes toward Nonmarital Sex, 1972–1998." *Sociological Perspectives* 45.3 (2002): 267–83.

Via, Dan O. and Gagnon, Robert A. *Homosexuality and the Bible: Two Views.* Minneapolis: Fortress, 2003.

Wanamaker, Charles A. *The Epistles to the Thessalonians: A Commentary on the Greek Text.* NIGTC. Carlisle: Paternoster/Grand Rapids: Eerdmans, 1990.

Webb, William J. *Slaves, Women & Homosexuals: Exploring the Hermeneutics of Cultural Analysis.* Downers Grove: InterVarsity Press, 2001.

Wekesser, Carol, ed. *Pornography: Opposing Viewpoints.* San Diego: Greenhaven Press, 1997.

Wier, Terry, with Mark Carruth. *Holy Sex: God's Purpose and Plan for Our Sexuality.* New Kensington, Penn.: Whitaker House, 1999.

Yarbrough, O. Larry. *Not Like the Gentiles: Marriage Rules in the Letters of Paul.* SBL Dissertation Series 80; Atlanta: Scholars Press, 1985.

Yarbrough, Robert W. "Sexual Gratification in 1 Thess 4:1–8." *Trinity Journal* 20ns (1999): 215–232.

* Special thanks to Erin Langhoser of Azusa Pacific University for assisting me with the resources in this bibliography.

3 Woman's Place or Women's Spaces: Intertwining History, *Her*story, and Christianity

Georgia A. Newman

What is the first question a person asks on learning that a new baby is about to be born: "Is it a boy or a girl? Today, when most Americans would concur in principle, if not in fact, that "*all* are created equal," why and how does this question of gender at birth matter?

The fact that major courses at universities today have grown up around the topic "Gender Studies"; that test scores of achievement in science, math, and reading, from pre-school to college, continue to be classified by gender; that companies spend fortunes targeting their products and their advertising to gender-specific audiences; and that religious institutions themselves continue to wrestle with the question of what roles are appropriate for men, which suitable for women—all testify to just how much *maleness* and *femaleness* matter in our society as well as how firmly notions of gender are embedded in our psyches.

However, do we not claim that our legal system and social customs blur, if not erase altogether, formerly established gender boundaries? Indeed, nearly a half-century after the advent of that post-WWII socio-political phenomenon popularly known as the Women's Movement, we can point objectively to dramatic shifts in how our society has come to regard little boys and little girls, how men's and women's roles in both public and private spheres have been redefined, and how laws and courts have put a new face on the concepts of "fair and equitable."

Old stereotypes that once saw little boys as competitive and athletic, and little girls as cooperative and demure, are fast becoming obsolete. When Title IX of the Civil Rights Act of 1964 promoted both literally and figuratively a leveling of the playing field for male and female athletes, its impact extended far beyond the walls of schools and colleges targeted by this federal legislation. Female athleticism, once spurned in the term "tomboy," became desirable. Today, female toddlers are more likely to appear in rompers than in frilly dresses.

A blurring of gender boundaries is also apparent in the marketing of children's toys. Dolls now compete with skateboards and soccer balls for the attention of little girls. Barbie herself has been forced into an extreme makeover—with breast reduction rather than augmentation; with astronaut and GI Joe uniforms added to her wardrobe; and with a surfboard replacing a purse—as she fights to stay atop Santa's wish list for the tough, little short-haired girl in blue as well as for her pig-tailed or Goldilocks friend in pink.

The past thirty years have seen women in record numbers finding employment in jobs and career paths in professions once considered appropriate only for men. Today, Jane Doe, granddaughter of Rosie the Riveter, may well be a truck driver, a physician, an engineer, or a combat veteran. She is also capable of earning a living as a professional tennis player or golfer, although her earnings are not yet on par with her male counterparts. Careers once considered "women's work"—nursing; elementary school teaching; secretarial work, and the like—are attracting men as well. (However, one cannot help noting how the term "administrative assistant" has coincided with the arrival of men in the "secretarial" field.) Partnerships are now being forged between men and women in both law enforcement and the food sciences, on the battlefield, as well as in the home.

Even within the context of traditional marriage, the word *partnership* seems to be taking on new meaning. While the home continues to be seen primarily as a woman's responsibility (How often have you heard Bob exclaim, "Susie is so much help to me in the kitchen!"), men are increasingly visible in homemaking roles once relegated exclusively to women—from cooking to housecleaning to childcare. Even the birthing process itself (which in mid-twentieth century relegated husbands to a hospital waiting room until a male doctor at last announced to an anxious dad, "You've got a ____!") now presumes the presence of most dads-to-be as helpers and coaches in the delivery of Baby "Jamie." Moreover, John Smith may well choose to be a stay-at-home dad while wife Nancy brokers stocks.

The role of women in religious institutions too has seen dramatic change in our society over the past thirty years. On July 29, 1974, at the Church of the Advocate in Philadelphia, eleven Episcopal women were ordained as priests. They were not ordained, however, by the official church hierarchy, but by three retired bishops acting "irregularly"—— other words, in violation of canonical law—with the conviction that this act on behalf of women was, as one of the "Philadelphia Eleven," Suzanne Hiatt put it, "taken as a right from God."[1] That moment in history was met with great controversy and concern, certainly by opponents of women's ordination, but even by some proponents as well. One of the latter, the Rt. Rev. Ned Cole, Bishop of Central New York, worrying about the consequences of an act not sanctioned by the corporate body, wrote: "I am for the ordination of women to the priesthood and the episcopacy, but I will not ordain a woman to the priesthood until the General Convention of 1976 authorizes me to do so."[2] The patriarchal order was needed to approve the breakdown of patriarchy!

That highly controversial General Convention of 1976 did proclaim formally the right of women to enter the Episcopal priesthood. Interestingly, within that context, however, the "irregular" ordination of those women priests, now known as the Philadelphia Eleven, was not overturned. Thus, despite protests accompanying the donning of clerical robes and collars by these new priests, the women did not have to be re-ordained. With their entry into the priesthood, the whole notion of apostolic succession—the episcopacy itself—was redefined.

In succeeding years, however, society has alternately embraced and pulled back from the social force giving impetus to this new world order. Marking its thrust at the beginning of the twenty-first century, twenty-five years after the historic ordination of the first women priests, the *Episcopal Clerical Directory* listed ordination dates for more than 2,000 women priests.[3] Schools of theology serving mainline Presbyterian, Methodist, ELCA Lutheran, and other Protestant churches over this same period of time have also seen women in growing numbers preparing for clerical roles.

In these and other Christian denominations, such church organizations as the Women's Ordination Conference of the Roman

Catholic Church have advocated a new place for women in religious vocation. However, the movement forward has also met with counterthrust. Of interest, particularly in retrospect, is a 1978 address given by Mary Hunt at the Second Conference on the Ordination of Roman Catholic Women. In that address, Hunt, a prison chaplain and advocate for the ordination of women to the priesthood, commented on what she viewed as a major shift already underway, a new paradigm already emerging:

> From a Feminist Liberation Theology perspective, the evidence is overwhelming that the paradigm has shifted. No longer is clerical, celibate, hierarchical ministry adequate to the pastoral needs of our day. The decline in male applicants to the priesthood, the exodus of men from the clerical ranks, the growing number of women in theological schools, the general ferment around the ordination question in the United States and elsewhere, tell us loudly that the people are more than ready. The need is real; the response is genuine. We are responding to the Spirit's expression of pastoral need. We are the people who have suffered from the delayed vocations of perhaps thousands of women. There is hint of miracle about it all. Women, "faithing" in a future of jobs unseen, insist that we too are called to ministry.[4]

Despite these claims of need and possibility, however, the future that Hunt envisioned for the Catholic Church nearly three decades ago has yet to unfold.

The rapid expansion of women's roles and women's rights in the early to mid-seventies—an expansion that no doubt fueled Hunt's hopes and vision—began to be opposed in the late seventies by a powerful counterthrust in politics as in religion. In 1972, two years before the Philadelphia Eleven pushed boundaries in church practice, both the U.S. Senate and House of Representatives passed a proposal for an Equal Rights Amendment to the U.S. Constitution, an amendment written to give women equal protection under the law by prohibiting the denial of equal rights on the basis of sex. Twenty-two of a required thirty-eight states ratified the amendment during the first year; twelve more followed in the subsequent three years. Opposition mounted, however, and by 1982, the proposed amendment had failed to secure more than one of the four additional votes required for ratification.[5] While many argued at that time that equal pay and other statutes in existing federal legislation were adequate to prevent gender discrimination, a 2004 Census Report reported that women wage earners were being paid only $.76 for each dollar earned by men.[6]

The issue of equal pay for equal work, however, is more than an economic or political issue. Indeed, it is rooted deeply in religious sensibility as well, in the question of whether or not women are called by God into full partnership with men and, if so, what sort of partnership, what types of roles. Imbedded in this discussion are issues of whether women *ought* to work outside the home; in the question of how gender *difference* should be addressed; and, for many religious feminists (both men and women), in the larger questions of how or even if the feminine principle is reflected in the Godhead.

Addressing the need, particularly of women, to see feminine aspects of God, Rosemary Radford Ruether in the early nineteen eighties posed this question: "Can a male savior save women?"[7] While her own answer to that question was a qualified "yes" in her contention that Jesus himself was a feminist (i.e., one who breaks old patriarchal patterns of hierarchy and subjection, and establishes a new paradigm of mutuality and interdependence), there are other religious scholars who question whether images of Jesus, shaped over centuries within a masculinist culture, can ever speak truly to women today.

In 1993, a conference sponsored by the Presbyterian Church USA addressed the theme "Re-Imagining God." Bringing together representatives of a host of denominations within the World Council of Churches (to recognize the Council's "Ecumenical Decade: Churches in Solidarity with Women"), this conference ignited momentous controversy in its celebration of God as *Wisdom* (feminine *Sophia*) of Old Testament and apocryphal scriptures. Applauded by many for its boldness and vision in recognizing dimensions of God that church tradition over centuries had systematically eliminated, the conference horrified others, who saw it instead as an attempt to "upstage Jesus with Sophia" and/or to inject into Christianity a pagan, cultic practice.[8]

Joining voices speaking at and emerging from this conference in subsequent years, scholars and theologians have continued the debate about the image of God. One among a number of feminist perspectives is that, in Christ, a person finds a synthesis of male and female principles (both *Logos/Word/*male and *Sophia/Wisdom/*female). Some identify the Holy Spirit/Comforter as the feminine presence of God in unity with "true man" in the person of Jesus. Other points of view have also been debated in the quest to see how Christianity can speak in new ways to people who may have felt alienated from or by more conventional representations of God.[9]

One effect of this wider debate has been the emergence of new translations and paraphrases of the Bible in gender-neutral, inclusive language. As some theologians wrestle with the question of how or whether traditional Trinitarian terminology—*Father*, *Son*, and *Holy Spirit*—adequately communicates the fullness of *Creator*, *Redeemer*, and *Comforter*, so translators themselves have looked afresh at such phrases as "*sons* of God" or "*brothers* in Christ" and translated more inclusively (as, for example, "*children* of God"; "brothers *and sisters* in Christ") to speak for a contemporary age.

The degree to which gender is emphasized in such textual changes, of course, varies from translation to translation, but not even the most minor adaptations have come without controversy. Particularly notable is the recent opposition from some thirty-five evangelical scholars who have challenged word and phrase changes made to the 1978 text of the New International Version of the Bible (NIV), changes authorized by the International Bible Society (IBS) to insure a Bible in "the language of the day." Defending the decision of IBS to go forward with Today's New International Version (TNIV) in 2004–5, IBS Communications Director Larry Lincoln pointed out to critics that minor changes had been made for clarification, and that less than 2% of these changes were gender-related. Nevertheless, dissenting scholars consider the newer version "distorted"; indeed, "Focus on the Family" theologian James Dobson has called the TNIV "a step backward."[10] Acknowledging this dissent, but noting too that William Tyndale was burned at the stake in 1536 for daring to translate the Latin Vulgate Bible into English and that the Pilgrims refused to bring the then controversial, now quite popular, King James Bible aboard the *Mayflower,* Jane Lampman, staff writer for *The Christian Science Monitor*, announced the release of the TNIV with these words: "Tinkering with the Bible has always been controversial."[11] Indeed, even proponents of change differ in their attitudes towards the degree to which gender-neutral, inclusive language can alter old attitudes—some seeing linguistic change as solution to a once pervasive problem of locating women in silent spaces; some see change in language as a good but incomplete first step; others criticize most of these efforts as inadequate attempts to "fix" a broken faith, one whose centuries-old tradition still maintains a "place" for women, not in partnership with, but in submission to men.

Certainly debate about woman's place and women's spaces is gaining greater and greater ground in religious discussion and religious practice. However, even among those who champion efforts to achieve gender equality, many today are still unaware of how subtly the female has yet to be fully embraced. Consider, for instance, the naming of Catholic and Anglican/Episcopal churches as just one small example. While both of these denominations commonly name churches for a religious saint, it is noteworthy that few such churches bear the names of women saints. St. Joseph, St. Stephen, St. Thomas, St. Paul, and other men of faith continue to be honored. Yet, apart from homage to the Virgin Mary (and occasional reverencing of the Virgin's mother Anne), how many churches can claim to celebrate the life of such "ordinary" women of faith as a St. Claire, St. Catherine, or St. Mary Magdalene?

It is also curious to observe the differences in societal attitude toward male and female sinner-saints. Mary Magdalene, a woman from whom "seven devils had gone forth"[12] and clearly one of Jesus's closest friends, may well find her male counterpart in the person of Augustine of Hippo, a man who turned from a life of debauchery to one of discipline and devotion to Christ; nonetheless, church tradition seems to perpetuate a double standard in elevating Augustine to revered saintly status while paying mild, often embarrassed homage to the woman whose "scarlet past," as it is popularly conceived (and despite scholarly disputations to the contrary[13]), remains with her to the end.

Indeed, beliefs about and attitudes toward woman's sexuality, many of them rooted in either-or thinking, continue to define the role and "place" of women in the church. An oversimplified dichotomy of vixen vs. virgin limits options even as it calls into question notions of female agency vs. female receptivity. Personifying the vixen or siren is Eve, source of original sin, a beguiling female who lures an otherwise innocent Adam to partake of fruit expressly forbidden by God. Eve's antithesis is found in Mary, the humble woman of Galilee who accepts, with wonder but without question, the role she is to play in giving birth to the promised Messiah. In subtle but important ways, these images continue to shape attitudes toward women today, and create powerful implications for roles expected of and/or forbidden to women.

That the appellation *virgin* is wedded to the role of *mother* in the figure of Mary may well suggest that the feminine ideal is, quite simply, unattainable for women. Such is not the case for men. While one could argue that the paradox of *true man* being *true God* in the person of Jesus Christ establishes an equally impossible standard for men (as for women) called to "be perfect," men are not branded as categorically evil for falling short of the mark. Unlike the figure of Eve, the "old Adam" is generic "sinful man" who points to and finds redemption in Christ, the "new Adam." There is no "new Eve," except as the old treachery associated with Eve's persona is re-inscribed in other wicked women, a Delilah, perhaps, or a Salome. The figure of Eve also raises a question about free agency. Can a woman assert free agency, a trait heralded in the self-actualized individual, without also running afoul of humble obedience to God? In a similar way, does "obedience to God" translate of necessity into a submissive role for woman within the church itself?

The "Catch 22" dilemma of a one-dimensional vixen-virgin dichotomy for females is markedly absent in representations of men. Consider, for example, King David—every bit as conniving as Delilah, as lustful as Potiphar's wife, as murderous as Salome—yet lauded as "a man after God's own heart,"[14] the king from whose lineage the Messiah was to come. Trickster Jacob, who betrays brother and father, typically evokes sympathy when he himself is tricked into marrying the "ugly sister" of his desired bride, Rachel. However, in contrast to such women as Hagar or Tamar, much less the daughters of Lot (who are "branded" but never converted), Jacob, accepted as both sinner and saint, is enshrined in the church as the "new Israel," the father of God's chosen people. A New Testament exemplum in the Gospel of John tells of a Samaritan "woman at the well," a woman who has been wed to five husbands and is living with another out of wedlock when she encounters Jesus in a startling, life-changing moment. Despite her redirected apostolic zeal, though (she is said to have told the whole town of her experience), is this woman remembered as another "good Samaritan?" Is she appreciated for her quick wit; her boldness in speaking to a stranger; her willingness to argue a theological point; her humility in recognizing the Messiah; her eagerness to speak the good news; her decision to point the way for others? Would this woman, in personality not so different from the Apostle Paul (formerly Saul, the "Pharisee of Pharisees"), be accepted in clerical collar today? Certainly not without friction. As Elaine Pagels has pointed out in *Adam, Eve, and the Serpent*, one cannot overestimate just how strongly notions of sexuality and power influenced early church fathers to place restrictions on women while establishing a hierarchy that imbued men with decision-making authority.[15]

Women of faith must thus continue to search for biblical and other religious models who can speak to today's economic realities, to the experiences of violence and abuse from which so many suffer, and to a gospel that calls Christians surely to make disciples not just of all *men*, but of all *people*. In his message for the 1995 World Day of Peace ("Women Teachers of Peace"), Pope John Paul II called women to a "new feminism" that rejects the violence often associated with male domination while also fulfilling the life-giving, life-sustaining, life-nurturing role traditionally associated with female experience:

> In transforming culture so that it supports life, [women] occupy a place in thought and action which is unique and decisive. It depends on them to promote a "new feminism" which rejects the temptation of imitating models of "male domination," in order to acknowledge and affirm the true genius of women in every aspect of the life of society, and overcome all discrimination, violence and exploitation.[16]

For many women, however, the Pope's call stops short of an all-important *how*.

If discrimination, violence, and exploitation are to be overcome, then how must the world see and understand God? What spaces must women occupy to find a "place" in which the uniquely feminine is truly at one with the uniquely masculine? Clearly, a new movement—a reformation—is at work in the Church. However, as socio-political and religious pressures and debate continue the thrust-pull patterns in evidence over centuries, and especially visible within the past thirty years, this question is not likely to be answered except in the actual experiences of men and women willing to live and work within these tensions, willing to embrace the notion of a female as well as a male Jacob wrestling with God in quest of the "Who are you?" and the "Who am I?"

Notes

[1] Suzanne Hiatt, Interview. Philadelphia Eleven Papers. Archives of Women in Theological Scholarship, The Burke Library, Union Theological Seminary. Cited in Claire McCurdy, Leslie Reyman, and Letitia Campbell, "Processing the Papers of Women Religious Figures: The Archives of Women in Theological Scholarship (AWTS) Project." *Annotation: The Newsletter of the National Historical Publications and Records Commission.* 30.1 (March 2002). *http://www.archives. Gov/grants/annotation.march_2002/women_theological_scholarship.html.*

[2] "Why I will not ordain a woman/until General Convention authorizes me." *The Ordination of Women: Pro and Con*, ed. Michael P. Hamilton and Nancy S. Montgomery (New York: Morehouse Barlow Co, 1975), 70–80. *http://www. womenpriests.org/ classic/cole.htm .*

[3] Louie Crew, "Female Priests in the Episcopal Church," 1998. *www.dioceseofnewark.org/GC97/womenpr.html.* Crew reports that the 1998 *Directory* listed ordination dates for 1,954 women priests (13.8% of all priests). By 2001, the percentage had increased more dramatically to 20.3%, and the number has grown steadily since.

[4] Mary E. Hunt, "Roman Catholic Ministry: Patriarchal Past, Feminist Future." New Woman, New Church, New Priestly Ministry. *Proceedings of the Second Conference on the Ordination of Roman Catholic Women, www.womenpriests. org/classic2/hunt.asp.*

[5] Roberta W. Francis, Chair, ERA Task Force, National Council of Women's Organizations. *The History Behind the Equal Rights Amendment, www. equalrightsamendment.org/era.htm.*

[6] "Women's Earnings Fall; U.S. Census Bureau Finds Rising Gender Wage Gap." *U. S. Newswire.* Aug. 2004. *http://releases.usnewswire.com/GetRelease.asp?id=35313.*

[7] Rosemary Radford Ruether. *Sexism and God-Talk: Toward a Feminist Theology* (Boston: Beacon Press, 1983).

[8] For a strong position in favor of multiple views of God that also embrace the feminine, see Johanna W. H. van Wijk-Bos, *Reimagining God: The Case for Scriptural Diversity* (Louisville: Westminster John Knox, 1995). For opposing viewpoints, see John H. Adams (Presbyterian), "ReImagining God Movement Will Observe Tenth Anniversary," *The Layman Online* (Nov. 2002), *www.layman.org/layman/news/ news-around-church/reimagining-god-movement-10-years.html.* See also Harold S.

Martin (Brethren), "Paganism at the Minneapolis Re-Imagining Conference in Minneapolis (1993)," editorial. BRF *Witness.* 29.3 (May-June 1994), *www. brfwitness.org/Articles/1994v29n3.html.*

9 See Elisabeth Schüssler Fiorenza. *Jesus, Miriam's Child, Sophia's Prophet: Critical Issues in Feminist Christology* (New York: Continuum, 1994); Denis Edwards, *Jesus the Wisdom of God: An Ecological Theology* (Maryknoll, NY: Orbis, 1995); Karen Trimble Alliaume, "The Risks of Repeating Ourselves: Reading Feminist/Womanist Figures of Jesus." *Cross Currents.* Association for Religion and Intellectual Life, *www.aril.org/alliaume.htm*; Dolores Williams, *Sisters in the Wilderness: The Challenge of Womanist God-Talk* (Maryknoll, NY: Orbis, 1993).

10 Jane Lampman, "Bible's language Riles Evangelicals," *Christian Science Monitor, www.csmonitor.com/2002/0411/p13s01-lire.html.*

11 Ibid.

12 Luke 8:2.

13 For a discussion of biblical ambiguity in linking Mary Magdalene conclusively with the "sinner" of Luke 7: 36–50, see Hugh Pope, "St. Mary Magdalen," *Catholic Encyclopedia.* Vol. IX (Appleton, 1910). Online edition by K. Knight, *www. newadvent.org/cathen/09761a.htm.*

14 I Samuel 13:14.

15 Elaine Pagels, *Adam, Eve, and the Serpent* (New York: Random House, 1988).

16 *Evangelium Vitae* (1995), cited in Leonie Caldecott, "Sincere Gift: The Pope's New Feminism." *Communio: International Catholic Review* (Spring 1996), *www.ewtn. com/library/ISSUES/SINCGIFT.TXT.*

Bibliography

Adams, John H. "ReImagining God Movement Will Observe Tenth Anniversary." *The Layman Online* (Nov. 2002). *www.layman.org/layman/news/news-around-church/ reimagining-god-movement-10-years.html.*

Alliaume, Karen Trimble, "The Risks of Repeating Ourselves: Reading Feminist/Womanist Figures of Jesus." *Cross Currents.* Association for Religion and Intellectual Life. *www.aril.org/alliaume.htm.*

Caldecott, Leonie. "Sincere Gift: The Pope's New Feminism." *Communio: International Catholic Review* (Spring 1996). *www.ewtn.com/library/ISSUES/SINCGIFT. TXT.*

Crew, Louie, "Female Priests in the Episcopal Church." 1998. Online report. *www. dioceseofnewark.org/GC97/womenpr.html .*

Edwards, Denis. *Jesus the Wisdom of God: An Ecological Theology.* Maryknoll, NY, Orbis, 1995.

Fiorenza, Elisabeth Schüssler. *Jesus, Miriam's Child, Sophia's Prophet: Critical Issues in Feminist Christology.* New York, Continuum, 1994.

Francis, Roberta W. *The History Behind the Equal Rights Amendment.* National Council of Women's Organizations. *www.equalrightsamendment.org/era.htm.*

Hunt, Mary E. "Roman Catholic Ministry: Patriarchal Past, Feminist Future." *New Woman, New Church, New Priestly Ministry. Proceedings of the Second Conference on the Ordination of Roman Catholic Women. www.womenpriests.org/classic2/ hunt.asp.*

Lampman, Jane. "Bible's Language Riles Evangelicals." *Christian Science Monitor. www.csmonitor.com/2002/0411/p13s01-lire.html.*

Martin, Harold S. "Paganism at the Minneapolis Re-Imagining Conference in Minneapolis (1993)." Editorial. BRF *Witness.* 29.3 (May-June 1994). *www. brfwitness.org/Articles/1994v29n3.htm.*

McCurdy, Clair, Leslie Reyman, Letitia Campbell, "Processing the Papers of Women Religious Figures: The Archives of Women in Theological Scholarship (AWTS) Project." *Annotation: The Newsletter of the National Historical Publications and Records Commission.* 30:1 (March 2002). *www.archives.gov/grants/annotation/ march_2002/women_theological_scholarship.html.*

Pagels, Elaine. *Adam, Eve, and the Serpent.* New York, Random House, 1988.

Pope, Hugh. "St. Mary Magdalen," *Catholic Encyclopedia.* Vol. IX (Appleton, 1910). Online edition. *www.newadvent.org/cathen/09761a.htm.*

Ruether, Rosemary Radford. *Sexism and God-Talk: Toward a Feminist Theology* (Boston, Beacon P), 1983.

vanWijk-Bos, Johanna W.H. *Reimagining God: The Case for Scriptural Diversity.* Louisville: Westminster/John Knox, 1995.

Williams, Dolores. *Sisters in the Wilderness: The Challenge of Womanist God-Talk.* Maryknoll, NY: Orbis, 1993.

4 The Lord Gave, and the Lord Hath Taken Away: A History of Mormon Polygamy

David D. Peck

Members of the Church of Jesus Christ of Latter-day Saints (more commonly known as "Mormons") openly practiced polygamy between 1852 and 1890. Since then, observers have struggled to comprehend why men—and particularly women—would advocate and willingly participate in such an exotic marriage arrangement.[1] Nineteenth-century critics of Mormon polygamy ignorantly ascribed participation to over-sexed Mormon men, fantasizing hordes of male-dominated harem slaves reminiscent more of a Turkish *seraglio* than of reality.[2] When faced with Mormon women who defended its practice, detractors dismissed them as "those wretched and deluded women."[3] Twentieth-century historians employ more sophisticated analyses, but the concept that the participants were *willing* (particularly women) presents a serious challenge, particularly to modern feminist scholars.[4] Voluntary participation is compounded by the fact that women in the Territory of Utah enjoyed greater political liberty than virtually any other place in America, transforming a mere challenge into a more serious paradox. Some academics assign an almost subversive motivation to polygamist wives, that they embraced polygamy as a means to political (voting) power, which would then be employed as a means to undermine male power at the poll booth.[5] However, in their own words, those Mormon women and men were not over-sexed, deluded, or subversive; they practiced polygamy because they believed that God commanded them to do so. Their perspective deserves to be told on those terms.

The Doctrinal Foundations of Mormon Polygamy

Mormon plural marriage was the product of the theocratic restructuring of monogamous marriage based upon modern divine revelation.

Knowledge of three key Mormon doctrines and practices is necessary to understand the theological justifications for plural marriage: Direct contemporary revelation from God; the existence of an extensive lay clergy; and the Mormon patriarchal system of eternal family organization.

Joseph Smith (1805–1844) was the first prophet and founder of the Church of Jesus Christ of Latter-day Saints. Persons unacquainted with the Mormon Church often experience difficulty understanding the significance of a living prophet in Latter-day Saint culture. A living prophet acts as an oracle, a conduit for divine revelation. Living prophets are comparable to Moses having returned from Mount Sinai. They receive and expound the very words of God, including new commandments and social orders. Thus, modern revelation carries at least equal weight with ancient revelation, the current living prophet acting in his day as Moses did for the ancient Israelites. In a revelation ascribed to Joseph Smith in 1831, Jesus Christ declared, "What I the Lord have spoken, I have spoken and … my word shall not pass away, but shall all be fulfilled, whether by mine own voice or by the voice of my servants, *it is the same* (Doctrine & Covenants 1:38, emphasis added). Rejection of revelation pronounced by the living prophet in the name of God is for devout Mormons a rejection of Jesus Christ's message. The faith associated with modern revelation cannot be overstated, and the ability of modern revelation to mold the behavior of Mormons must be factored into any discussion of a practice as unique as polygamy.

Mormons claim that Prophets exercise apostolic priesthood authority received from Jesus. Latter-day Saints maintain that this authority was given to Joseph Smith in 1829. They teach that Smith was ordained both to an "Aaronic" (or Levitical) order of priesthood by John the Baptist, and later in the same year to a higher, or "Melchizedek" priesthood order through a visitation from the ancient apostles Peter, James, and John. This priesthood authority was (and is) dispersed through a formal church organization including a Quorum of Twelve Apostles, and an extensive lay clergy that potentially includes all worthy male members over the age of eleven years. Because only males are invested with priesthood authority, the system of church government is fundamentally patriarchal.

Furthermore, priesthood authority extends potentially into most households because nearly every adult male is an ordained priest. Revelations pronounced by the prophet are thus maintained down through the hierarchy of the church and into the household itself. A uniformity of patriarchal religious practice emerges that is unique in modern Christianity, allowing for a comparatively high degree of clerical consensus concerning polygamy that may confound persons unfamiliar with Mormon priesthood organization.[6]

The Mormon doctrine of plural marriage developed in the 1830s and 1840s within this priesthood and patriarchal context. The LDS church, organized in upstate New York on April 6, 1830, soon began to develop unique practices as the result of constant revelations on a wide variety of subjects. Many of these revelations address explicitly the intentional "restoration" of the same ecclesiastical organization as the ancient Christian church under the Apostles. Likewise, revelations re-established doctrines and practices associated with the Old Testament but which were compatible with ancient Christianity. Joseph Smith taught that God directed him to restore true forms of Christianity as instituted by Jesus Christ and the first apostles in order to fulfill the Pauline prophecy "That in the dispensation of the fullness of times he might gather together in one all things in Christ, both which are in heaven, and which are on earth; even in him" (Eph. 1:10). The central question faced by Smith as he organized the new church was exactly which institutions, organizations, doctrines, and practices must be restored or gathered "together in one." In 1831, Smith received revelations correcting certain portions of the Bible that had been textually corrupted, through multiple translations for example, and came across Old Testament passages referring to the numerous wives and concubines of Abraham, Jacob, David, and Solomon, raising the issue of whether or not "plurality of wives" was an ancient practice that should be restored in the Latter-days.

Although Joseph may have formulated the question of plural marriage in his own mind as early as 1831, there was no official revelation pronounced by him on the subject until July 12, 1843, in what is called "Section 132" of the LDS scripture "Doctrine and Covenants" (D&C). The revelation was privately circulated among selected Mormon leaders in Nauvoo, amid rumors that Joseph was practicing "spiritual wifery" in secret, having married other women in addition to his first wife, Emma Hale. It was unclear up to that point whether or not "spiritual wifery" involved sexual contact or was instead an ordinance intended to establish a heavenly order of marriage without its terrestrial "consummation." In fact, he was already married privately to two sisters, Emily and Eliza Partridge, months prior to the public announcement of the revelation. There are reasons to believe that Smith considered himself in an impossible position: He believed that he had received a revelation concerning plural marriage and a commandment to live it, even in private if necessary, but feared public reaction. Emma, having learned about the sealings,[7] whereby one man and, at that time, one or more women were married both for all time and for all eternity, was alternately angered and assuaged by Joseph's entreaties about the divine commandment to marry other women. His brother, Hyrum Smith, was also concerned, and begged Joseph to make the revelation official for the good of the community and of Emma. Pursuant to Hyrum's request, Joseph dictated the revelation.[8]

The doctrinal implications of "sealing" or "celestial marriage" set forth in the revelation were profound, sharply dividing the Mormon community. The revelation, commonly referred to as "Section 132," at a stroke addressed the modern restoration of an old Testament patriarchal marital practice, the continuance of the marital order of the Melchizedek Priesthood into the eternities, unveiled the crowning purpose for Mormon temples, pronounced the eternal endurance of family ties based upon marriages made in Mormon temples as well as the transitory nature of all covenants made outside of the temple. It is no exaggeration to suggest that Section 132 was among the most significant pronouncements made by Joseph Smith, and that no other pronouncement has evoked more religious faith while simultaneously creating a greater trial of faith for Mormons, particularly during the next fifty years. As if anticipating the coming socio-political storm associated with polygamy, the revelation, written in the voice of Jesus Christ, warns, personally to Joseph, but by extension to every Mormon:

> *Prepare thy heart* to receive and obey the instructions which I am about to give
> unto you; for all those who have this law revealed unto them must obey the

same. For behold, I reveal unto you *a new and an everlasting covenant;* and if ye abide not that covenant, then are ye *damned*; for *no one can reject this covenant and be permitted to enter into my glory.*" (D&C 132: 3–4, emphasis added)

From the date of this revelation onward, the "sealing" marriage ordinance performed in Mormon temples is formally referred to as the "new and everlasting covenant of marriage." The revelation further clarified that only one living person holds the priesthood "keys" necessary to govern the performance of sealings (just as Peter was given the "keys" of the kingdom in ancient times to bind—or *seal* together—on earth and in heaven, and to loose on earth and in heaven). It specifically stated that Joseph Smith was anointed to hold the keys of sealing for his day. Sealings were considered to be the same order of marriage known and practiced by ancient and venerated patriarchs like Abraham, Isaac, Jacob, Moses, David, and Solomon, restored in modern times by a living prophet. Its religious implications went far beyond the marital relationship per se:

If ye abide in my covenant [of marriage ... ye] shall pass ... to ... exaltation and glory in all things, which glory shall be a fulness and a continuation of the seeds [i.e., a continuation of children] forever and ever. (D&C 132:19–20)

Thus, marriage made through a temple sealing promised the faithful Mormon not only individual salvation, but a fullness of glory in connection with a literal continuation of families after death and ultimate resurrection. The revelation ends with the statement "verily, verily, I say unto you, I will reveal more unto you, hereafter; therefore, let this suffice for the present. Behold, I am Alpha and Omega. Amen" (D&C 132:66). From the point of view of the faithful Latter-day Saint, to disregard the revelation was to disobey Jesus Christ. Many felt compelled to choose between their faith in Joseph Smith as a living prophet, and their cultural convictions about the propriety of monogamy.

During the next year, which led to the murder of Joseph Smith by a mob in June 1844, the Mormon community was increasingly divided over the issue of plural marriage. As one indication of the coming internal strife, the revelation addressed Emma directly: "Let my

Handmaiden, Emma Smith, receive all those that have been given unto my servant Joseph" (D&C 132:52, 54). Her subsequent recorded remarks about the revelation, particularly after Joseph's death, revealed a near-continual struggle to alternately accept the revelation and then reject it, a struggle common to many other Mormons.[9]

Openly violent opposition to the practice of sealings increased in frequency and ferocity, and in 1847 a sizeable portion of the LDS community began its pilgrimage to the Salt Lake Valley under the leadership of the senior Apostle, Brigham Young. These were pilgrims searching for a safe place where, in the words of a popular Mormon hymn penned during the 1847 exodus to Utah, "none shall come to hurt or make afraid."[10] For many, the privations of the thousand-mile journey validated their perceived right to practice Mormonism, including the right to practice polygamy.

From an LDS perspective, institutionalized polygamy was not the product of cultural evolution (or devolution, as some would have it), it was not principally a matter of political freedom, or the release of sexual repression, or the institutionalization of patriarchal power. It was a matter of faith and commandment. Emmeline Wells, seventh wife of Apostle Daniel H. Wells, and editor of *The Women's Exponent*, restated the deeply religious motivations of many polygamist wives:

> These noble [polygamist] women are like other good, pure, virtuous women, industrially, morally and intellectually. Religiously they are far above them in the graces which elevate and adorn human character. It is no wonder that contemplating these noble-minded women many are let to exclaim, "It is not possible that you are like us, for if you were you could not live in such relationships." ... The women who entered into these sacred covenants of marriage for time and all eternity accepted this holy order as a divine revelation and commandment, and in all sincerity, with the purest motives obeyed the same.[11]

Devout Mormon men shared the same religious motivations. For many practitioners of polygamy, rejection of plural marriage constituted a form of rejection of all faith in living prophets and in Jesus Christ. It should come as no surprise that non-Mormon scholars have difficulty accurately identifying the factors that prompted Mormons to practice plural marriage so long as their studies were based upon the premise that religious faith alone was not sufficient motivation.

Polygamy in Utah (1847–1910)

The history of polygamy in Utah is a subject that has received considerable treatment by a number of prominent scholars.[12] The essential theme is that public opposition to polygamy did not end with the Mormon exodus to Utah but was transformed into an issue of national import. Powerful national attacks on polygamy eventually forced Mormons to either seek additional revelation regarding the continued practice of polygamy or fight the insistent military and legal might of the United States. From the Mormon perspective, the local persecutions and mob violence endured in Ohio and Missouri in the 1830s and in Illinois in the 1840s were merely a prelude to a subsequent national design to end the religion altogether. In light of the federal government's determination to end polygamy, the remainder of the essay attempts to answer the question: Because polygamy was primarily practiced in consequence of deep religious conviction, how could Mormons bring themselves to eventually abandon it without renouncing their faith?

The issue of Mormon polygamy became one of national import immediately after Brigham Young and a few hundred Mormons arrived in the Salt Lake Valley in 1847. At that time, the region was officially part of Mexico, although under the effective control of the United States. Having already organized Mormon volunteers for the Mexican War—the famous "Mormon Battalion"—Young was aware that the territory probably would not long remain Mexican. Young and other Church leaders proposed to Congress the creation of the "State of Deseret," and began drafting a constitution to that effect in December 1848. Concurrent with the petition for admission to the Union, Brigham Young was selected as the governor of the proposed state, and the selection was later approved by President Millard Fillmore. The draft constitution included a bill of rights with strongly worded guarantees regarding the freedom of religious practice, particularly aimed at securing the right to practice plural marriage. Eventually, congressional debate over the proposed state and the issue of Mormon polygamy was joined with debate over the issue of Southern slavery within the context of the Kansas-Nebraska Act of 1854. The official pronouncement regarding the open practice of polygamy in 1852 joined the issues of slavery and polygamy together in Congress. By 1856, the Republican party cemented the debate in place by adding a platform plank calling for the termination of the "twin relics of barbarism," namely, slavery and Mormon polygamy. Democrats, seeking to keep the issues of slavery and polygamy separate, distanced themselves from the Mormons, although they opposed anti-polygamy legislative proposals insofar as they were viewed as supporting a subsequent attack on slavery. Stephen Douglas, so strong a supporter of popular sovereignty that one would have thought him a natural supporter of the Mormon right to practice polygamy should it represent the popular will, responded by declaring Mormons "subversive aliens who recognized Brigham Young and the government of which he is the head above that of the United States … [prosecuting] a system of robbery and murders upon American citizens."[13] Although his comments were wholly unsupported by fact (most Mormons were in fact U.S. citizens, and there was no evidence of systemic murder and robbery), such rhetoric, combined with the "twin relics" position of the Republicans, inaugurated a prolonged confrontation between the Church and the United States government.

Beginning in the early 1850s, the federal government dispatched territorial agents to the Utah in response to the request for statehood and appointment of a governor. The agents returned speculative and, at times, wildly inaccurate reports to Washington about Mormons in general and polygamy in particular. This prompted the dispatch of an army of several thousand troops under the command of Albert Sydney Johnston to Utah in 1857, beginning the "Utah War." Young mobilized a guerilla force which harassed, albeit without bloodshed, the troops as they advanced across what is now part of Wyoming. Johnston discerned that there was no nascent Mormon rebellion, and based upon an understanding negotiated with Brigham Young, elected not to provoke a confrontation by camping the army about 40 miles to the south, establishing Camp Floyd. Due to the commencement of the American Civil War, the army was recalled. Johnston's regulars were replaced by "Patrick O'Connor's California Volunteers" in 1862. The Mormons and the troops soon learned to co-exist, although the obvious potential for military action at the president's order did not pass unnoticed. Mormons were placed on notice that the federal government intended to have its way in the coming years.

The Morrill Act of 1862 was the first serious legal attack on Mormon polygamy. The provisions of the act made bigamy a territorial crime, punishable by five years' imprisonment and a fine. Although the act addressed bigamy generically, it was designed to end Mormon polygamy. The law was difficult to enforce because evidence of a second "marriage" was almost impossible to secure. Mormon polygamists did not bother to register for plural marriages, considered invalid under any condition, nor was registration required by law until the 1880s. One prosecution, however, produced the first and one of the most famous decisions of the U.S. Supreme Court on the subject of the First Amendment and the free exercise of religion. George Reynolds, husband to two wives, was convicted in 1875 of bigamy under the Morrill Act, although he was able to vacate the conviction on procedural grounds. He was subsequently re-tried, convicted, and sentenced to two years in prison and a fine of $500. Reynolds appealed the conviction to the U.S. Supreme Court on the grounds that the Morrill Act violated the free exercise guarantees of the First Amendment, "Congress shall make no law … prohibiting the free exercise [of religion]." The Court concluded that there existed a critical difference between religious belief and religiously motivated action. The opinion held that "Congress was deprived of all … power over mere opinion, but was left free to react to actions which were in violation of social duty or subversive of good order" (98 U.S. 164).[14] The Reynolds Court did not rely upon empirical evidence in reaching its conclusions. Instead, the unproven theories of "Professor [Francis] Lieber" were all the evidence necessary to demonstrate the social evil called polygamy.[15] The court advanced incredible hypothetical examples—such as a religion that required human sacrifice—clearly in conflict with other constitutionally protected rights, including the due process provisions of the Fifth and Fourteenth Amendments. All this legal activity clearly demonstrated that while the government was not particularly concerned with defining social duty associated with marriage, or with the preservation of good order through monogamy, there was a clear intention to abolish Mormon polygamy.

Congress moved to exercise direct political control over the Utah Territory through a series of acts passed between 1874 and 1887. The Poland Act of 1874 removed criminal proceedings, which included bigamy trials, from local courts to federally controlled courts. The Edmunds Act of 1882 attacked the civil rights of polygamists, prohibiting them from voting or from holding public office. Finally, the Edmunds-Tucker Act of 1887 covered a broad range of anti-polygamy measures, requiring an anti-polygamy oath as a prerequisite to voting and for holding public office, disbanded the territorial militia, disenfranchised women in the Utah Territory, dissolved the Corporation of the Church of Jesus Christ of Latter-day Saints, seized a sizeable amount of Church-owned property, took control of public education, and dissolved the Church's "Perpetual Emigrating Fund" which was designed to assist Mormon converts abroad to pay the expense of relocating to Utah. Although the Supreme Court upheld the Morrill Act as a permissible regulation of religious action rather than religious belief, the Edmunds Act and the Edmunds-Tucker Act contained provisions aimed directly at religious belief. Their common purpose was more than the mere extinction of polygamy; it included the extinction of the Church itself. The actual confiscation of Church property was upheld by the U.S. Supreme Court in *The Church of Jesus Christ of Latter-day Saints v. United States* (136 U.S. 1, 1890).

The events referred to simply as "The Raid" took place within this military and legal milieu, which included the confiscations and chilling of civil rights already mentioned. Additionally, federal law enforcement began the wholesale arrest and imprisonment of Mormon priestly leadership. Over 1,000 Mormon males were imprisoned in the Utah Territorial Penitentiary between 1884–95.[16] Most were charged with "UC," formally called "Unlawful Cohabitation." It is not inconceivable that at least two thousand marriages were thus sundered, and many thousands of children left without fiscal support. Many Mormons unsurprisingly considered the anti-polygamy "crusade" hypocritical. Eliza R. Snow, former wife of Joseph Smith, and later wife of Brigham

Young, spoke at an "indignation rally" of about 1,500 women in Salt Lake City, aiming her remarks at the vices Mormons perceived among the members of Congress: "I truly believe that a congress composed of polygamic men who are true to their wives ... would perform better service to this country than a congress composed of monogamic unreliable husbands."[17] Although her comments came on January 13, 1870, and were aimed at post-Morrill Act hypocrisies, these same sentiments were repeatedly directed at the Edmunds Act because enforcement of its UC provisions targeted Mormon polygamists exclusively, even though the provisions applied with equal force to prostitution (a habit frequently indulged in by the officers and judges charged with enforcement of the Edmunds Act, as polygamists were quick to point out). The government contention that the Edmunds Act was intended to improve the moral climate generally didn't hold in light of such hypocrisies.

Instead of encouraging the abandonment of polygamy, the imprisonments hardened Mormon resolve. One of the most famous, and obdurate, "UC" inmates, Rudger Clawson, reemphasized that the practice of polygamy was considered a matter of the deepest religious devotion for Mormons, when he addressed the judge at his sentencing on November 3, 1884:

> I regret very much that the laws of my country come in conflict with the laws
> of my God, but whenever they do, I shall invariably choose to obey the latter. If
> I did not so express myself, I should feel unworthy of the cause I represent.[18]

In addition to the arrests and convictions mentioned, Church President John Taylor, Brigham Young's successor, moved from place to place in order to evade arrest. Mormons and federals were now engaged in an increasingly desperate struggle, one believing that faith and integrity to the U.S. Constitution was at stake, the other that their faith in God and eternal exaltation lay in the balance. There seemed little hope for a peaceable resolve at the close of the 1880s.

Realizing that the Church was in increasingly desperate straits, President Wilford Woodruff, Taylor's successor, sought and received a revelation on the matter of practicing polygamy, referred to as the

"Manifesto of 1890." This Manifesto contained a declaration of President Woodruff's intention to submit to anti-polygamy laws and to use his influence to induce Church members to do the same: "I hereby declare my intention to submit to those laws … and I now publicly declare that my advice to the Latter-day Saints is to refrain from contracting any marriage forbidden by the law of the land" (Doctrine and Covenants: Official Declaration 1, adopted October 6, 1890). Woodruff addressed the Church membership in 1891 and in 1893, explaining the circumstances under which he elected to write the Manifesto of 1890, describing the revelation he received:

> The Lord showed me by vision and revelation exactly what would take place if we did not stop this practice…all the [temple sealing] ordinances would have stopped throughout the land of Zion. Confusion would reign throughout Israel. … and we would have been compelled [by the federal government] to stop the practice. Now, the question is, whether it should be stopped in this manner, or in the way the Lord has manifested to us … when the hour came that I was commanded to [write the Manifesto of 1890], it was all clear to me. I went before the Lord, and wrote what the Lord told me to write.[19]

This declaration resulted in deep concern on the part of Mormons, many of whom had suffered imprisonment or other privations for the cause of polygamy as an act of religious devotion. President Woodruff's speeches assuaged some but failed to convince others. Now, polygamists were being commanded to abandon the practice for the same reasons that they had adopted it: As a matter of faith. When the closing sentences of Section 132 provided that The Alpha and Omega "will reveal more to you hereafter," most Latter-day Saints probably did not anticipate subsequent revelation to take the form of an instruction to *stop* practicing plural marriage (D&C 132:66).

Although President Woodruff "advised" the Saints to "refrain from contracting any marriage forbidden by the law of the land," clandestine plural marriages were still being solemnized after 1890. President Woodruff did possess the "keys" governing the sealing ordinance, but those keys were shared with all the members of the Quorum of the Twelve Apostles, some of whom resided outside of the United States. President Woodruff had publicly declared his own intention not to contract plural marriages and had publicly discouraged the Saints from so doing, but the practice did in fact continue.[20] For example, some Mormons believed that the Manifesto was limited only to marriages made within the United States, and saw no reason why plural marriages would not be made in Mormon colonies in Alberta, Canada, or Juarez, Mexico, countries that either had no anti-polygamy laws, or where polygamy could be practiced beyond the effective reach of law enforcement. Others considered the Manifesto a temporary measure, allaying the concerns of the federals until such time as the practice could be lawfully resumed.

Rumors in Washington that new plural marriages were being affected persisted over the next decade, continuing through Utah's statehood (1896) and into the early 1900s. Prominent Mormon Reed Smoot was elected to the U.S. Senate but met with immediate opposition to being "seated" as a full member. A series of hearings followed in 1904, at which President Joseph F. Smith, Woodruff's successor, denied under oath that new and additional plural marriages were taking place. When he later discovered that the accuracy of his statements had been compromised, he issued a second statement, the "Manifesto of 1904," which declared in the complete prohibition of polygamy throughout the church and made offenders subject to official discipline, including excommunication.[21]

It was now the Church's turn to test the loyalty of its leaders to the declarations of Presidents Woodruff and Smith as adopted as the official doctrine of the Church. Two apostles residing in Canada, Mathias Cowley and John W. Taylor, tendered resignations from the Quorum of the Twelve Apostles, rather than travel to Washington and testify in the Smoot Hearings, and the resignations were accepted in 1906. Smoot was finally seated in the Senate, where he served for nearly 30 years. The matter was not, however, put to rest. Taylor and Cowley apparently continued, in their apostolic capacities, to perform plural marriages outside of United States territory. Both were eventually summoned to appear before the president of the Church as insubordinates. Taylor did not appear, and was subsequently excommunicated. Cowley did appear, disavowed polygamy and stated unequivocally his support for the position of the Church against the practice of polygamy, avoided excommunication but was not reinstated as an apostle (although his son, Matthew Cowley did serve later as an Apostle).[22] Even as the adoption of polygamy was considered a test of faith, so its discontinuance proved the believer's commitment to core LDS doctrines, particularly the doctrine of living prophets and modern revelation.

Polygamy Since 1910

From 1910 onward, the Church of Jesus Christ of Latter-day Saints not only officially but effectively abandoned the practice of polygamy, enforcing its position until the present through prompt excommunication of any member that enters into plural marriage or even advocates its practice. Several Mormons have resisted this policy and have formed their own church organizations. Referred to by historians of Mormonism as "fundamentalists," they thus have perpetuated the practice of polygamy, declaring it a matter of religious conviction. One noteworthy group has established a "colony" in Short Creek (now Colorado City), Arizona. Determined to root out the remnants of polygamy in America, law enforcement officials in Arizona and Utah cooperated in conduction of the "Short Creek Raids" in the 1940s. Polygamous husbands went to jail, and perhaps hundreds of children were separated from mothers and placed in foster homes. Eventually realizing that this response created more problems than it solved, many families were eventually reunited, and parents obeyed the anti-polygamy law ... for a time. Other fundamentalist groups became increasingly violent as rival claimants to "prophethood" resorted to gangster tactics to enforce their power. In a notable example, Rulon Allred, his brothers, and Joseph Musser formed their own church called the United Apostolic Brethren, while a former associate, Ervil LeBaron headed the Church of the Lamb of God. The divisive split between the groups came to a head in 1976, when Rulon Allred was murdered in his office by two of LeBaron's plural wives.[23] At present, polygamy continues to be practiced semi-clandestinely by fundamentalists in Utah, Arizona, and elsewhere outside the United States, although not by members of the Mormon church. As recently as July 23, 1998, Utah governor Mike Leavitt essentially admitted that anti-polygamy laws are not being actively enforced in Utah.[24] Focusing instead on what he termed "civil rights violations," some of which may be considered more likely in fundamentalist polygamist environments, the governor's position was seen by some as a realization that separating families of polygamists creates problems for children and women that cannot be resolved effectively by state social services agencies. This probably will not change in the foreseeable future. Small-scale polygamy will continue as long as fundamentalists are committed to its practice.

Conclusion

Mormon polygamy was not the manifestation of cultural evolution or devolution, a problematic appendage to women's suffrage movements, or the institutionalization of unmanageable male libido. From the Mormon perspective, the doctrine underlying its practice was unsolicited, but once revealed in Section 132, it was practiced by about one-fifth of the nineteenth-century Utah Mormon population in spite of the practical difficulties it posed, and in spite of personal qualms about its propriety. It was practiced primarily as a matter of faith. When the time came to abandon the practice, the overwhelming majority of Mormons made what they considered a significant sacrifice of faith in order to obey those persons they considered living oracles of God. The very small minority that persisted in practicing polygamy were excommunicated from the Church of Jesus Christ of Latter-day Saints. The difficulties in prosecuting polygamy reveal the limits of the state in eliminating completely what is still considered an issue of deep religious conviction.

Notes

[1] Technically, the term here is "polygyny." Mormons also referred to the practice as "plural marriage" or "plurality of wives." The Church of Jesus Christ of Latter-day Saints is popularly referred to as the Mormon Church, but also as the "LDS Church," a reference that interested researchers are likely to encounter.

[2] Andrea G. Radke, a Mormon scholar of women's history, categorically rejected such motivations in clear terms: Much to the disappointment of observers then and today,

"Contrary to popular nineteenth century notions about polygamy, the Mormon harem, dominated by lascivious males with hyperactive libidos, did not exist." Andrea G. Radke, "The Place of Mormon Women: Perceptions, Prozac, Polygamy, Priesthood, Patriarchy, and Peace," paper presented at the Foundation for Apologetic Information and Research Conference, August 2004, 20, citing also Richard van Wagoner, *Mormon Polygamy: A History* (Salt Lake City: Signature Books, 1986), 81. Van Wagoner's monograph is considered the standard historical narrative on Mormon polygamy. Another excellent study is Kathryn Daynes, *More Wives Than One: Transformation of the Mormon Marriage System, 1840–1910* (Urbana and Chicago: University of Illinois Press, 2001).

[3] Mary Ryan, "Proto-feminism or Victims of Patriarchy: Two Interpretations of Mormon Polygyny," *Feminist Studies*, 10 (1984), 470.

[4] See Raymond Lee Muncy, *Sex and Marriage in Utopian Communities* (Bloomington: Indiana University Press, 1973) and Lawrence Foster, *Between Two Worlds: The Origins of Shaker Celibacy, Oneida Community Complex Marriage, and Mormon Polygamy* (Ph.D. Dissertation, University of Chicago, 1976). Both authors performed excellent research in the quest to uncover a cultural source for the emergence of Mormon polygamy but failed to provide a cultural explanation for its emergence, or more significantly, for willing participation. This avenue of research has been effectively abandoned.

[5] Joan Iverson, "Feminist implications of Mormon Polygyny," *Feminist Studies*, 10 (1984), 504–24.

[6] The term "patriarchal" is stereotypically equated with "male domination" or "oppression" in the popular mind. The reader should be aware that modern Mormon revelation strongly cautions priesthood holders against such tyranny. In fact, it is grounds for excommunication from the Church: "No power or influence can or ought to be maintained by virtue of the priesthood, only by persuasion, by long-suffering, by gentleness and meekness, and by love unfeigned; By kindness, and pure knowledge, which shall greatly enlarge the soul without hypocrisy, and without guile…" (D&C 121:41–42).

[7] The term "sealing" refers to the performance of the ordinances connected with the "new and everlasting covenant of marriage," consummated in LDS temples only. A sealing could only be performed by an LDS prophet, apostle, or other Melchizedek priesthood holder specifically ordained to that authority by a prophet or apostle. Mormon men could not simply take on an additional wife without the involvement and supervision of these priesthood leaders.

[8] The entire revelation, complete with LDS cross-references to other scriptures is available online at http://scriptures.lds.org/dc/132.

[9] Van Wagoner, 50–59, 72–78.

[10] William Clayton, "Come, Come Ye Saints," *Hymns of the Church of Jesus Christ of Latter-day Saints* (Salt Lake City, Utah: Deseret Book Company, 1985), 30. Clayton wrote the hymn while participating in the first Mormon expedition to the Salt Lake Valley in the summer of 1847.

[11] Emmeline B. Wells, "Is It Ignorance?" *The Women's Exponent* (July 1, 1883).

[12] See Van Wagoner's book and the *Encyclopedia of Mormonism*, Daniel H. Ludlow, ed. (New York: Macmillan Publishing Company, 1992) are highly accessible sources. For a review of sources up to 1977 see David Bitton, "Mormon Polygamy: A Review Article," *Journal of Mormon History*, 4 (1977), 101–18.

[13] "Politics: Political History," *Encyclopedia of Mormonism*, 1100–01.

[14] "Reynolds v. United States," *Encyclopedia of Mormonism*, 1229–30; van Wagoner, 200–22. The holding was modified in 1940, and religious activity was brought under the protection of the First Amendment in *Cantwell v. Connecticut*, 310 U.S. 296. An excellent study of the Reynolds case is found in John David Pulsipher, *The Americanization of Monogamy: Mormons, Native Americans and the Nineteenth-Century Perception That Polygamy was a Threat to Democracy* (Ph.D. dissertation, University of Minnesota, 1999).

[15] The opinion of Chief Justice Waite states "Professor Lieber says, polygamy leads to the patriarchal principle, and which, when applied to large communities, fetters the people in stationary despotism, while that principle cannot long exist in connection with monogamy." The Professor's dictums were taken as entirely dispositive, ignoring the fact the Mormon polygamy was a novelty whose societal consequences were unknown and unpredictable.

[16] Evans, 209–31.

[17] Janet Peterson and Larens Gaunt, *Elect Ladies* (Salt Lake City: Deseret Book, 1990), 38; John Henry Evans, *Joseph Smith: An American Prophet* (New York: Macmillan Company, 1933), 275.

[18] Larson, 41.

[19] Wilford Woodruff, "Excerpts from Three Addresses by President Wilford Woodruff Regarding the Manifesto," *The Doctrine and Covenants of the Church of Jesus Christ of Latter-day Saints containing the Revelations given to Joseph Smith, The Prophet with Some Additions by His Successors in the Presidency of the Church* (Salt Lake City: The Church of Jesus Christ of Latter-day Saints, 1985), 292–93.

[20] "Manifesto of 1890," *Encyclopedia of Mormonism*, 852–53; van Wagoner, 150–54.

[21] Van Wagoner, 170–74.

[22] Van Wagoner, 186–89.

[23] One of the wives, Rena Chynoweth, revealed details of the murder in her memoirs. Rena Chynoweth, *Blood Covenant* (New York: Diamond Books, 1990).

[24] Mike Carter, Utah Governor, cited in "Mike Leavitt in Political Minefield," *Associated Press*, August 2, 1998.

Bibliography

Bitton, David. "Mormon Polygamy: A Review Article." *Journal of Mormon History.* 4 (1977), 101–18.

Carter, Mike. "Mike Leavitt in Political Minefield," *Associated Press*, August 2, 1998.

Chynoweth, Rena. *Blood Covenant.* New York: Diamond Books, 1990.

Clayton, William. "Come, Come Ye Saints." *Hymns of the Church of Jesus Christ of*

Latter-day Saints. Salt Lake City, Utah: Deseret Book Company, 1985.

Daynes, Kathryn. *More Wives Than One: Transformation of the Mormon Marriage System, 1840–1910.* Urbana and Chicago: University of Illinois Press, 2001.

Evans, John Henry. *Joseph Smith: An American Prophet.* New York: Macmillan Company, 1933.

Foster, Lawrence. *Between Two Worlds: The Origins of Shaker Celibacy, Oneida Community Complex Marriage, and Mormon Polygamy.* Ph.D. Dissertation, University of Chicago, 1976.

Iverson, Joan. "Feminist Implications of Mormon Polygyny." *Feminist Studies.* 10 (1984), 504–24.

Ludlow, Daniel H., editor. *Encyclopedia of Mormonism.* New York: Macmillan Publishing Company, 1992.

Muncy, Raymond Lee. *Sex and Marriage in Utopian Communities.* Bloomington: Indiana University Press, 1973.

Peterson, Janet, and Larens Gaunt. *Elect Ladies.* Salt Lake City: Deseret Book, 1990.

Pulsipher, John David. *The Americanization of Monogamy: Mormons, Native Americans and the Nineteenth-Century Perception that Polygamy was a Threat to Democracy.* Ph.D. Dissertation, University of Minnesota, 1999.

Radke, Andrea G. "The Place of Mormon Women: Perceptions, Prozac, Polygamy, Priesthood, Patriarchy, and Peace." Paper presented at the Foundation for Apologetic Information and Research Conference. August 2004.

Ryan, Mary. "Proto-feminism or Victims of Patriarchy: Two Interpretations of Mormon Polygyny," *Feminist Studies.* 10 (1984), 470–504.

van Wagoner, Richard. *Mormon Polygamy: A History.* Salt Lake City: Signature Books, 1986.

Wells, Emmeline B. "Is It Ignorance?" *The Women's Exponent.* July 1, 1883.

Woodruff, Wilford. "Excerpts from Three Addresses by President Wilford Woodruff Regarding the Manifesto." *The Doctrine and Covenants of the Church of Jesus Christ of Latter-day Saints Containing the Revelations given to Joseph Smith, The Prophet with Some Additions by His Successors in the Presidency of the Church.* Salt Lake City: the Church of Jesus Christ of Latter-day Saints, 1985.

*　I wish to thank Dr. John David Pulsipher for commenting upon his essay, *The Americanization of Monogamy,* prior to its publication.

5 The Oppressed Self: Desire, Sexuality, and Religious Cinema

Douglas MacLeod

In the 1997 film, *Shakespeare in Love*, a character by the name of Makepeace the Preacher spouts anti-entertainment rhetoric from his doorframe. Later in the film, he does so from the front of the Curtain Theater, where young Shakespeare's *Romeo and Juliet* is going to make its theatrical debut:

> Theaters are handmaidens of the devil. The players breed lewdness in your wives and wickedness in your children. And a rose smells thusly rank by any name! I say, a plague on both their houses.

> Licentiousness is made a show! Vice is made a show! Vanity and pride likewise made a show! This is the very business of show!

In the latter scene, Makepeace is swept away by the determined and excited crowd and placed in the theater, a building that he equates to a den of inequity. *Romeo and Juliet*, a play that exudes pure and unadulterated desire, is then performed with great intensity and is followed by thunderous applause. In a brief but unforgettable shot, Makepeace the Preacher, in the midst of the now boisterous crowd, is seen in tears and applauding the players. It is as if he has finally realized that the theater can, in fact, portray true love and desire. Although seemingly insignificant to *Shakespeare in Love*, a romantic comedy about the great Bard and his secret lover, the scenes with Makepeace are quite important inasmuch as they say something about how religious figures are often represented on-screen. They are human beings who experience internal conflicts with sexuality, demons that must be warded off but cannot be. As media specialist Teresa Blythe suggests, it is the "titillating 'Oh, my!' reaction that filmmakers look for," and "the clergyperson indeed might be prone to the kind of emotional highs and lows that make for visual interest in films."[1]

This chapter features themes of sexuality and sexual desire, and how they are used in films about members of the clergy and other religious figures. Considering specific cinematic texts, both American and foreign, we will attempt to show how contemporary religious figures are in constant conflict with their sexual self for conflict's sake and for the sake of a captivated viewing—and participating—audience.

Repressed Sexuality?

When speaking of fictionalized sexual conflict in the movies, many assume that much of the inhibition a religious figure has in regard to feelings of desire is caused by repression. David G. Myers defines repression as "the basic defense mechanism that banishes anxiety-arousing thoughts, feelings, and memories from consciousness."[2] In other words, repression is a way of warding off problematic situations that originate, and are hidden from, within; it is a conflict what one desires and what one believes cannot be fulfilled. Repression is what Sigmund Freud calls a way of avoiding "conflict with the id."[3] For example, in the 1991 film, *Defending Your Life,* Daniel Miller finds himself in a limbo state somewhere between life and death, with the only way to move to Heaven being a successful courtroom defense of his own life. Daniel must prove that his life was worth something to two steadfast judges, a menacing prosecutor, and Bob Diamond, Daniel's hapless defense attorney. More importantly, he must prove that he was unafraid of accomplishing the goals he sought out for himself. In a series of scenes, the audience is privy to both great acts of courage as well as moments of great fear and loathing in Daniel's life. His earthly existence is filled with anxieties, frustrations, and fear that eventually hinder his movement forward to a more heavenly existence. These scenes, presented to Daniel in several moments of reflexive genius, are wrought with repressed desire, things that Daniel wishes he could have done but did not do such as speak in front of a large crowd or tell his new employer that he wanted to start with a higher salary or sleep with his newest friend in Judgment City, Julia. It is his inability to go to Julia's room that seals Daniel's fate, leaving him at the hands of his two unsympathetic judges. Daniel represses his desire for Julia due to his fears of failure, rejection, and judgment, thus giving his judges no other choice but to vote against Daniel's acceptance to Heaven, whereas Julia is quickly accepted. He must go back to Earth and try again, a fate that is later recanted when Daniel triumphs over his repressed desire for Julia and jumps from his bus to be with her for all eternity.

Despite its comic elements, *Defending Your Life* can be considered a religious film because it contains many motifs usually associated with various religious beliefs, i.e., judgment, purgatory, angels, heaven, reincarnation, and so on. However, this film differs from other religious cinematic texts in that it perpetuates the notion that repression is the reason why religious figures suppress their desires. In this respect, they, albeit unintentionally, mislead audience members into believing that this takes place in all religious cinematic texts. *Defending Your Life* stands out among other religious texts because it takes a different approach toward sexuality and desire.

Feelings of desire are usually created when religious figures or icons in religious cinematic texts are both obligated to their beliefs as well as oppressed by them. What we mean by this is that the sexual desire, or the desire for a love-bound relationship, is hindered not by repression but by the oppressive forces of Christianity or Judaism, religious forces that are considered oppressive by much of the cinematic community. Repression is something that comes from within; it is a conflict with one's self about what one wants or desires. Oppression, on the other hand, comes not only from the self but from an outside entity; the person knows what he or she wants but cannot have it due to societal or religious obligations. Although recognized in a different context, Paulo Freire calls this a "prescription" that "represents the imposition of one individual's choice upon another, transforming the consciousness of the person prescribed to into that which conforms with the prescriber's consciousness."[4] Thus, the conflict is not solely perpetuated from within but from the outside world, "following as it does the guidelines of the oppressor,"[5] which makes the situation all the more frustrating and debilitating. With repression, one has to wrestle with oneself where the rules can be played with or manipulated and one's desire can (or may not) be fulfilled to one's own satisfaction. With oppression, the rules cannot be broken, and hence one's desires, sexual or otherwise, cannot be fulfilled. If their desires are fulfilled, then one's beliefs and obligations are no longer considered truthful or committed, and one gets shunned from the particular community that abides by those rules, whoever or whatever they may be. Freire states:

> The oppressed suffer from the duality which has established itself in their innermost being. They discover that without freedom they cannot exist authentically. Yet, although they desire authentic existence, they fear it. They are at one and the same time themselves and the oppressor whose consciousness they have internalized. The conflict lies in the choice between ejecting the oppressor within or not ejecting them; between human solidarity or alienation; between following prescriptions or having choices […][6]

As Freire's ideological standpoint toward oppression—a standpoint that is associated with pedagogy—pertains to religious-based cinematic texts, the oppressive entity or oppressor is religion itself, and the oppressed person or entity is usually completely obligated to his or her own faith. Indeed, it is that faith, whatever it may be, along with its obligated/oppressed follower, that brings about the necessary conflicts.

> Sometimes I'm fed up with my spiritual existence. Instead of forever hovering above, I'd like to feel a weight grow in me, to end the infinity and to tie me to earth. I'd like, at each step, at each gust of wind, to be able to say "now!" "Now and now" and no "forever" and "for eternity." … No, I don't have to beget a child or plant a tree but it would be rather nice coming home after a long day, to feed the cat, like Philip Marlowe, to have a fever, and blackened fingers from the newspaper, to be excited not only by the mind but, at last, by a meal … by the line of a neck … by an ear. To lie! Through one's teeth! As you're walking, to feel your bones moving along. At last to guess, instead of always knowing … to be able to say "ah" and "oh" and "hey" instead of "yea" and "amen."[7]

One of Germany's more memorable post-World War II filmic texts is the 1988 Wim Wenders classic, *Wings of Desire*. Damiel and Cassiel are guardian angels on Earth attempting to provide solace to an angst-ridden German population ravaged by political division and moral anxieties. Wearing black overcoats and sporting small ponytails, they fly over the German countryside traveling through closed windows, moving car doors and even the Berlin Wall (an impossibility for German mortals prior to the Wall's destruction in 1989), listening to the thoughts of anyone with whom they come into contact. Damiel and Cassiel look at the world in black and white; they do not have the ability to see in color. They never truly experience the physical world; they seem to only have a distinct *desire* to experience it.

The monologue above is proof that the guardian angel in Wenders's (and writer, Peter Handke's) imagination has a definite "need" for physical contact, especially that of Damiel who recites the speech with passion and longing. While he and Cassiel sit in a car dealership and talk about the events of the day, Damiel gets distracted by two lovers kissing, pointing at them with childish glee and fascination. He longs to be the kisser or the one kissed. However, Damiel cannot be either; he is thoroughly oppressed by his angelic way of life. He desires to have, as Freire puts it, an "authentic existence" filled with love and physically passionate relationships but is unable to because of his Heavenly existence.

Damiel's desire becomes enflamed later in the film when he sees, for the first time, Marion (played by Solveig Dommartin), a trapeze artist wearing angel's wings high above the big top. She is, to Damiel, a vision of beauty and an object for infatuation. He even goes as far as to follow Marion into her dressing room/trailer to watch her. As she takes off her clothing, Damiel takes his finger and traces the line of her neck, her shoulder and the top of her arm with his inauthentic fingers. She can feel his presence, but cannot see him. Damiel's desire is strong, but the only way he can connect with her is by listening to her thoughts and, later, by entering her dreams where he grabs her hand and makes himself known to her. His oppression is absolutely physical. Although he is seemingly free because of his angelic abilities, he is instead very much oppressed by his situation. It is because of his inability to be seen and to be caressed that he cannot be with the woman he loves.

This point is later reiterated in a dance sequence where Marion is seductively moving to the music of an underground band in what is now the torn down Esplanade ballroom in Berlin. Damiel stands next to her, barely moving as she moves, and lifting his hands to grab hers in a futile gesture of pure agonizing desire. Once again, she can only feel his presence. It is understood that Damiel would do just about anything to be with this woman, even give up his status as a guardian angel; he would become a fallen angel and turn away from his heavenly existence just to be with this woman for all eternity.

Finally, Damiel gets his wish when his desire to become a mortal grows so strong that nothing can stop him, not even his being oppressed by Heaven above. He is placed on earth by his good friend Cassiel and is able to finally see the world in color. He is no longer oppressed by his angelic status, the almost disembodied thoughts of the German people he guards or by his lack of flesh, blood, and bone. Damiel's desire can now be fulfilled and finally is, at the end of the film, where he gets together with Marion at the Esplanade, the ballroom where they had their first dance. The conflict is now over. Satisfaction for Damiel, and for the audience, can now set in.

The satisfaction that transpires while watching *Wings of Desire* is only fleeting in the American version of the Wim Wenders masterpiece entitled *City of Angels* (Warner Brothers, 1998). This second version, directed by Brad Silberling, takes place in the over-crowded city of Los Angeles, California. Rather than barren streets, Los Angeles is a hubbub of activity. Rather than sitting on a large angel that hovers above the center of Berlin, the guardian angels sit on a freeway sign, closer to the noise that surrounds them and the seemingly superficial people below. Rather than mortals thinking in poetic prose about their humble existence, they think about sex, money, sex, whether they left the iron on and sex. Rather than them spending most of their time in the library, the guardian angels look out into the ocean, pleased more by the aesthetics of Earthly existence than by what may be lying beneath that type of existence. In *City of Angels* both the mortal and the eternal are the same—seeing only the surface, not realizing that life has more to offer, that everyone has the power of free will and is able to use that power at any time.

Seth (played by Nicolas Cage) sees the world differently and knows that there is more than just visual pleasure sustaining us and his celestial race; that living a life of immortality, or being human, means more than just viewing life as it continues to pass us by. He, however, also believes that he does not have the power of free will and feels oppressed by the

God who gave him a life without death. Like Damiel in *Wings of Desire*, Seth cannot see in color, feel, taste or experience mortality. But his desire to do so is strong, especially after seeing Doctor Maggie Rice (played by Meg Ryan) as she tries to save the life of a patient who eventually dies while on her operating table. He envies her, desires to be like her, wants her, needs her, desires to be with her, is in love with her. These emotions are expressed only by the way he looks at her. Like Damiel, Seth watches her undress, longs for her from afar, stays with her when she needs comforting and gives her the ability to move on after not being able to save her dying patient.

Unlike Damiel, however, Seth cannot only be seen in dreams. Seth can be seen if he wants to be seen; he can take human form and is able to touch. His oppression is not as physical as Damiel's, even though his ability to touch can only go as far as the act itself. In other words, he cannot feel what he is touching, thus making *City of Angels* even more frustrating than the original. Seth is able to kiss Maggie, touch Maggie's face, even caress Maggie's hand, but it is all in vain. It is not until Seth meets Nathaniel Messenger (played by Dennis Franz), a construction worker with a heart problem and taken care of by Maggie, that Seth understands angels can fall from eternity if they wish; that angels can give up their wings because they too have the free will to do so. Messenger recognizes that Seth "has no fear, no pain, no hunger" and that he "hears music in the sunrise," but, because of Seth's desire, he would give it all up for Maggie like he did for his wife and the possibility of having a family (a possibility that eventually took place).

Seth, later in the film, comes to terms with himself when he realizes that the oppression he feels comes only from within; that his love for Maggie is neither repressed nor oppressed by the God who created him, but that his feelings of obligation to God are his own. With this insight, he takes a literal leap of faith and becomes a man, flesh and blood. He hitches a ride to Lake Tahoe where Maggie is staying to get away from the world … a world filled with a man whom she does not love, an angel she loves with all of her heart, and a past experience with a dying patient that also allows her to see more than just the surface of life. Then, while bruised and battered, Seth knocks on her closed door. Maggie lets him into her home and they make love in front of a crackling fireplace. Their sexual encounter is much more explicit than in the original version of the film, filled with light kissing, sweet caressing and verbal affirmations that he can, in fact, feel what she is doing to him. The audience is made privy to the sexual fulfillment of Seth's desire and feels somewhat relieved because of it.

City of Angels, though, only satisfies the audience's need for the fulfillment of desire for a short time. While riding her bicycle, feeling the wind at her fingertips and thinking about the future, Maggie careens into a log truck and dies in the arms of the man who emotionally saved her. The audience participates in these two individuals' experience, both the fulfillment of desire and its being oppressed again by the lack of the physical. Seth does go on to experience mortal life—as is clear at the end of the film when he jumps into the ocean to feel the waves crash against his body—and shows that becoming a fallen angel has not been in vain. He tells his former eternal colleague Cassiel (played by Andre Braugher), that at least he got to touch Maggie's hair, her skin, and make love to her once. In other words, Seth's desire may now continue because of her death, but emotionally he will always have that experience of fulfillment to remember and cherish.

Wings of Desire and *City of Angels* are both films about angelic anguish, about the oppressed religious and spiritual self being torn in two because of a want, need, and desire for physical human contact. However, what happens when a mortal dies in religious cinema? Is desire suppressed and oppressed by religious institutions and rules? If one were to watch Vincent Ward's *What Dreams May Come* (Polygram Films, 1998), one would be correct to assume that the answer is yes; that one's physical/emotional desire transcends the boundaries of religion and mortality, and can enter into the kingdoms of God and the Devil.

Doctor Christopher Nielsen (played by Robin Williams) is a married man with two beautiful children. He loves his entire family—he is a faithful husband to his wife Annie (played by Annabella Sciorra), an adequate (but sometimes absent) father to his children and an excellent friend to the patients he cares for—and tries desperately to fill his world with witty, colorful dialogue and smiling faces. The happy existence Christy lives, however, is shattered when a truck hits the car that carries his two children to school, killing them instantly. This sets off a chain of events that lead to his distancing himself from Annie, Annie's attempt at suicide, her placement into a mental institution, and their decision to get divorced. Annie and Christy are literally pulled apart by the tragedy, and it almost destroys their marriage, but they manage to stay together, coming to the realization that they are soul mates.

Four years later, after successfully getting through their deadly tragedy, Christy gets killed in a car accident as well, trying to help someone trapped in a car that flipped onto its roof. His death leads him to Heaven, a place where everything is yours to create and the experiences you have are only good. Even if he misses Annie, at least he can learn to adjust; that is until Annie decides to kill herself and, after taking her own life, gets placed into the bowels of Hell, a place ridden with lost souls and people who do not understand or know what has happened to them. No longer oppressed physically by his death, Christy's desire gets the better of him, and he wants to go see her. Annie, however, is trapped in Hell, and the only way to get her out is to prove to her that she is dead and, although almost out of her reach, that eternity is at hand. He gets told by his companion Albert (played by Cuba Gooding, Jr.) and by The Tracker (played by Max Von Sydow), that his desire will not be strong enough, that his will is not resilient enough and that the evils of Hell will stop him from his intended goal. As one could see, Christy is not the only one who has tried to infiltrate Hell. Others have, but with no success. The unlucky or less intelligent ultimately get stuck there forever to wallow in misery for all eternity.

In *What Dreams May Come*, like in *City of Angels*, free will prevails. Christy is able to do anything he puts his mind to. He, at first, has the freedom to do as he wishes. However, his freedom only goes as far as what occurs in Heaven above. In Hell, the rules are different. If one is in Heaven, one can enter Hell but at the risk of losing one's mind and one's freedom. The rules, regulations, and restrictions that are placed on these eternally damned individuals become oppressive and persuasive, thereby preventing the fulfillment of one's desires. Christy understands what may happen to him, but his desire and passion lead him as far as he can go, finding Annie wallowing in her own misery, trapped in the remains of a home created in her tortured mind and broken apart by death. Christy's desire to regain Annie's love brings him to the brink of insanity; she does not know that the person she is speaking with is Christy, and he so desperately wants her to finally see past her sorrow. Not succeeding, he decides to stay with her, even though her oblivion overrules her. It is only then that Annie realizes who he is and that their desires can indeed be fulfilled. Their love for each other and their relationship as soul mates are once again reaffirmed.

In all three of these films, it is explicitly stated that both the mortal and the immortal have free will. All people on Earth, in Heaven, and in Hell have the ability to move about as freely as they wish. However, for Christy, Annie, Seth, and Damiel, their physical and spiritual status is a hindrance. They desire love, passion, and satisfying relationships, but they are unable to fulfill their desires. Passionately charged sexual conflict is what drives these stories and allows audience members to identify with the protagonists, even though the films deal with subject matters far past the realm of human and mortal understanding. At the end, in true conventional cinematic form, that conflict is squelched and desire is no longer oppressed, cannot be oppressed due to free will.

Moving away from the realm of immortality, mortal religious figures in religious cinema are even more oppressed by their spiritual beliefs than immortals. Priests, evangelists, rabbis, and even Jesus are all used for the purposes of desire-filled, sexually based conflict. Their desire, however, is unlike that of the angels or the dead because their desire cannot be fulfilled physically, but it may be fulfilled spiritually. These religious figures are oppressed beings, frustrated, angry, and in need of physical pleasure but unable to provide or accept that pleasure for fear of excommunication or congregational backlash. Instead they grow to understand that they must deal with their desires without completely destroying their relationship with God.

For example, one of the more controversial films of the 1990s is Antonia Bird's *Priest* (Miramax Pictures, 1994), a film that delves into the fictional heterosexual and homosexual love affairs of Father Matthew Thomas (played by Tom Wilkinson) and Father Greg Pilkington (played by Linus Roache), as well as the sexual abuse of children by their parents. According to Teresa Blythe, the most prominent leitmotif in *Priest* is the "treatments of celibacy, homosexuality, confessional confidentiality, child sexual abuse (by a layman against his daughter; not clergy sexual abuse), and the perils of hiding one's true nature in order to serve God as a priest."[8] The "authentic" self thus becomes the oppressed self, suppressed by the rules and regulations created by the Vatican and by Catholicism.

In *Priest*, however, the line is much less clearly demarcated between what is the "authentic" self and what is the "inauthentic" self. In contrast to the films discussed above, where being an angel or a deceased person was a hindrance towards their authenticity, *Priest* deals more specifically with the possibility that there may, in fact, be two "authentic" selves at work: The sexual being and the religious being. Although Father Greg falls in love with a young man named Graham (played by Robert Carlyle) after meeting him in a gay bar, and Father Matthew is having a passionate love affair with the church's hired help, both priests are still very much embedded in their priestly existence. In one scene, after realizing the consequences of his sexual actions and being told by another exiled priest that he should leave the clergy, Father Greg states, "I can't get out. God wants me to be a priest. I don't think it. I don't just believe it. I know it."

Father Greg understands that his sexual being is a reality, that it is certainly something that drives him and is "authentic" in nature. However, God has also given him a sign, letting him know that this is what he should be doing as a profession. He was called by God regardless of his sexuality and his sexual preference to preach the Gospel. The same conclusion can be made when discussing Father Matthew who is in touch with his sexual and priestly self, and does not allow the pressures of Catholicism to deter him from taking advantage of both. Father Matthew, rather than being in conflict with himself, embraces both "authentic" selves and reassures Father Greg that it is okay to do the same, constantly goading him to once again say Mass to his former congregation.

The pedophilic father also embraces his own restricted sexuality. In one disturbing scene, Father Greg talks to the father in the confessional, and the father claims that it is perfectly natural to love one's daughter in that way. Sexuality and desire are moved to the forefront and are used to further Father Greg's own conflicts and oppression. He not only has to fight the sexual demons he has inside himself, but he must also keep quiet about the physical demon that has taken over the father of this young girl he teaches. He cannot expose his own sins and he cannot expose the sins of others, even though it would be healthier for everyone involved if all these sins were placed out in the open. What is exposed instead is the oppressive nature of the Catholic Church, and how that oppression can affect clergy members in similar predicaments. One's complete "authentic" self is broken in two not by the priests themselves, but by the atmosphere in which they exist.

A more lighthearted version of the same sexual conflict between clergy and secular forces comes in the form of Edward Norton's *Keeping the Faith* (Touchstone Pictures, 2000), a romantic comedy that depicts three friends in a complex love triangle. Jake Schram (played by Ben Stiller) is an aspiring rabbi, considered by his congregation to be a funny, cute, warm soul in desperate need of a wife. Brian Finn (played by Edward Norton) is a fledgling but popular priest, considered by his congregation to be a funny, cute, warm soul in need of God. Anna (played by Jenna Elfman) is a friend to both and is just a funny, cute, warm soul. Jake and Brian both desire Anna. Anna desires Jake knowing full well that Brian is a priest and is unable to be with a woman sexually; in fact, although stating in one scene that she is in need of human physical contact on occasion, her desire for Jake goes much deeper than that. Anna wants companionship and friendship from Brian, who unfortunately receives mixed signals from her and feels romantically passionate toward her. However, it is Jake with whom Anna is in love. For these two, it appears love is meant to be.

Keeping the Faith depicts the relationships and love all three characters have one for another. The film is about their bond since childhood. As with most cinematic religious friendships, though, their unstoppable trio must be wrought with conflict and oppressed feelings. Jake cannot marry Anna because she is not Jewish and it could jeopardize his status as a rabbi. Brian cannot fall in love with a woman or have sexual feelings for a woman because of his vow of celibacy. Anna cannot be with either because of their backgrounds and their emotional insecurities. These are certainly not repressed characters; they all know what they desire and want. These are people trapped in what they think are oppressive situations, contemplating the alternative to their spiritual lifestyles: abandonment, excommunication and shunning. It is not until Jake's mother, Ruth (played by Anne Bancroft) and Brian's monsignor, Father Havel (played by Milos Forman), tell them that their feelings are normal that they realize that their spiritual self and secular self are not oppressive, but rather that they would make them more complete individuals. This realization leads to Jake's reaffirmation of love towards Anna, to her decision to become Jewish, and to Brian's choice to live happily ever after as a man of the cloth. Desire and sexual feelings are normal to have; it is how you act when presented with those feelings that matter.

Judaism in *Keeping the Faith* is an open religious practice compared to Hasidim, as it is depicted by Sidney Lumet in *A Stranger Among Us* (Buena Vista Films, 1992). The film takes place in Brooklyn, N.Y., and follows the life of Detective Emily Eden (played by Melanie Griffith), a sexy rogue police officer in search of a killer amongst the Hasidic community. She wears revealing clothes, has a torrid love affair with her partner, and continuously exudes a need for passion and sexual pleasure. As Jay Boyer states, Emily "thinks she is liberated sexually and professionally."[9]

This feeling of liberation, however, is later challenged by her desire for Ariel (played by Eric Thal), a Hasidic man who also has feelings for Emily but is not allowed to express them due to his oppressive religious beliefs. On several occasions, Ariel even goes as far as to tell Emily that he cannot be in the same room with her by himself because it is not acceptable in the Hasidic faith. This hesitation makes Emily even more interested in him; she feels compelled to be with him and teach him how to be in lust for a sexually appealing and active woman. Boyer recognizes this as well when he states that "Emily taunts Ariel about his virginity" and "Ariel acknowledges that her sexual experience is far greater than his own."[10] Even when he almost gives in to her, however, Ariel understands that his faith will not allow this to take place. Rather than throwing everything he cherishes away, Ariel marries a Hasidic woman, thereby leaving Emily to see her own flaws. Emily can still feel desire, but she now realizes after meeting Ariel that it must be more meaningful and involved than just having sexual fulfillment. His oppression (an oppression that he takes control over and begins to embrace) is her liberation.

Sexual liberation can very well be considered a prominent motif of Martin Scorsese's *The Last Temptation of Christ* (Universal Pictures, 1988), a film that expresses sexuality in several key moments of Jesus' life and the oppressive nature of religious belief towards that sexuality. Jesus (played by Willem Dafoe), in *The Last Temptation of Christ*, is not just the Son of God, he is a human being, a man who "had to possess all of the weakness of man, to be prey to all of the temptations"[11] to which human beings are exposed. In one scene, he goes to a brothel where Mary Magdalene (played by Barbara Hershey) is having sex with a large amount of men. As Jesus watches, he wonders what it would be like to be with her, to caress her, to make love to her. He is seduced by her and by her naked body. However, his spiritual self holds him back from doing anything with her.

Mary's seduction is a temptation later manifested in a fantasy created by the Devil as Jesus dies on the cross. He imagines making love to her, having children with her, getting married and growing old with her. Mary becomes his one true sexual fantasy; he desires to have a life where free will can take over and he can be a man rather than the Son of God. Sexual free will, however, does not prevail. Jesus realizes that his fantasy is only perpetuated by Satan and Satan's own desire to see Jesus fail God. Jesus escapes from the Devil-induced fantasy and dies with the knowledge that God is his Father. Spiritual free will lives forever.

The Last Temptation of Christ is the penultimate religious text about the conflict of sexuality, desire, and oppression in the spiritual self because it delves into the mind of Jesus. Audience members are allowed to feel as if even the Son of Man has the ability to be tempted, to be sexually desired and to desire. Jesus is one of us—morally conflicted and oppressed by our beliefs and spiritual feelings. In addition, after conquering his moral ambiguity, Jesus uses his free will as a way to destroy Satan's temptations and live the life that he knows is right. Similar to most of the other religious figures mentioned above, the conflict no longer exists, and everyone can rest easy.

Before concluding this essay, we look at Giuseppe Tornatore's *Cinema Paradiso* (Miramax Films, 1989), where we see an old Italian priest named Father Adelfio (played by Leopoldo Trieste) ringing a bell whenever two characters passionately kiss on-screen. The ringing bell is a sign for Alfredo, the projection booth worker (played by Philippe Noiret), to remove the kisses from the final cut. The oppressive Catholic Church thus makes sure that the so-called immoral acts projected on film are not presented to an easily stimulated young audience who are more than willing to follow the actions that the fictional characters perform. These scenes are later followed by the death of the priest and Alfredo. What survives, however, is the film stock. Alfredo decides, in the end, before he passes away, to create a montage of kisses for everyone to see; the oppression of the Church destroyed while the cinema lives on.

What this essay has highlighted is the fact that American and foreign- based religious cinema uses religion as an oppressive entity for the sole purpose of conflict (sexual or otherwise) and audience satisfaction following the resolution of the conflict. For a cinema set on showing need, desire, love, passion, sexual pleasure, and sexual free will, one's conflicts become enhanced and are much more interesting when they are made manifest in fictional characters that are not repressed beings, but have oppressive religious backgrounds dictating their lives and their sexuality.

Notes

[1] Teresa Blythe, "The Collar and the Bottle: Film Portrayals of Drinking Clergy," in *Religion and Alcohol: Sobering Thoughts*, ed. C.K. Robertson (New York: Peter Lang, 2004), 79.

[2] David G. Myers, *Exploring Psychology*, 3rd ed. (Hope College: Worth Publishers, 1996), 247.

[3] Sigmund Freud, *Inhibitions, Symptoms and Anxiety* (New York: W.W. Norton & Co., 1989), 7.

[4] Paulo Freire, *Pedagogy of the Oppressed*, trans. Myra Bergman Ramos, 20th Anniversary Ed. (New York: Continuum, 1998), 29.

[5] Ibid., 29.

[6] Ibid., 30.

[7] Ibid.

[8] Blythe, "The Collar and the Bottle," 85.

[9] Jay Boyer, *Sidney Lumet*, (New York: Twayne Publishers, 1993), 141.

[10] Ibid., 143.

Roger Ebert, Review for *The Last Temptation of Christ*, *Roger Ebert's Video Companion* (Kansas City: Andrews and McMeel, 1996), 405.

Bibliography

Blythe, Teresa. "The Collar and the Bottle: Film Portrayals of Drinking Clergy." In C. K. Robertson, editor. *Religion and Alcohol: Sobering Thoughts.* New York: Peter Lang, 2004, 79–83.

Boyer, Jay. *Sidney Lumet.* New York: Twayne Publishers, 1993.

Cinema Paradiso. Dir. Giuseppe Tornatore. Perf. Philippe Noiret, Jacques Perrin. Miramax, 1989.

City of Angels. Dir. Brad Silberling. Perf. Nicolas Cage, Meg Ryan, Andre Braugher, Dennis Franz. Warner Brothers, 1998.

Defending Your Life. Dir. Albert Brooks. Perf. Albert Brooks, Meryl Streep, Rip Torn. Warner Brothers, 1991.

Ebert, Roger. *Roger Ebert's Video Companion.* Kansas City: Andrews and McNeel, 1996.

Freire, Paulo. *Pedagogy of the Oppressed.* New York: Continuum, 1998.

Freud, Sigmund. *Inhibitions, Symptoms and Anxiety.* New York: W.W. Norton & Co., 1989.

Keeping the Faith. Dir. Edward Norton. Perf. Edward Norton, Ben Stiller, Jenna Elfman. Touchstone, 2000.

Last Temptation of Christ, The. Dir. Martin Scorsese. Perf. Willem Dafoe, Harvey Keitel, Barbara Hershey. Universal, 1988.

Myers, David G. *Exploring Psychology.* 3rd ed. Hope College: Worth Publishers, 1996.

Priest. Dir. Antonia Bird. Perf. Linus Roache, Tom Wilkinson, Robert Carlyle. Miramax, 1994.

Shakespeare in Love. Dir. John Madden. Perf. Gwyneth Paltrow, Joseph Finnes, Judy Dench. Miramax, 1997.

Stranger Among Us, A. Dir. Sidney Lumet. Perf. Melanie Griffith, Eric Thal. Buena Vista, 1992.

What Dreams May Come. Dir. Vincent Ward. Perf. Robin Williams, Cuba Gooding, Jr. Annabella Sciorra, Max von Sydow. Polygram, 1998.

Wings of Desire. Dir. Wim Wenders. Perf. Bruno Ganz, Solveig Dommartin, Peter Falk. MGM, 1988.

6 Out of Bounds: The Clergy and Sexual Boundaries
John W. Gamble

Any complete discussion of clergy sexual boundaries and their violation would require two books, one book devoted to the church history of the topic and a second book examining the issues from a comparative religion point of view. This chapter will offer a brief survey of both of these areas along with a look at the current situation in the United States.

Today, in the first years of the twenty-first century, the impetus for any discussion of clergy sexual boundary violation owes a considerable debt, if one can use that word in this context, to the explosive exposure of the Catholic priest pedophilia scandal. That development has placed the topic squarely into the public awareness. At the same time, these initial years of the century have seen a second sexual boundary-relevant controversial development that has claimed considerable public attention. That is the ordination of the Rt. Rev. V. Gene Robinson as the Episcopal bishop of New Hampshire. Bishop Robinson is a formerly married openly gay man living with his male partner. Both developments nicely bracket the tensions between and within denominations that characterize issues of sexual boundaries in the United States. In the final analysis it is possible to view both developments as a sign of the maturing and the democratization of congregations and certain denominations in the United States as they relate to their culture both religious and secular.

Historical View

Tempting though it is to approach the topic of clergy sexual boundaries from the point of individual clergy sexual transgressions, to do so would be to miss the complexities and traditions that influence present problems and denominational struggles. The issues of clergy sexual boundary behavior occur at a number of levels. These levels range from problematic church-sanctioned actions to the behavior of individual clergy that violate the teachings of their particular faith group. The story of clergy boundaries and sex cannot be separated from a particular religion's historical attitude toward women, beginning with early scriptures/teachings where the foundational proscriptions are proclaimed.

Christianity

For Christians and Jews that story begins immediately in the Bible in the early chapters of the Book of Genesis, as God confronts Adam and Eve after they have eaten the forbidden fruit:

> "Have you eaten from the tree of which I commanded you not to eat?" The man said, "The woman whom you gave to be with me, she gave me fruit from the tree, and I ate." Then the LORD God said to the woman, "What is this that you have done?" The woman said, "The serpent tricked me, and I ate."
> … To the woman he said, "I will greatly increase your pangs in childbearing; in pain you shall bring forth children, yet your desire shall be for your husband, and he shall rule over you." And to the man he said, "Because you have listened to the voice of your wife, and have eaten of the tree about which I commanded you, 'You shall not eat of it,' cursed is the ground because of you; in toil you shall eat of it all the days of your life; 18 thorns and thistles it shall bring forth for you; and you shall eat the plants of the field. By the sweat of your face you shall eat bread until you return to the ground, for out of it you were taken; you are dust, and to dust you shall return."
> … And the Lord God made garments of skins for the man and for his wife, and clothed them.[1]

The Genesis story had been handed down from ancient Hebrew tribes well before the time of Christ. Elaine Pagels points out in her influential book *Adam, Eve, and The Serpent,* that this story presents its imbedded values as universally valid rather than as an isolated incident for a particular couple.[2] However, the interpretation of the story has not resulted in universal agreement as to its meaning. Some have chosen to focus on both the sexual and the obedience issue while others have focused essentially on the obedience issue alone. At the same time some interpreters have highlighted the role of the woman as instigator and cause of man's downfall while others have chosen to appreciate the mutuality of the decision and its act. Today, as in the intervening centuries, the creation story is taken by many to validate their own social and sexual attitudes. The role of the woman and the results of her actions have influenced Christian teachings and attitudes over the millennium and continue to do so in various denominations today. While some sects have used the creation story as a justification for a condemnation of women and sexuality, the generally prevailing Christian view seeks to understand the story in terms of the couple's behavior and refuses to absolve Adam for his decision to eat of the forbidden fruit.

Despite the potentially dubious presentation of women in the creation story, Genesis commends the institution of marriage and procreation in the command to "be fruitful and multiply, and fill the earth" (Genesis 1:28). The Jewish religion has always accepted this commandment without question, However, with the advent of the teachings of Jesus there was born the idea of the institution of marriage and sex as an impediment to entering the Kingdom of Heaven. Jesus noted that it was better not to marry and praised "those who have made themselves eunuchs for the sake of the Kingdom of Heaven" (Matthew 19:12). Celibacy for the sake of salvation became an issue of debate among early Christians. Later the disciple Paul, while not condemning marriage as a sin, extolled the virtue of the celibate life, noting that the celibate life frees men and woman to devote their energies "to the Lord" (1 Corinthians 7:1–35). Paul expressed his desire for church members to be voluntarily celibate for the sake of the Kingdom, and he encouraged those who were married to live as though they were unmarried. One of the obvious and accepted implications of these admonitions among various early Christian groups was that carnal knowledge rendered one unfit for the Kingdom of Heaven.

The question of the appropriateness of marriage versus celibacy continued to be debated through the history of the early church. As Pagels notes, "For many Christians of the first four centuries and ever since, the greatest freedom demanded the greatest renunciation, above all celibacy. ... As the early Christians saw it, celibacy involved rejection of "the world" of ordinary society and its multitudinous entanglements and was thereby a way to gain control over one's own life."[3] At the same time, with freedom came the idea of avoiding the taint of carnal sin.

In the late fourth and early fifth centuries, Augustine, responding to his own passionate nature, emphasized the sinful aspect of sexual desire. Augustine viewed the arising of sexual desire without the active wish of, and at times in spite of, one's will as proof of man's essential nature having been damaged from the original sin of Adam and Eve's disobedience of God's commandment in the Garden. He equated the willfulness of the body with the willfulness of the original couple's behavior. In addition, Augustine came to believe that although woman was originally created to be man's helper, she instead had become his temptress, resulting in God proclaiming the husband's authority over the woman. While Augustine's thoughts were not the universal view before and at the time of his writing, the influence of these ideas have, according to Pagels, "surpassed that of any other church father."[4] The issue of celibacy and sexuality continued to be a source of conflict within the church. Despite the controversy many priests, bishops and popes were legitimately married. However, in 1139 a papal decree required that any candidate for Holy Orders be single with the attendant implication of celibacy both upon acceptance and in the life that followed. The results of this decree have been an increasing source of stress and conflict within the Catholic Church. Today the issue has reached crisis proportions.

Judaism

Jewish teachers historically focused on the portions of the Genesis story that commanded marriage and procreation. The tribal survival issues that characterized the life experiences of a wandering people in a harsh climate made an emphasis on procreation a necessity. This emphasis colored an abhorrence of some of the sexual practices of their pagan neighbors. The historical status of women in ancient Jewish society has in recent years been undergoing some degree of revision brought about in part by feminist-inspired research. However, as with women in the Moslem religion, from the vantage point of modern western society the status of women in ancient Hebrew society has been viewed as that of a second-class citizen. In some respects this is unfair as the demands of family and home required different roles. Nevertheless, we find women in large measure excluded from a public religious role in the synagogue. Divorce was proscribed for a barren woman after a certain period of time and those who could afford it practiced polygamy. Finally we are informed that stoning of women for sexual transgressions was present in early Jewish societies:

> The scribes and the Pharisees brought a woman who had been caught in adultery; and making her stand before all of them, they said to him, "Teacher, this woman was caught in the very act of committing adultery. Now in the law Moses commanded us to stone such women. Now what do you say?"[5]

Islam

The creation story has had much less influence in Islam than in Christianity. Scholars agree that with the inception of the teachings of the Prophet Muhammad and the advent of the Qur'an the condition and status of women improved significantly in Arab countries. Apologists for the Moslem faith note that the Qur'an granted women many rights that were only given in the West at much later dates. The historical role of women in Islam is complicated and varied. It is interesting to note that at the present time Islamic feminism has its own flavor. For example there is an increasing tendency of young Islamic women to choose the wearing of the historically proscribed veil and other symbols of their religion proudly in their own countries and in western countries. Although Westerners are generally disquieted by the harshness of the penalties prescribed for behavioral transgression in the Qur'an—such as flogging with 100 stripes for fornication—they are generally quite ignorant of the basic teachings of Islam. Moslems point with pride to the fact that the original texts and teachings are in many aspects respectful of women and place no onus on them for original sin. Differences in proscribed behavior between men and women in the initial teachings are based on the perceived psychology of women and the requirements of the society and family. As with Judaism, the result of this perception of differences in psychology and the requirements of home and family resulted in practices that, when viewed from the vantage point of modern western society, appear to place women in an unfavorable status as contrasted with men. In addition, in practical terms in many areas of today's Islamic world, men treat the majority of women as second-class citizens. The proliferation of Islamic laws based in part on certain interpretations of the Qur'an and certain sayings of The Prophet have resulted in a body of religious-based laws that have in fundamentally Islamic societies significantly affected the status of women in negative ways. The struggle between moderate and fundamentalist factions of the religion is more intense in those countries where Islam plays a major role and where there is also political unrest. The tension resulting from these differences is the source of an ongoing struggle within the Moslem community at large.

Sexual Boundary Violations
Sanctioned and Initiated by the Church

Within a particular body of religious ideas and their interpretations there are instances when the question arises, "At what point does that which passes for orthodoxy become the violation of a sexual boundary?" The answer, or course, depends on where the questioner stands with respect to a particular religion, spiritual practice, and/or cultural identity. So far the issues presented here have had more to do with the formation of general attitudes toward sex and the sexes. These attitudes may or may not be viewed as sexual boundary violations depending on the orientation of the viewer. They do not clearly violate established boundary issues. However, whether due to religious laws adopted since the original teachings, or due to a particular interpretation of the original teachings, religions have at times initiated practices that are viewed in modern western industrialized society as clear sexual boundary violations. The most obvious example in Christian history was the practice during various periods of branding certain women as witches. The labeling and hunting of "witches" reached its zenith in the sixteenth and seventeenth centuries. Here we encounter a practice against women initiated and conducted by the established clerical hierarchy that clearly violates our own sense of boundaries. Achterberg notes that the church's stance was that since women were not allowed to study curing, any knowledge they had in that practice could only have come from the devil. The official church position was, "that if a woman dare to cure without having studied she is a witch and must die."[6] In actuality, healing was not a necessary and sufficient cause for a woman to be accused, and once accused the confession-gathering techniques almost guaranteed a guilty verdict. The result of such a verdict was burning at the stake. The actual number of women killed is unknown, but estimates range from two hundred thousand to nine million. Men were also accused and executed as witches, but in far fewer numbers. Feminist apologists have labeled the witch-hunting craze, "the hunting of women who do not fulfill the male view of how women ought to conduct themselves."[7]

Although Europe witnessed the most ferocious period of witch burnings, other countries such as Russia were characterized by similar practices. In the United States, the most notorious witch trials and burnings occurred in Salem, Massachusetts, in 1692. The witch hysteria in Salem arose from church tensions and the frenzied behavior of some children, one of whom was the daughter of a local pastor. By the time the townspeople came to their senses nineteen people had been hanged, one pressed to death with stones, and four had died in prison. Those who were imprisoned numbered between one hundred and two hundred people. In time, the practice died out on both sides of the ocean, but not before thousands had been tortured and burned. In retrospect, the Church's responsibility for these events and the subtle influence of the creation story on the view of women cannot be avoided. Other instances of Christian boundary violations occurred during the Inquisition, as well as during the Crusades.

There has been a growing interest in the Moslem Arab countries by people in the western industrialized countries. This is due in part to the oil dependency of the West and, in the first years of the twenty-first century, to the sharply increased level of conflict with certain groups and elements claiming allegiance to Islam. The result of this growing awareness is a belief among westerners that the status of women in fundamentalist-dominated societies does not compare favorably with women in western societies, regardless of the subtleties of interpretation and positive situations in moderate Islamic societies. The issue of education for women, along with general rights, remains problematic in the fundamentalist societies. These issues of rights and education are generally viewed in western "first world" countries as sexual boundary violations that have been mandated by ultra-orthodox religions. This view is held in spite of political-social-cultural pressures that are intrinsic to such arrangements. At the same time, some of these issues resonate with the attitudes of certain western fundamentalist-oriented Christian denominations, in particular the ascendancy of men over women in matters of obedience and "appropriate" behavior. There are, however, certain elements of modern Islamic law and practice that are universally viewed as sexual boundary violations by inhabitants of western countries. In 2004, international attention was focused on the plight of a woman in Nigeria who had been sentenced to stoning. The woman had been convicted and sentenced in March 2002, after giving birth to a baby girl more than nine months after divorcing. She claimed that the father of the baby had promised to marry her but did not. Despite her protestations, she was sentenced to be buried in the ground up to her neck and then stoned until dead. Under the strict Shariah (Islamic) law, pregnancy outside marriage constitutes sufficient evidence for a woman to be convicted of adultery; the penalty is stoning in strict fundamentalist societies, although the Qur'an only stipulates 100 lashes (24:2). In February 1998, thirty thousand spectators at the Kabul sports stadium watched while a teenage girl received a hundred lashes for walking with a non-related male. These extreme measures of control over women echo more general measures of control that fundamental Islamic societies have instituted or are trying to institute in various countries. As these societies strive to implement literalistic interpretations of their religion, they have created prohibitions against dancing, music, education of women, and social relations, and they have initiated severe penalties for criminal transgressions, including amputation for stealing and execution for adultery and many other offenses. Similarly, in the realm of sexual boundaries that have a religious element, the Human Rights Information Packet of 1997 notes that female circumcision—or female genital mutilation, as it is known in the West—has acquired a religious dimension in some Muslim societies. It should be noted, of course, that female genital mutilation predates Islam and is not practiced by the vast majority of Muslims.

Individual Sexual Boundary Violations

So far we have examined in a very brief survey early attitudes toward the feminine that have influenced subsequent behavior and some of the specific religion-inspired practices that provoke a clear sense of sexual boundary violation in a western industrial society audience. However, the issue of boundary violation has lately become a far livelier topic in the United States as it relates to the individual clerical violator, that is, the pastors who violate their own denomination's prohibitions while simultaneously they may be violating the civil and criminal standards of the culture in which they live.

It is important to appreciate that denominational and secular societal violations do not occur within a vacuum. They are most often the result of stresses that affect individual pastors or in the case of Catholic priests, stresses that attend the Church's unique requirements. Within this context it will be helpful to have an appreciation of the pressures under which the typical modern pastor usually operates. While this general description of pressures may not be universal for all congregations in all places and at all times, it is sufficiently common to stand as an overview of professional occupational demands.

The role of the modern pastor in the United States varies in some respects with the religious denomination with which he or she is affiliated, however, there are many commonalities. Just as in the rest of society workloads tend to be high and job demands stressful, modern pastors are expected by their congregations to be on call 24 hours a day, seven days a week. Although lip service is given to family life, the actual requirements of the job tend to place a burden on the family. Modern churches are also modern businesses. They usually have significant budgets, expansion plans, and concomitant debts. The pastor operates in a corporate structure usually in the form of a group of volunteers who exercise power in varying degrees and also, in most denominations, in a hierarchical authority structure (e.g., diocese, synod, convocation, region). These structures will assist the pastor and, in the final analysis, often ultimately control the finances of the church. However, it is the pastor who is viewed as ultimately responsible for the business of the church. They are seen as the ones responsible for creating sufficient income to sustain the church and its employees as well as furthering any improvement or expansion plans the church might have. Although the pastor position is similar to that of a CEO of any business, the option of making significant changes or firing those who are sharing financial and administrative responsibility is often problematic, and at times simply impossible, as a result of the politics and congregational power structures in any given church.

The pastoral job, in fact, is somewhat schizophrenic in nature. While pastors are the primary responsible officers, they are viewed as the respective congregation's employee, there to serve them. Unlike secular leadership positions, pastors are expected to have a greater than average capacity for generosity, understanding, and spiritually inspired wisdom, as well as equanimity in all of their dealings. In addition, because most members in a congregation see the pastor only at church during scheduled worship services, they often have no idea of the demands of the job and thus see the pastor as not working particularly hard and therefore having plenty of free time.

Interchurch life in a modern community tends to have a certain competitive flavor fueled by the natural tendency of groups to compete and their desire to be the most popular and influential. The same competitiveness may exist within a particular denomination. Pastors are acutely aware of the "numbers," that is, the number of people registered in their church and the number of people regularly attending services. Those pastors that are able to bring in the most new members are rewarded monetarily and with perks. They may also come to wield considerable influence in their communities. In those denominations with a hierarchal structure successful pastors are rewarded with promotions to larger more impressive churches with attendant larger remuneration packages. In some cases there are interdenominational antagonisms. These elements of church relationships tend to isolate the pastor from fellow pastors, thus robbing him of potential sources of support from members of his own profession. The experience of isolation is exacerbated by the attitudes of congregations and their concomitant expectations. The pastor functions as spiritual leader, counselor, confessor, and exemplary person for their congregation. The natural life/maturation struggles that characterize the vast majority of individual lives and relationships are, for the pastor, a burden that frequently must be contained quietly within the family and at times just within oneself.

Although pastors begin their careers with a set of beliefs and practices as well as expectations, the wear and tear of the "business" of being a pastor frequently exerts a considerable toll. The combination of the personal cost of the job and normal maturing that occurs with increasing age and experience in life may result in a natural change in pastors' attitudes toward their job and their denomination. This change in attitude may include maturation in their spiritual vision and life. However, that maturation may or may not fit into the teachings of a particular denomination. Unfortunately, by the time the process of maturation occurs a particular pastor may have devoted the best working years of his or her life to the profession and have achieved an income level that may not easily be put aside. At the same time, the unique training that characterizes pastoral education and experience does not easily translate into another profession without considerable retraining or education. While this process can and does occur with all denominations, the most obvious example occurs with those Catholic priests who come to realize that the celibate life does not fit with their personal life vision.

These expectations, pressures, and stresses place a heavy burden on pastors and on their families. That burden coupled with the isolation from congregations and other pastors for the above stated reasons have the potential to result in a multitude of stress related problems ranging from job dissatisfaction, marital difficulties, alcoholism, and sexual transgressions.

Pastoral malfeasance is not new. It may take the form of a financial, authoritarian, or sexual nature. Until the 1990s, such malfeasance tended to remain in the shadows. Since then, though, the public has become increasingly aware of the existence of clergy transgressions. Two related factors have played a prominent role in this new awareness. The first factor involves an historical movement that has been occurring in the western industrialized first world countries in general, and the United States in particular, for several decades. That factor is the empowerment of minorities and the concomitant appreciation of victimization. These movements began in the late 1950s with the crusades led by ordinary black citizens and black leaders to stand up and fight for a measure of heretofore denied recognition and equality. With the general success of that movement the vision of equality and recognition began to take on a genuine sexual boundary element as it spread to women who launched a struggle for feminine empowerment. Both the African-American movement and the women's movement contained a significant understanding and uplifting of the victimization inherent in the status quo that had preceded these movements. These struggles were followed by a demand for recognition and equality by gay and lesbian groups. Today struggles continue for each of these groups. However, the present status of each group is tremendously improved from its original point of departure. This general success of the women's movement and the gay-lesbian movement has resulted in a heightened cultural sensitivity to issues of sexual victimization and, perhaps more importantly, an appreciation of the fact that something can be done to rectify the situation.

The second factor that has contributed to public awareness of clergy malfeasance relating particularly to sexual boundary violations arose from the revelations involving the Catholic clergy pedophilia scandal. On January 6, 2002, *The Boston Globe* began publishing a series of reports detailing the abuse of children by Fr. John Geoghen, a Catholic priest. 150 victims were numbered. However, the behavior of this one particular priest was not the most explosive issue in the news revelations. There had been previous reports of priest abuse, most notably the case in 1992 of Fr. James Porter in Fall River, Massachusetts. Instead of focusing on the accused priest, the investigative team of the *Globe* began to detail the manner in which the Church's hierarchy conspired to keep sexually abusive behavior by priests a secret in order to protect the clergy. In fact, when complaints of abuse came to the attention of certain bishops, their response of simply transferring the guilty party in question to another parish virtually assured the continuation of abuse. The result of such revelations was the beginning of an avalanche of reports of abuse going back for decades, the filing of civil and criminal suits, outrage among faithful Catholic parishioners, and confrontation with church authorities. This particular struggle shows few signs of abating; instead, there are signs that the Catholic Church will undergo some forms of major change.

Together these two events—the one historical and affecting large elements of the general population and the other quite specific, brought about by a unique group, and affecting a large but limited number of victims—have placed the conduct of all pastors under the spotlight of public scrutiny. That scrutiny had not been limited to the United States but has accompanied a demand for rights and empowerment of minorities and victims in the majority of western industrialized nations. In addition, there has been an increase in the number of reports of sexual abuse of minors by priests in other countries.

Clergy sexual boundary violations tend to fall into a number of levels. Bromley and Cress detail four types of sexual coercion scandals:

Sexual Harassment—Referring to any attempted or completed sexual relationship by one individual within an organizational context that impedes occupational performance or opportunity of another individual.

Sexual Exploitation—Referring to attempted or completed relationships in the context of treatment of clients by professional service providers.

Sexual Abuse—Referring to attempted or completed coercive sexual activity in the context of covenantal role relationships.

Sexual Molestation—Referring to attempted or completed coercive sexual activity in the context of relationships involving socialization or care.[8]

Pastoral sexual boundary violations can and do involve each of the categories above. With issues of rights violations and pedophilia, the final arbiter and rectifier, to the degree such is possible, has been civil and criminal courts. However, the vast majority of instances of boundary violation do not qualify for such remediation. For example, it may be morally inappropriate for a pastor to become sexually involved with a woman he is counseling, but it is not a violation of criminal law as it is for licensed counseling professions in most states. The same is true for adultery, viewing pornography, and other activities that may be banned by a particular religion but condoned or tolerated by civil authorities and the secular culture. The same may be said for homosexuality when practiced by consenting adults. However, homosexuality represents a special case with which various denominations and the general society is currently engaged in a vitriolic struggle.

Any discussion of clergy sexual boundary violation in the early years of the twenty-first century must begin and perhaps end with the Catholic pedophilia scandal. However, clergy sexual boundary violation is not limited to Catholicism. Over the years there have been individual isolated reports of sexual malfeasance that have caught the public's attention. These reports ranged from relatively innocuous behaviors such as a pastor being caught looking at pornography and then being publicly chastised by his congregation, to adulterous relationships that destroyed marriages and divided congregations, to severe predatory behavior. However, because of the nature of religious institutions and public attitudes toward those institutions there has been little official or scholarly attention paid to these incidents until very recently. Stacey, Darnell, and Shupe conducted an initial survey that attempted to look at the issue of "how much clergy malfeasance is really out there?"[9] Their research took a two-pronged approach toward beginning to answer questions of quantity. The first approach involved a detailed review of what they considered to be a limited but extensive collection of publications, books, and articles available on the topic. Although they note the difficulties inherent in drawing accurate numbers from this collection of varied data, they are confident that the general directions and implications are correct. They also note that there were no previous data with which to compare their findings. They report 337 victim-reported cases of sexual abuse inflicted by clergy. The number of cases reported annually increased each decade. The authors are unable to state whether this increase is due to a greater number of instances of abuse or increased media interest. The majority of perpetrators were Catholic; however, 27 percent were Protestant and 11 percent unknown or unspecified. The majority of the victims were young males. The geographic spread throughout the United States included 38 states. Stacey et al. also examined this issue on an international level; again, they found clergy sexual abuse to be a problem in a number of countries. Their research dispelled the notion that the issue of clergy abuse is due to a few "bad apples" in isolated locations.

The second focus of their research involved the question, "How widespread is self-reported victimization by clergy within a sample of one Bible Belt region's general population?"[10] This element of their research was not limited to the question of sexual misconduct but included mental and physical abuse. In addition, the survey looked at clergy malfeasance in the areas of financial and authoritative excesses. To answer these questions the authors conducted a survey in the Dallas-Fort Worth metroplex. They balanced their sample, which included 1067 respondents, to be representative of the general population of the area. Results revealed that 2.8 percent of those interviewed had personally experienced mental, sexual, or physical abuse by a clergyman, and 7.4 percent of those interviewed had intimate knowledge from friends, coworkers, or relatives reports or from their own experience of one of the forms of clergy abuse examined. The percentage of 2.8 compares favorably with a poll conducted by the *Twin Cities Star Tribune* in February 1993, in which 2 percent of Minnesotans claimed to have been physically touched by church workers "in a way that made them feel uncomfortable."[11] Significantly in the Stacey et al. survey of those who had personally experienced clergy abuse of a sexual, physical, or mental nature, only a very small percentage had reported it to religious authorities and even smaller percentage to civil authorities.

We may be assured that these figures, which precede the Catholic pedophile scandal, are on the low side for the reasons that will be discussed below. Experts agree that clergy sexual boundary violations are vastly underreported, as victims, for perhaps quite understandable reasons, are hesitant to reveal their victimization and file a complaint. However, with the publications of *The Boston Globe* investigation in 2002, the public sensitivity to issues of clergy sexual abuse in particular and clergy malfeasance in general burgeoned.

The issue of celibacy and its possible contribution to clergy malfeasance represents a rather special situation for those involved in religious practice that requires it. Wherever it is encountered, mandatory celibacy places a special demand on the practitioner. Hartsuiker's pictorial study of India's mystic sadhus (religious holy renunciates) displays photographs of men wearing elaborate chastity belts and going to extreme levels of penile mortification in an effort to suppress their sexual nature.[12] As noted earlier celibacy was a live issue for the early Christian church having been given impetus by the teaching of Jesus, Paul, and Augustine as well as others. Because the practice of celibacy is required by the Catholic church, any violation of that vow would constitute a sexual barrier violation for the church whether or not it was considered such by the general public.

A. W. Richard Sipe is a former Catholic monk, priest, psychotherapist, and the author of books and articles dealing with celibacy. His particular concern is the mandatory requirement of celibacy for priests in the Catholic Church, in particular, and mandatory celibacy as it is encountered anywhere in a religious tradition such as in Buddhism and Hinduism. Sipe defines celibacy "as a freely chosen dynamic state, usually vowed, that involves an honest sustained attempt to live without direct sexual gratification in order to serve others productively for a spiritual motive."[13] Sipe provides an estimate of the sexual behavior of Catholic priests based on his own counseling practice, clinical treatment records, church records to which he had access, and personal communication with fellow church officials. His sample population numbered 2,776 priests. He estimates that at any one time 50 percent of priests are practicing celibacy; of the other 50 percent, Sipe believes that 30 percent are involved in heterosexual relationships, 15 percent involved in homosexual relationships or experimentation, and the other 5 percent involved in problematic sexual behaviors such as transvestitism, exhibitionism, pornography, or compulsive masturbation. These figures do not specify pedophilic activity; however, Sipe notes that in 2003 a validated list of over 2,100 priests guilty of sexual abuse was in the process of completion and categorization by Dallas lawyer Sylvia Demerest.[14]

At this point, the question arises as to how clergy sexual boundary violations could have gone on for so long without the general public becoming aware of it? One answer to that question lies with the overall growth in the general culture's sensitivity and willingness to deal with issues of victimization. Prior to the 1960s there were few reports of child abuse and fewer still instances of legal intervention. Although sexual abuse of minor females was not unheard of, the idea of male sexual abuse was thought by experts in the field to be quite rare. Despite the paucity of reported abuse there is no particular reason to suspect that the steady increase in the number of reported instances is entirely due to changes in the general cultural behavior and attitudes. One has only to think back to the early days of the Industrial Revolution in this country with its attendant treatment of children as miniature adults employed in factories and other venues of adult work to suspect that sexual exploitation is hardly new. However, with the empowerment of minorities and the attendant uplifting of issues of victimization following the enactment of civil rights legislation there has been a steady increase in the number of civil and criminal court rulings in the favor of victims of various types of sexual injury. By the end of the 1960s every state had enacted child abuse legislation. Child welfare officials and physicians became increasingly sensitive to the warning signs of child sexual abuse. Concomitantly mandatory reporting procedures were developed with appropriate safeguards for reporting individuals.

Despite these developments in the secular society the church and clergy remained relatively immune from legal oversight and legal proceedings. Bromley and Cress note that the particular nature of clergy boundary violations has been unclear as these violations have both elements of a violation of a contractual relationship resulting from the managerial/counselor roles of clergy and a violation of a family-church alliance where clergy is viewed as the shepherd head of a church family.[15] Also relevant is the fact that civil regulatory agencies have traditionally tended to take less interest and therefore less control over churches than other secular entities. In addition both the Catholic and Mormon churches have elaborate internal judicial systems that were viewed by the general public and civil authorities as adequate to the task of policing and adjudicating boundary violations. At the same time, denominations did not have in place a formal readily accessible means for congregants to present complaints regarding clergy. Even when complaints were made and reached a level where they might have been addressed, the complaints were invariably handled internally in a manner that tended to protect the church and its reputation rather than the congregant. Only in the rarest of cases were outside civil authorities brought in by church authorities. The procedure of handling complaints internally within the church governance has been the most important factor in keeping the fact of clergy sexual boundary violations out of the public eye.

The *Boston Globe* revelations documented the active collusion and cover up by church authorities in the case of abusing priests. As Sipe notes, "By exposing the dynamic that supported and conspired to keep secret the individual priest abusers they tapped into the lifeblood of Boston Catholic Power, the pope's representative, Cardinal Law. They unfolded the *pattern,* almost a template, that was being used generally in American dioceses to hide abusing priests, and silence victims."[16]

Who Abuses?

A profile of priest sexual abusers is slowly emerging from therapists and from centers that specialize in treating abusive priests. A tentative and overgeneralized picture would be of a man who is "self-centered, in need of reassurance or adulation, insecure about his sexual identity, somewhat isolated in adult relationships, poor at controlling impulse, dependent, and inept at handling his anger."[17] While this description is based on Sipe's extensive experience with Catholic priests who have abused and who have taken a vow of celibacy, it is not off the mark for clergy in general who violate the sexual boundaries of their profession. In fact, this description is appropriate for clergy who engage in each of the categories of malfeasance including sexual, mental, and physical abuse, as well as financial and authority abuse.

Priests who have taken a vow of celibacy form a rather exceptional case. Another unique case involves the charismatic religious leader. Charismatic leaders are found in all of the major religions including Christianity, Buddhism, Hinduism, and Islam. Certainly, the characteristic of charisma is not inappropriate or injurious in and of itself. However, some of the most egregious cases of sexual exploitation and abuse have occurred in cults led by charismatic males. Research by Janet Jacobs determined that the perceived relationship of the leader of a charismatic cult with the divine provides the basis for authoritative control over religious followers. She quotes the remarks of a devotee of a Christian fundamentalist movement as follows:

Pastor Jim was feared and revered. He was the leader of the thing. He was responsible for bringing them together. Pastor Jim's word was law. ... The people followed him completely, worshiped him. He made the decisions and when anyone challenged him, he would say they were in with the devil, the cloak of evil had been pulled over their eyes.[18]

Such devotion and authority are ready made for boundary violation of all sorts and particularly those that are sexual in nature. In the 1970s, David Berg of the Christian-based Children of God required that female followers prostitute themselves for God and for the Group. Berg's female members were required to sexually seduce potential converts as a means of bringing them into the group. He couched his explanation for the required behavior in Christian terms. The decades since the late 1950s have seen a significant rise in the west in interest in Hindu and Buddhist teachings. Concomitantly, the number of sexual transgressions by teachers with their student-followers has increased. These teachers have frequently couched their seductive rationales in terms of meditative practices that will lead to spiritual realization. The revelations following the destruction of the Branch Davidians compound demonstrated that the absolute authority inherent in the charismatic cult leader's position can, on occasion, extend to the abuse of children. A similar instance of the revelation of child sexual abuse by a cult leader became public in 2004 with the arrest and conviction of Dwight York of the United Nuwabian Nation of Moors, an African-American religious cult located near a small town in central Georgia.

Homosexuality

The very controversial issue of homosexuality between consenting adults in a stable relationship represents a particular case of clergy boundary violation as defined by many denominations and elements of the secular culture. Homosexuality has been a provocative issue throughout church history, though, for the most part it was simply condemned and in those instances where it was practiced it was done so in secret. But with the advent of the gay-lesbian liberation movement and the attendant public awareness and debate, it was only a matter of time before the issue of homosexual clergy would arise. The debate over the acceptability of homosexuality has always had a religious flavor. Many of those who condemn the practice believe that they find support for their condemnation in their basic texts and in the early teachings. Most denominations in the United States condemn the active practice of homosexuality.

The Catholic pedophilia crisis may have heightened the tension regarding the practice, if that were possible. In 2003 and 2004 the issue took on political overtones with the passage of statutes that legalize gay and lesbian marriages in some locales of the United States. In response, some state legislatures and some leaders at the national level have pushed for state and national constitutional changes that would limit marriage to a man and a woman.

In 1998, the Anglican Communion, including the Episcopal Church in the United States, passed the Lambeth Resolution which calls for the Church to "listen to the experience of homosexual persons, and ... to assure them that they are loved by God and that all baptized, believing and faithful persons, regardless of sexual orientation, are full members of the body of Christ." On June 7, 2003, the Rev. Canon V. Gene Robinson was elected Bishop of the Episcopal Diocese of New Hampshire. Robinson is a divorced priest with two grown daughters. At the time of his consecration he was living with his male partner in a long-term, committed gay relationship. Regarding his relational life changes, he stated:

> Risking the loss of my children and the exercise of my ordained ministry in the Church was the biggest risk I've ever taken, but it left me with two unshakable things: my integrity and my God. ... The Living Christ walked with me on that journey: telling the truth about my life and daring me to be the person God created me to be in service.[19]

His election received the necessary consents of members of the House of Deputies and of the House of Bishops at the General Convention of the Episcopal Church in 2003. His investiture, which occurred on June 7, 2004, only added to the furor of debate and controversy that had surrounded the whole process of Bishop Robinson's journey to that office. The controversy was most virulent among those denominations that actively oppose homosexuality as a sin. However, that opposition included elements within the Episcopal denomination in the United States and in other parts of the world.

In March, 2004, the Rev. Karen Dammann of the United Methodist Church was acquitted by church jury in a small central Washington State town of violating church doctrine by living in a lesbian relationship. The United Methodist Church's Book of Discipline declares homosexuality to be "incompatible to Christian teachings." The controversy is on going in the United Methodist Church as various regional conventions struggle with these events.

Women

The issue of homosexuality practiced among consenting adults highlights the ongoing struggle of minorities to gain acceptance and freedom from victimization both in the culture at large and in specific denominations. A final area of controversy that has the flavor of a sexual boundary issue is that of woman officiates in the clergy. The Rt. Rev. Barbara Harris, an African-American woman, was ordained an Episcopal priest in 1980, and then consecrated a bishop in 1989. She was the first woman to become a bishop in the worldwide Anglican Communion. In 2003, at the time of the Rev. Gene Robinson's consecration to the episcopacy, Bishop Harris reflected on her experiences leading up to, and following, her own consecration. Her consecration was celebrated by liberals and vehemently criticized by conservatives.

The appointment was controversial not only because of her gender, but also because she was black, divorced, outspoken, and did not have a traditional seminary degree. Bishop Harris recalled that she had received death threats before her ordination and for years after and had to change her telephone number several times to avoid harassing phone calls. She noted that at the time of her consecration, there were the same dire threats of schism within the church that are occurring now with the Robinson investiture and, rather ironically, the same worries of worsening relations between the Anglican and Catholic denominations due to the Catholic view of homosexuality as a sin. She pointed out, however, that in 2004 the appointment of women priests is common and a matter of routine in at least 23 of the 38 Anglican provinces around the world, and Canada and New Zealand have elected women bishops.

Although the ordination of women into the clergy is common in much of the Anglican Communion, that is hardly the case in all denominations. Today, when successful gender discrimination lawsuits occur frequently in secular life, certain denominations continue to hold the line or, as in the case of the Southern Baptists, to reverse the trend. Although the Southern Baptist Convention has about 1,600 ordained women filling various roles, in May of 2000, following the rise to power of the conservative faction, the Convention released a document stating that the "office of pastor is limited to men as qualified by Scripture." That statement was consistent with the Southern Baptist Convention's earlier 1989 ruling that a wife should, "submit herself graciously to the servant leadership of her husband." Predictably the denomination's female clergy has struggled within the denomination to ameliorate the effects of the pronouncement against women clergy.

Catholicism, Eastern Orthodoxy, and the Church of Jesus Christ of Latter-day Saints restrict the role of women in clergy posts. These groups base their decision to discriminate on their interpretations of biblical passages viewing the Bible as prohibiting female clergy. Other denominations in addition to the Episcopal Church have welcomed female clergy including the American Baptist Church, The United Methodist Church, liberal Jewish groups, Native American, Unitarian Universalist Association, and in some neo-pagan sects, women officiates have more authority than men. However, despite acceptance in these organizations, there are instances where remuneration is not on a par with that of male pastors.

Sexual equality and homosexuality are very much in the forefront of denominational concerns today. The debates that surround them are invariably defined in terms of boundaries. They represent a far cry from instances of individual sexual boundary violations, and yet they are as controversial and provocative for various denominations as are the instances of clergy sexual malfeasance.

Preventing Abuse

When it comes to preventing sexual boundary violations, the question emerges as to who is defining the act as a boundary violation, and what is the framework within which the act or acts in question are taking place. For example, what is known in the west as female genital mutilation has cultural and at times religious acceptance in most of the countries in which it is practiced. Any efforts to alter the practice involve dealing with a particular culture in a particular country with its own history, beliefs, and laws. There are, though, ongoing international efforts to alter these practices, and these appear to be having some degree of success. Conversely, the prevention of the sexual abuse of minors by clergy when it is reported to secular authority immediately becomes a civil-criminal matter. The investigation and prosecution of this kind of transgression may result in significant monetary awards for the victim and incarceration for the perpetrator. Sexual harassment and sexual exploitation may also be addressed by legal proceedings.

Instances of individual clergy sexual boundary violations are undergoing a process of increasing awareness on the part of the public. Various denominations are beginning to consider ways in which to develop appropriate channels for complaints and various procedures for involving civil authorities in matters of criminal abuse. At this writing, most denominations have a long way to go in that direction. However, public demand for reform, particularly in the matter of dealing with abusing clergy, will eventually prevail. Sipe has raised the very difficult issue of the Catholic Church's consideration of celibacy as a mandatory requirement. He has also called for the development of a theology of sexuality as a preparation for priests. The instance of the relatively isolated self-contained charismatic cult leadership that begins to cross the lines of sexual boundary will unfortunately remain a possibility. By the same token, the individual pastor who becomes involved in an adulterous relationship or some other problematic sexual activity that crosses the boundaries of propriety will continue to be a problem for individual congregations. Even so, the generally heightened scrutiny and sensitivity to these issues will provide a greater safeguard than has existed in the past.

Conclusion

In these first years of the twenty-first century a drift toward fundamentalism or literalism in scripture has occurred in many cultures. These movements have not been limited in their efforts to simply controlling religious practices but have affected whole areas of secular societal behaviors. The movement is invariably aligned against liberal theologies and liberal interpretations. At the international level the struggle is particularly virulent in Islamic countries. In the United States the struggle is playing out with respect to the roles of women and attitudes toward homosexuality. The outcome of these boundary role issues will be determined by the cultures involved. The rightness or wrongness of the particular issues will then be defined by the position of the judge or dominant forces in the society.

Finally, it is important to put the issue of clergy malfeasance in perspective. One way to do that is to compare statistics of abuse by other professions. Stacey et al. found 2.8 percent of their sample had personally experienced mental, sexual, or physical abuse by a clergyman and 4.6 percent of the respondents knew someone who was a victim. The figures for teacher, coach, or school administrator were 2.5 personally experienced and 8.9 for knew someone, for a lawyer, policeman, judge or public official 11.2 knew someone and 12.8 personally experienced, and for abuse or exploitation in business and industry 43.4 knew someone and 21.4 personally experienced. While these categories are quite loose, they are helpful in putting the issue of clergy sexual boundary malfeasance into perspective. It is simply not true that the clergy as a profession is out of control and violating sexual boundaries at an inordinate rate. In fact, it would appear that as a profession the clergy has a better record than other professions, despite the fact that the role of the pastor is particularly demanding and less financially rewarding.

Notes

[1] Genesis 2:15–17; 3:6–21.
[2] Elaine Pagels, *Adam, Eve, and the Serpent* (New York: Vintage, 1988).

[3] Ibid, 78.

[4] Ibid, 125.

[5] John 8:3–5.

[6] Jeanne Achterberg, *Woman as Healer* (Boston: Shambhala, 1991), 81.

[7] Ibid., 82.

[8] David G. Bromley and Clinton H. Cress, "Narratives of Sexual Danger: A Comparative Perspective on the Emergence of the Clergy Sexual Violation Scandal," in Anson Shupe, William Stacey, and Susan Darnell, editors, *Bad Pastors: Clergy Misconduct in Modern America* (New York: SUNY Press, 2000), 39–68.

[9] William Stacey, Susan Darnell, and Anson Shupe, "How Much Clergy Malfeasance Is Really Out There? A Victimization Survey of Prevalence and Perceptions," in Anson Shupe, William Stacey, and Susan Darnell, editors, *Bad Pastors: Clergy Misconduct in Modern America* (New York: SUNY Press. 2000), 187.

[10] Ibid., 196.

[11] Ibid., 201.

[12] Dolf Hartsuiker, *Sadhus: India's Mystic Holy Men* (Rochester, VT: Inner Traditions International, 1993).

[13] A. W. Richard Sipe, *Celibacy in Crisis: A Secret World Revisited.* (New York: Brunner-Routledge, 2003), 32.

[14] Ibid., 227.

[15] Bromley and Cress, "Narratives of Sexual Danger."

[16] Sipe, *Celibacy in Crisis,* 200.

[17] Ibid., 228.

[18] Janet L. Jacobs, *Divine Disenchantment: Deconverting from New Religions* (Bloomington: Indiana University Press. 1989), 94.

[19] V. Gene Robinson, "The Diocese of New Hampshire," found online in 2004 at www.nhepiscopal.org.

Bibliography

Achterberg, Jeanne. *Woman as Healer.* Boston: Shambhala, 1991.

Bromley, David G. and Clinton H. Cress. "Narratives of Sexual Danger: A Comparative Perspective on the Emergence of the Clergy Sexual Violation Scandal." In ed. Anson Shupe, William Stacey, Susan Darnell. *Bad Pastors: Clergy Misconduct in Modern America.* New York: SUNY Press, 2000. 39-68.

Hartsuiker, Dolf. *Sadhus: India's Mystic Holy Men.* Rochester, VT: Inner Traditions International, 1993.

Jacobs, Janet L. "Charisma, Male Entitlement, and the Abuse of Power." In ed. Anson Shupe, William Stacey, Susan Darnell. *Bad Pastors: Clergy Misconduct in Modern America.* New York: SUNY Press, 2000. 113-130.

———. *Divine Disenchantment: Deconverting from New Religions.* Bloomington: Indiana University Press, 1989.

Pagels, Elaine. *Adam Eve and the Serpent.* New York: Vintage, 1989.

Shupe, Anson, William Stacey, Susan Darnell. *Bad Pastors: Clergy Misconduct in Modern America.* New York: SUNY Press, 2000.

Sipe, A.W. Richard. *Celibacy in Crisis: A Secret World Revisited.* New York: Brunner-Routledge, 2003.

Stacey, Willliam, Susan Darnell, and Anson Shupe. "How Much Clergy Malfeasance Is Really Out There?" In ed. Anson Shupe, William Stacey, Susan Darnell. *Bad Pastors: Clergy Misconduct in Modern America.* New York: SUNY Press, 2000. 189–213.

Robinson, V. Gene. "The Diocese of New Hampshire." www.nhepiscopal.org. 2004.

"Status of Female Ordination," Women as Clergy: Priests, Pastors, Ministers, Rabbis. Ontario Consultants on Religious Tolerance. Religious Tolerance. Org. 2002.

"Some in Gay Pastor's Congregations Celebrate Win." Associated Press. March 21, 2004.

"Stop Violence Against Women." Female Genital Mutilation. A Human Rights Information Pack. Amnesty International, New York: 2004.

"Woman Sentenced to Stoning Freed." CNN.com. Feb. 23, 2004.

7 Eunuchs for the Kingdom: The Origin and Discipline of Clerical Celibacy

Deborah Vess

Clerical celibacy is one of the most controversial customs of the Roman Catholic tradition. Newspaper headlines routinely proclaim the latest sexual scandals in the Church and often cite celibacy as the root cause. While being quick to criticize a custom that sets the clergy of the Catholic Church apart from a society that is increasingly fixated on sexuality, few commentaries in the mass media seek to understand the profound theological basis of celibacy. Although significant differences in practice between the eastern and western churches suggest that celibacy is an innovation introduced by the west, it can be argued that it dates to the apostolic era. In a similar way, from earliest times the Church was fully aware of the difficulties posed by the celibate life. Indeed, there are numerous instances of the breakdown of Church discipline in this matter. Throughout the history of the western Church, but especially in the years following Vatican II, clergy have demanded that the Church reconsider its position on celibacy. According to some priests, the continued insistence on legislated clerical celibacy threatens to make the Church an "atrophied curiosity."[1] The Vatican, however, continues to reaffirm its importance.

Celibacy is and always has been a cherished form of spirituality. Although it is not for everyone, the presence of celibates among us serves as a model of total devotion to Christ and his people. The celibate is a special icon of a life consecrated to God, a life that cannot be mandated but must be freely chosen. Celibacy is not the only model for a deeply spiritual life, but it continues to be a powerful one that should be valued.

A Brief History of Clerical Continence

The word *celibacy,* from the Latin word *caelebs,* means "unmarried." According to Church teachings on chastity, living in an unmarried state also implies renunciation of sexual relations. From this point of view, the debate in the early Church was really over the requirement of continence for clergy. The word *celibacy* itself is in some ways unreflective of the actual history of the discipline, as in fact, in the apostolic and later medieval *oikos* Church. Historically, many members of the clergy had either been married and widowed before ordination or were married at the time of ordination. The important distinction here is to what extent these clerics continued the "use" of their marriage, and herein lies the crux of the matter. For most of the early history of the Church, we should be talking about laws of mandatory continence rather than celibacy.

In the early Church, Paul tells Timothy that the cleric must be "the husband of one wife."[2] To be considered fit for the duties of bishop, a married man must keep his own house in order. This includes raising his children well (1 Tim. 3:2, 4–5; 3:12; Tit. 1:6–9). In fact, the early Church grew out of the *oikoi*, or households, of its followers. The made possible the travels of the apostles; without its support, their wanderings would have been impossible. Further, the *oikos* would have cared for the wives of apostles such as Peter in the absence of their husbands. Local churches were created out of combination of the *oikoi* of several followers. There was, then, a strong parallel between a cleric's care of his own household and his care of God's household.

There is no doubt, then, that in the early Church clerics were married and had children. In fact, many of the children of early clerics went on to enter the clergy. The second-century Bishop Polycrates of Ephesus had no fewer than seven relatives in the clergy. In the fourth century, the bishop Gregory Nazianzen the Elder ordained his son, Gregory Nazianzen the Younger, who later became his father's successor as bishop and a well-known theologian. The fourth-century Pope Damasus was the son of a priest. Julian, a bishop of southern Italy, was himself the son of a bishop and his father's successor. His wife was also the daughter of a bishop. That these were not uncommon occurrences is indicated by Origen's condemnation of priestly families that became in effect dynasties.[3] In fact, several canons of the Council of Carthage (397 C.E.) address the children of clergy.

There are even indications that the early Church sometimes broke the "husband of one wife" rule. It appears that the Church occasionally ordained clerics in their second or third marriages. Hippolytus, a priest in Rome in the third century, criticized Pope Callistus for ordaining "bishops, priests, and deacons who had been married two or three times ... even if a member of the clergy gets married he can remain a cleric, as though he had not sinned."[4] The Church justified such a practice by counting as valid only those marriages that were entered into after baptism. Baptism was widely viewed as enabling one to practice continence, even if one was previously unable to abstain.[5] Similarly, the fourth-century Apostolic Canon 17 bars from the higher orders of the clergy men who have married for a second time following baptism.[6] There were also several exegetes who criticized the Church's refusal to ordain those in second or third marriages. Jerome, for example, could not see how a man in his second marriage who chose continence following the loss of a wife was less perfect a candidate for ordination than a man married only once.[7]

The later Roman insistence on a celibate clergy, moreover, is *prima facie* at odds with an equally emphatic Christian insistence on marriage as a holy state. In the Jewish world, the unmarried were viewed with suspicion, as Jews were commanded to "be fruitful and multiply" (Gen. 1:28). Jesus, however, led an unmarried life and taught that some of his followers would be come "eunuchs for the sake of the kingdom of heaven." He also just as clearly pointed out that not everyone was able to live a celibate life (Matthew 19:9–12). Despite the example of Jesus, the apostle Peter was a married man, suggesting that celibacy itself was not a crucial precondition for one to become a eunuch for the sake of the kingdom, even among the first who followed Jesus.[8] Even the apostle Paul, who generally advocated celibacy as the most desirable state, as it freed one from worldly concerns, wrote that "concerning the unmarried, I have no command of the Lord" (1 Cor. 7:25).

Paul did have numerous things to say, however, on the mutual responsibilities of husbands and wives. These duties included sexual relationships, as Paul thought it nearly impossible to maintain abstinence within marriage. Paul allowed for abstinence at certain times, such as before and during the Divine Liturgy or even for a few months at a time, but he regarded this practice within marriage as dangerous. Paul argued that one who wished to live a perfectly continent life should not be married (1 Cor. 7:5),[9] but he prohibited a man from sending away his wife to achieve this goal (1 Cor. 7:11). The extent to which Christians valued the married life is also evident in patristic writings. Clement of Alexandria, for example, made the shocking assertion that Paul himself had been a married man at one point in his life, and Clement also vigorously defended the sanctity of marriage against Encratic tendencies of his day.[10] The Pauline veneration of celibacy, then, did not negate an equally strong insistence in the early Church on the sanctity of marriage.

These facts would seem to suggest that the law of celibacy of the clergy was primarily an innovation introduced in later times by the western Church. Scholars have often cited the famous legend of Paphnutius in support of such an argument. Paphnutius was bishop of Upper Thebes in Egypt, a region famous for its ascetic monks who lived in the desert. Allegedly, Paphnutius argued to the delegates at the Council of Nicaea in 325 C.E. that mandatory separation from one's wife was evil, as marriage itself was an honorable state. Further, he argued that to insist that a cleric separate from his wife would make it difficult for the wife to practice chastity. Imposing mandatory continence on married clerics was excessively severe.[11] The Council itself, following Paphnutius, did not issue an injunction against clerical marriage but only against marriage after ordination. The Second Council in Trullo in 692 C.E. reconfirmed the prohibition of marriage after ordination.[12] This applied both to clerics whose wives died and who wished to remarry as well as to those wishing to contract a first marriage. The council, however, also permitted priests and deacons to continue their marital relations with their wives but forbade bishops from exercising this right.[13] According to the thirteenth canon of the Council, clerics were to observe continence on liturgical days. This is the law of continence that continues to be followed in the east today.

For centuries, scholars accepted the story of Paphnutius as genuine, and on that line of argumentation, the development of mandatory celibacy of the clergy is a particularly harsh and cumbersome western invention. The legend of Paphnutius, however, is likely spurious. No one has ever succeeded in decisively proving the claim that there was a bishop in Thebes by this name, and there was not a delegate by this name listed at the Council of Nicaea.[14] While many modern sources continue to accept the story as genuine, doubts about the story do raise new questions as to the origin of the discipline of clerical continence and later, of celibacy.[15] There is no doubt though, that in the east, married priests continued to be a common occurrence, though as time went on, the Church preferred celibate clergy to married clergy.[16] Further, by the fourth century, a strongly ascetical trend had infiltrated the Eastern Church. Encratics and Montanists, for example, explicitly rejected marriage and sexual relations. The alarm that ran through the Eastern Church is evident in canons 5 and 51 of the Apostolic Canons, which condemn and remove from office priests who left their wives out of a desire to practice continence.[17] Canon 51 even mandates excommunication for priests who refuse to enter into marital relations "out of abhorrence, forgetting that all things are exceedingly good."[18]

Traditionally, scholars have argued that this ascetic strain that the east fought against eventually took root in the west and culminated in the mandate of perpetual clerical celibacy. While the east refused to mandate celibacy or even continence for priests and deacons, the west implemented ever more strict regulations.[19] Scholars who follow this line of argumentation insist that the first appearance of continence laws was in the fourth century C.E. in the western Church. The first generally accepted date for the introduction of mandatory clerical continence in the west is 306 C.E., at the Council of Elvira in Spain. According to Canon 33 of the Council, there was a "general prohibition for married bishops, priests, and deacons, or also for all clerics who have been appointed to ministry; they must not come together with their wives, and they must not beget children. Whosoever shall do the same shall be expelled from the ranks of the clergy."[20] The canon refers to married clergy and forbids them to have marital relations or to have children with their wives following ordination. This prohibition was also repeated in canon 29 of the Council of Arles (314 C.E.) and again in canon 2 of the Council of Carthage (390 C.E.). The fourth-century pope Siricius also mandated clerical continence even within marriage in his decretal *Cum in unum*.[21] Note that these councils and decrees did not forbid the ordination of married men but only forbade them to have sexual relations with their wives. Popes Leo the Great and Gregory the Great also extended the obligation of continence even to subdeacons. [22] Presumably the children of clerics mentioned earlier were born before the ordination of their fathers, as seems to be the case with Gregory Nazianzen the Younger.[23]

These Councils and decrees were often issued either in response to queries about clerical discipline or outright scandals where clerics were openly violating expectations of continence.[24] Alfons Maria Cardinal Stickler points out that it would be illogical to suppose that the decisions of these Councils represent entirely new innovations, when in reality they were clarifications of custom followed since the early Church and responses to open violations of ancient expectations.[25] In fact, Pope Pius XI also realized this when he argued that the written law of Elvira presupposed a pre-existent practice of continence.[26] Modern scholars, such as Cardinal Stickler, also emphasize the fact that written law only appears after long periods where particular customs were followed and passed down orally.[27] Elvira is the first written instance of a clear departure from the norms established in the east, which culminated in the Second Council in Trullo.

While earlier scholars regarded the events rehearsed above as new precedents arbitrarily set by the western Church, more recent scholarship suggests that the expectation of clerical continence had its origins in the apostolic era, and that the decrees of the Council in Trullo, in particular, were an aberration rather than the norm.[28] Beginning in the late nineteenth century, scholars began to emphasize indirect evidence of more ancient origins of the law of clerical continence. In the 1980s, the Jesuit scholar Christian Cochini and Roman Cholij, a Ukrainian Catholic priest, put forth the argument for the first time that mandatory continence went back to the apostolic age.[29] Their arguments and those of later commentators, such as Stefan Heid and Cardinal Stickler, rely upon indirect evidence and revolve around the biblical injunction against bigamy or the remarriage of ordained clergy who lose their wives. While most commentators today agree that the injunction in 1 Timothy that a man be "husband of one wife" clearly means remarriage is not permitted upon the death of the cleric's wife, what they do not all agree on are the assumptions that may underlie such a prohibition.[30] Heid, for example, insists that the prohibition of bigamy also implies that once ordained, a married man did not continue the "use" of his marriage. In other words, he and his wife practiced continence after his ordination Heid argues that the prohibition against a second marriage was effectively a prohibition against ordaining those who were constitutionally unable to practice continence, and he finds support for this interpretation in the so-called Pastoral letters.[31] For Paul, marriage is a licit remedy for sexual desires. Someone whose desires are not satisfied through one marriage demonstrates desire to continue to have children (1 Tim. 5:14). Someone who is compelled to marry again following the death of his or her spouse is someone who was viewed by the early church as constitutionally unable to practice abstinence from sex. Even widows who wished to take a formal vow of widowhood had to be over sixty years of age and married to only one man (1 Tim. 5:9–12.). Further, widows also vowed not to remarry while listed on official Church rolls as a widow (1 Tim. 5:16).[32] While the Church did not officially condemn second marriages for all, it did for those seeking holy orders or wishing to take vows of widowhood (1 Tim. 5:14 and 1 Cor. 7:8ff).

Similarly, Apostolic Canon 18 forbade clerics to marry widows or women who had been divorced by their husbands, even if the marriages occurred before ordination. If continence were the primary issue behind remarriage, then logically complete continence was also required *within* marriage as well, even for those clerics in their first marriages. As Heid puts it, "If someone as a widower believed himself unable to resist sexual desire and therefore remarried, how would be ever be able to practice together with his wife this *total* abstinence, which a widower without a spouse must also practice?"[33] This interpretation of the Pauline texts is, in fact, also supported by medieval commentaries, such as Gratian's twelfth-century *Glossa Ordinaria* and the thirteenth-century commentaries on the *Decretals* of Gregory IX by Hostiensis, or Henry of Susa.[34]

Just as the apostles left behind their wives and family to travel with Jesus, so too, early clerics left behind the care of their *oikos* and entrusted it to their wives. Although Paul suggests that the apostles traveled with women (1 Cor. 9:2–6), there is no indication that they had physical relations with these women, who may or may not have been their wives. Certainly Clement of Alexandria believed that the apostles practiced continence even within their marriages in order to devote themselves to their ministry.[35] Jerome also maintained that the apostles were either virgins or lived continently with their wives.[36] The law of continence often meant that wives became the heads of their *oikoi* or, in New Testament times, were cared for by the *oikoi*. The New Testament contains the stories of numerous women who were the heads of their households, such as Lydia (Acts 16:14–5, 40), and the early Christian community relied upon them for support. Such a precedent made possible the acceptance of wives of continent clergy as heads of the households. It was also likely the case that women might more effectively manage the increased responsibilities of a household where the male head had taken on apostolic or clerical responsibilities if they ceased to bear children. Hence, the expectation of continence within marriage is consistent with the account given in the Bible of the requirements for the priesthood. In fact, the legend of Thecla makes it clear that what separated Christians from the pagan world was the valuation of continence. The rage of Thecla's husband-to-be over the loss of his future bride illustrates just what Romans believed to be most reprehensible about Christianity: It broke down the unity of *oikos* and the husband/wife relationship through the practice of continence.[37]

If there is indirect evidence of the expectation of clerical continence in the apostolic era, there is more direct evidence in the patristic period. Clement of Alexandria believed that the perfect Christians were married people who chose to renounce relations after raising their families.[38] Origen also supported the perpetual continence of the married priest, and Heid cites his work as evidence that clerical continence was a well-established and well-known practice even in the east.[39] Unlike the Old Testament Levite priests, who were continent only when serving,[40] Christian priests prayed without ceasing[41] and so perpetually offered the sacrifice of their bodies through perpetual continence.[42] Christian priests can, like their Levite predecessors, beget children, but theirs are spiritual children only begotten through the Word.[43] Pope Siricius also made this argument in his *Directa* of 385 C.E. He rejected the claim that priests should be continent only on days of service and asserted that priests were bound by continence from the instant they were ordained.[44]

Another telling bit of evidence that the early Church insisted on clerical continence is the continuous reference to the priest's wife as his *soror*, or sister. According to Gregory the Great, "The priest from the moment of his ordination will love his priestess [i.e., his wife] as a sister."[45] In 517 C.E. the Council of Gerona argued that in its sixth canon that, for the priest who was married upon ordination, "She who was a spouse has become a sister."[46] Similarly, in 535 C.E. the Council of Auvergne dictated that a married priest or deacon "becomes a brother to his former wife."[47] The Church rigorously enforced continence laws and punished those who broke them. According to canon 1 of the Council of Neocaesarea (315 C.E.), clergy who commit adultery were not only removed from office but also excommunicated. Similarly, Canon 25 of the Apostolic Canons mandates the removal of clergy convicted of lewd conduct. Just what constituted lewd conduct may surprise the modern reader. Jerome, for example, considered instances of clergy who had intercourse with their wives not only to fall under the rubric of lewd conduct but also to be defined as adultery.[48]

So important was the expectation of continence that one's behavior before ordination must also be above suspicion. Origen, for example, is clear that men, whether married or not, who are guilty of any kind of lewd behavior after their baptism, cannot later become clergy. This is true whether or not they performed acts of penance for their behavior.[49] This is not surprising, as Paul also rejects for the priesthood those who had a lapse in morals requiring public penance (1 Tim. 3:2).

The strict interpretation of continence rules resulted in the insistence that the Church admit priests to holy orders only after they reached a mature age, when transgressions were less likely to occur. The *Ecclesiastical Canons of the Holy Apostles* (ca. 300 C.E.), for example, allowed for the ordination of married priests who were already advanced in years. Canon 11 of the Council of Neocaesarea forbade ordination of any priest less than thirty years of age. Pope Siricius also insisted that married deacons be at least thirty, while priests were to be at least thirty-five and bishops forty-five.[50] The *Codex Justinianus* similarly declared that priests should be a minimum of thirty-five years of age.[51] The view that age might contribute to a person's ability to practice continence was well supported in ancient philosophers, including Zeno.[52]

So great was the concern for the continence of the ordained cleric that even his wife was subject to canonical restrictions. The *Didascalia* of Syria mandate that even a candidate's wife be chaste,[53] and the eighth canon of the Council of Neocaesarea bars a candidate whose wife is a proven adulteress from ordination. Neocaesarea also ordered a priest to leave a wife who committed adultery after his ordination.[54] Should he not do so, he could not continue to function as a priest. Upon the ordination of married priests and deacons, it was made clear that even their wives were to be continent.

Various councils also condemned the practice of *syneisagein*, or spiritual marriage, where a cleric lived with a woman called a *subintroducta* who was not his wife. Both pledged perpetual continence. Although the practice did not violate conciliar decrees on continence, nevertheless, many councils, including even Nicaea in its third canon, saw the practice as inherently dangerous. The Council of Antioch in 260 C.E. condemned Bishop Paul of Samosata for, among other things, leaving a legitimate wife and cohabiting with several *subintroductae*. As the Council pointed out, it was difficult for Bishop Paul to serve as an example of continence under such circumstances. Canon 27 of the Council of Elvira forbade clerics to live with any woman not a daughter or sister who was already consecrated a virgin.

If clerical continence indeed goes back to the apostolic era, then eastern practices were actually an aberration in the early Church and not the other way around. According to Stefan Heid, the eastern custom of allowing priests and deacons to continue conjugal relations was "a downright innovation that destroyed the intrinsic consistency of the other regulations."[55] Cardinal Stickler, in fact, insists that the Eastern Church modified the texts of the Council of Carthage and other African texts to suit its purpose at the Second Council in Trullo.[56] Consequently, eastern practice cannot be taken as indicative of norms that the west violated but rather just the reverse.

From Continence to Celibacy

While the east pursued a different path, clerical celibacy followed easily from the insistence on mandatory continence in the west. The Apostolic Canons allowed lower clerics to marry after ordination but not higher clerics.[57] According to the Apostolic Constitutions, however, bishops, priests, and deacons were forbidden to marry after ordination. The Council of Neocaesarea removed from office priests who attempted to marry after ordination. While the Council of Ancyra (314 C.E.) permitted candidates for the diaconate to declare their intention to marry or not before ordination, presumably ordination did not occur if they chose to marry.[58]

There is ample evidence, however, that discipline often broke down on this matter. A bishop of Liège remarked that he would have to dismiss his entire clergy to enforce church discipline.[59] The eleventh-century Pope Benedict VII preached vehemently against priests who were married or lived in concubinage.[60] The reforms of Gregory VII in the eleventh century spurred on the enforcement of clerical continence, and canonists began to argue that a *votum continentae* (vow of continence) was inherent in the sacrament of holy orders.[61] Consequently, at the First Lateran Council in 1123, Pope Callixtus II declared that martial bonds of the higher clergy must be broken.[62] The Church went further at the Second Lateran Council (1139), whose seventh canon of this Council declared marriages contracted by higher clerics and those under religious vows to be invalid.[63] Traditionally, scholars point to the Second Lateran Council as the first instance of the law of clerical celibacy. While some scholars argue that the decrees of this council were yet another innovation of the western Church, others, such as Heid, insist that this prohibition was a consequence of mandatory continence. What sense would it make for a cleric who could not consummate a marriage to be allowed to marry?

The Council of Trent also dealt with the issue of celibacy, particularly in Germany and England, where many priests left in the wake of the Reformation and contracted marriages. According to the canons of the Council, a priest in those areas who renounced his marriage might be readmitted to the ministry, which reaffirmed the expectation of continence. After Trent, the emperors Ferdinand and Maximillian II continued to beg the Church to make an exception in Germany, but the Pope refused to budge on the issue of celibacy. By far the most important of the Council's decrees was that dioceses establish seminaries to train potential priests.[64] The seminaries had the effect of moving the Church towards the exclusive ordination of unmarried men, and the numbers of married clergy declined consistently thereafter. The continuing decline of married clergy following Trent further distanced Roman practices from those of the Eastern Church. Despite obvious differences of practice, however, the Roman Church has always accepted eastern practices as valid.[65] In fact, the Council of Florence (1439 C.E.), which attempted to forge a reunion between the Greek Orthodox and Roman Catholic Churches, allowed for the preservation of Greek customs regarding clerical marriage.[66] The co-existence of two separate sets of customs often led to some interesting controversies in the Middle Ages and early modern period. For example, Pope Clement V in 1307 allowed missionaries in the east to permit their clergy who had married after ordination to continue their marriages.[67] In the eighteenth century, Pope Benedict XII allowed married clergy to minister to Greeks living in Italy who followed the Byzantine or eastern rites.[68] However, in the nineteenth century, the Church began to take a more negative stand on the issue of mixing customs within the areas governed by the Latin rite. Under Pope Pius XI, Armenian bishops reduced the number of married clergy within their dioceses and encouraged celibacy, despite their earlier toleration for eastern practices.[69] Another example occurred in 1929, when the pope decreed in *Qua sollerti* that priests of the Oriental rites who wished to minister to their faithful in North and South America and Australia must be celibate or widowers without children.[70] As a result, perhaps as many as 200,000 members of the Ukrainian-Byzantine rite in the United States and Canada left the Catholic Church.[71]

Despite growing reluctance to tolerate eastern practices in areas under western Church law, Pope Paul VI and Vatican II articulated a positive valuation of eastern rites and, in fact, openly praised the married priests of the east.[72] How is it possible for the western Church to legislate mandatory continence and clerical celibacy while openly praising eastern practices that violate those laws? If insistence on clerical celibacy can vary from region to region or if western practices represent an "innovation," as some have maintained, would we have any reason to think that celibacy is intrinsic to the nature of the priesthood? If, on the other hand, the origins of celibacy are apostolic, does the nature of the priesthood demand it?

The Nature of the Discipline of Celibacy

In fact, the question as to the origins of clerical continence and the later laws of celibacy in the western Church is not nearly as important as understanding what kind of law the Church imposes through its discipline of celibacy. To begin with, even the western Church acknowledges that the law of celibacy is an ecclesiastical law that can be changed. However, despite numerous protests throughout history, the Church has steadfastly refused to bend on this issue.[73] Largely this is because the Church maintains that there is an "affinity" between the priesthood and celibacy. While the Scriptures may not specifically command celibacy, Jesus himself established the internal logic of the priesthood. In Matthew 19:12, Jesus tells his disciplines that there are some who become "eunuchs for the sake of the kingdom of heaven." Jesus says that those who discover the kingdom of heaven are constitutionally unable to do anything but to leave everything and follow Jesus. The Greek word that is used for this inability to do other than abandon everything, *eunouchia,* means "incapacity for marriage." Those who leave everything become *eisin eunochoi.* So complete is the transformation that devotees can no longer return to their married lives or concern themselves with goods or material welfare. In the gospels, then, Jesus establishes celibacy as occurring when one cannot "existentially do otherwise."[74] Once having discovered the hidden pearl (Matt. 13:44–46), one can only live as a eunuch. From this point of view, the law of celibacy is "only a juridical formulation of the inner logic of a particular religious experience ... [it] is an attempt to reactivate the reception of holy orders into that original experience which intrinsically calls forth the spontaneous practice of celibacy."[75] Celibacy is a gift of grace, and Jesus made it clear that this gift was not given to all.[76] It is only for those whose love of God makes them "existentially unable to do otherwise." Continence and celibacy were part of many pagan cults' traditions, but pagans usually viewed continence as a form of heroic self-control.[77] The Christian ideals of continence and celibacy, on the other hand, are seen as gifts that come through grace. Because of the "existential inability to do otherwise" felt by those who dedicate their lives to the service of God, later commentators, such as Eusebius of Caesarea, for example, defined the relationship of celibacy, clerical continence, and the priesthood as "fitting" (prosèkei).[78]

In the wake of progressively strong conciliar and papal statements of mandatory clerical continence and celibacy, the canonists of the Middle Ages argued that the *ordo* or sacrament of holy orders itself contained a *votum continentiae,* or vow of continence. The law of celibacy is, then, founded upon the implicit vow of continence contained in the sacrament of holy orders.[79] On this view, continence was implicit in the inner nature of the priesthood, and it was, therefore, easy for the canonists to explain why ordination was an impediment to marriage.

Since Vatican II, however, celibacy has come increasingly under fire. Vatican II reaffirmed the sanctity of married life, but in so doing, it argued that the celibate and married lives were both equally viable ways of living a truly spiritual life. In previous centuries, the celibate life had been upheld as a special way of exhibiting union with God. Many religious found that in the wake of Vatican II, more questions arose for them over the difficulties of the celibate life, especially if that life did not carry with it any more special status than that of an ordinary lay person. When the question of optional celibacy as an option arose at Vatican II, Pope Paul VI reserved the matter to himself. The pope recognized many contemporary objections to celibacy, including the argument that it is "not only against nature but also physically and psychologically detrimental to the development of a mature and well-balanced human personality."[80] He also clearly indicated that "the teaching of Christ and the Apostles ... does not openly demand celibacy of sacred ministers."[81]

Nevertheless Pope Paul VI then reaffirmed the "affinity" of the priesthood and celibacy.[82] According to the pope, the choice of celibacy represents a more "direct imitation of the form of life which the Son of God accepted in entering the world to do the will of the Father. This state of life ... clearly manifests in a very special way that the kingdom of God and its needs are raised above all earthly considerations."[83] Vatican II also clarified the difficult nature of the choice to live a celibate lifestyle; it is precisely because marriage is so highly valued by the Church that the choice to renounce one's ability to marry is so profound. As Edward Schillebeeckx puts it, while married life is valued, celibacy remains a special "manner whereby a distinctive form is given to the one single universal call to evangelical holiness and apostolate."[84]

There is an affinity between the priesthood and celibacy because "by means of the sacrament of orders and the character it imprints, [priests] are configured to Christ and act in his name."[85] Priests act *in persona Christi*, as they "take the place of Christ himself, teacher, shepherd, and priest and act as his representatives (*in eius persona*)."[86] Celibacy allows priests to "devote themselves the more easily to God alone with undivided heart." [87] As Pope John Paul II put it in *Pastores dabo vobis*, "The priest is called to be the living image of Jesus Christ the Spouse of the Church ... in his spiritual life, therefore, he is called to live out Christ's spousal love towards the Church."[88]

Vatican II, however, raised more questions than it answered. For example, the Council reinstated the permanent deaconate and permitted the ordination of married deacons without expectation of continence. As some commentators point out, this admission alone raised new questions about the claim that there is an "affinity" between the priesthood and celibacy. If there are some in holy orders who are married and are effective ministers, why may not all be? Further, married laymen perform in an equally valid way many priestly activities such as baptism. If this is the case, then why must priests be celibate?[89]

Vatican II has also promoted new questions about the value of celibacy even as an ideal. While many modern commentators recognize the charismatic value of continence, or what they term "sacred virginity," they do not recognize the value of celibacy. From the point of view of eastern clerics, virginity is a positive term of "integrity, freedom and, above all, openness to the Triadic God," and, as a gift of grace, it cannot be legislated. Celibacy, on the other hand, is not only a negative term but also a canonical term. It implies the prohibition of sexual intercourse and also the canonical inability to contract a marriage. It "originates not from above, but from below." While virginity is a "pneumatic or spiritual sign of being open to and being united mystically with God," celibacy is "an artificially constructed somatic or bodily sign of being unmarried."[90] Further, virginity is a charism that can be followed voluntarily and later voluntarily renounced. Celibacy, however, is legislated in perpetuity, which seems to contradict the very ethos of the continent life.[91] Petro B.T. Bilaniuk has condemned celibacy for creating a closed caste of ruling priests, for creating a "fatherhood" rather than the "spiritual childhood" created by virginity. For Bilaniuk, celibacy is a sign of spiritual immaturity.[92]

Further, if continence is a gift of grace, then in what sense can the Church impose this gift on its priesthood?[93] St. Jerome argued that to force the virginal life on anyone was "against nature."[94] However, in order to be ordained, a man must accept the celibate life. While the Church maintains that those who choose ordination also choose to become priests and to accept celibacy freely, others find this explanation unsatisfactory. In *Popularum Progressio* the Church affirmed the right to marry as a human dignity, but the rigid stance on clerical celibacy appears to contradict this right for priests. Under current Church law, clerics do not have the right to marry and as one cleric put it, modern clergy have the right to ask the same question that the apostle Paul asked, "Am I not free?"[95]

Contemporary Reflections on Celibacy

More and more priests leave the priesthood every year, often out of a desire to marry. Many priests want to see celibacy made an option rather than a mandate. The debate within the priesthood first became public in 1965 when the *National Catholic Reporter* published an article requesting a review of Church policies on celibacy. Shortly thereafter, *The Saturday Evening Post* published a letter by "Father Nash," a pseudonym for a priest who asserted quite simply, "I want to marry." A survey by Joseph Fichter, published in 1966, indicated the growing support for choice on the issue of celibacy among Catholic priests, with sixty-two percent favoring an option and ninety-two percent wishing to readmit clergy who had left the priesthood to marry. While only five percent said they would unquestionably marry if given the option, clearly there was widespread support for an option.

According data collected by Fichter, clerics respond to the issue of mandatory celibacy differently based on their age and level of satisfaction with the Church. Only one-third of clergy over fifty favored a choice on the question of celibacy, whereas seventy-two percent of those under thirty-five clearly preferred a system of optional celibacy. Fichter's data also suggest that clergy more easily accepted the requirement of celibacy if they were over fiftty years of age upon entering the seminary. Ironically, Fichter's study may confirm medieval Christian assumptions about the ability of younger men and women to live a continent life. Fichter also reported that those who were content to live as celibates were also more satisfied that their talents were being used and generally had less formal education.[96] There is also support from the laity for change. According to the Harris poll published in *Newsweek* (1967), forty-eight percent of the laity favored allowing priests to marry.

As the Church has spread across borders and cultures, the custom of celibacy often proves extraordinarily difficult if not inappropriate to practice in places where manhood is tied to marriage. For example, one of the fastest growing areas in the modern Church is Africa. In many African cultures, a man is not considered to be a strong man unless he has a wife. Many African priests, consequently, live with women in a committed relationship without the benefit of marriage; if they did not, they could not hope to be accepted by their flocks.[97] The modern Church here again must discuss issues that arose in the early period of Christian history, where councils often wrestled with the nature of the relationship that might develop between priests and the women who keep their houses.

Nevertheless, the Church has consistently refused to modify its law of celibacy. Pope Paul VI's claim in *Sacerdotalis Caelibatus* that the current crisis of celibacy was due to priests who did not pray enough, seminaries that did not properly screen applicants, and supervisors who failed to recognize those unfit for orders before ordination angered many priests. Priests who struggled with celibacy believed they were labeled not so much as "bad celibates, but as bad priests."[98] Perhaps equally troubling on the other side of the argument is the suggestion that the desire to retain celibacy as a vital part of the priesthood serves an "ego-defensive function" for priests threatened by their own impulses.[99] An impasse has been reached between those priests who favor change and those who do not.

Celibacy and Sex Scandals

In recent years, the sex scandals in the Roman Catholic Church have intensified the debate, both in ecclesiastical circles and among the public at large. The case of Gilbert Gauthe was among the early instances of reported child abuse by Catholic priests. Gauthe molested possibly 100 boys in four parishes in the diocese of Lafayette. Although this was not the first reported case of sexual abuse by a Catholic clergyman, it opened the floodgates and many more cases were reported throughout the 1980s. In 1991, Chicago indicted one priest and six others were removed from parishes in the "October Massacre." Cardinal Joseph Bernardin openly admitted error and appointed a commission to investigate claims of sexual abuse. By 1992 the commission determined that claims against as many as thirty-two other priests had merit. In 1992, the James Porter case became public. Porter may have molested 200 to 300 children in Massachusetts before leaving the priesthood in 1974, with even more cases occurring in his later life.

The recent cases of John Geoghan and Paul Shanley have further fueled public outrage. Geoghan abused boys for over three decades in Boston and was repeatedly transferred to other parishes without warnings to the parishioners. Geoghan was convicted in 2002 and sentenced to ten years in prison, but another inmate strangled him before his term ended. The Boston archdiocese eventually settled with several victims for 10 million dollars. Shanley worked as a street priest and had publicly advocated sex between men and boys. Again, he was transferred from parish to parish and eventually to California, complete with a recommendation from the Boston archdiocese. The media relentlessly criticized Cardinal Bernard Law for allowing these incidents to continue unchecked, but in another public relations fiasco, the Church rewarded him with a lucrative position in Rome.

Not only do media reports suggest that there are more sexual abuse cases within the Catholic Church than in any other denomination, but they also invariably link sexual abuse to the discipline of celibacy. As the argument goes, if it were not for celibacy, there would not be so many cases of sexual abuse. Celibacy, it is argued, creates an unnatural condition that manifests itself in equally aberrant and dangerous behavior. However, is this really a fair picture of the matter?

According to Philip Jenkins, before 1984–85, the media and public policy makers paid little attention to sexual abuse by clerics. By 1992 or 1993, however, the situation had changed drastically, to the point where "it was difficult to find a mainstream periodical or news program that had not covered the phenomenon … often repeatedly and in detail."[100] For Jenkins, members of the media have created a far more serious problem than actually exists, misleading the public as to the "disproportionate" number of Catholic sex scandals as compared to Protestant incidents. The Catholic Church routinely collects and archives information, making it relatively easy to document cases of abuse, whereas many Protestant denominations have no such records.

Nevertheless, the numbers appear alarming. Andrew Greeley claimed that "blatantly active homosexual priests are appointed, transferred and promoted. Lavender rectories and seminaries are tolerated … perhaps a quarter of the priests under 35 are gay, and perhaps half of that group are sexually active."[101] James Berry asserted, for example, that there were 400 priests reported for molesting young people between 1982 and 1992. However, as Philip Jenkins points out, considering the entire number of priests in North America, this is only about .2 percent of the entire clergy.

Further, not all cases reported turn out to have merit, as illustrated by Cardinal Bernardin's commission. Of the fifty-nine clergy first investigated, only thirty-two cases were found to have merit. In Chicago, the number of priests first accused was 2.6 percent of the clergy, while the number whose behavior demanded further investigation was only 1.7 percent of the clergy.[102]

In fact, Jenkins argues that it is important to realize that the current sexual abuse crisis is "socially constructed," and, consequently, it "presents rich opportunities for understanding the fears, concerns, and prejudices of the society that comes to view a given issue as uniquely dangerous."[103] One example of the "social construction" of the sex crisis is the claim that the reported cases are instances of pedophilia. In fact, pedophilia can only occur with a prepubescent child, who is thought incapable of giving informed consent, while most of the reported victims are in their late teens with some even in their twenties, well beyond what is considered the minimum age of consent.[104] This makes the crisis more one of homosexuality within the priesthood than of pedophilia. Although homosexual activity is obviously itself a violation of clerical continence as well as other teachings of the Church, same-sex relations between two consenting people does not inflame the public as much as sex between a man and a prepubescent boy.

The choice of expert commentators with an explicit anti-Catholic agenda is another aspect of the social construction of the crisis. Many of those interviewed as experts are well-known activists for reform of the Catholic Church, who see the crisis entirely in Catholic terms. From this point of view, they see the crisis as a mandate for the changes in celibacy and other customs for which they have long advocated.[105] Although Jenkins does not argue that the media have a deliberate anti-Catholic bias, he has written eloquently in other venues about this "last acceptable prejudice" and its impact on the media, as well as many other areas.[106]

Perhaps most important, though, is the fact that it is a mistake to consider celibacy itself a fundamental cause of the abuse. If this were the case, one would not find widespread instances of sexual abuse by Protestant clergy. In fact, one of the earliest documented instances of sex abuse was that of a Pentecostal minister, Tony Levya, who in the 1980s abused as many as 100 boys. Although the *New York Times* covered the Levya affair, the case soon disappeared from public view "because it [did] not fit within the cultural frame that dominates public discourse, and that emphasizes the Catholic role to the virtual exclusion of others."[107] Many other cases of abuse by married Protestant ministers, such as several cases brought against Baptist ministers in 1992, suggest that celibacy itself is not to blame for the current crisis.[108] Jenkins argues that the framing of the stories and the questions asked tend to dictate answers that reflect negatively on the Catholic Church.

Anger over the callousness of a hierarchy that seemed to turn the other way in the face of a shocking and deeply immoral crisis, along with empathy for the victims of this current tragedy have made more people than ever before question the nature of the Church's authority and, in particular, the wisdom of maintaining its discipline of celibacy. However, it is also important to put this crisis into historic context. This is not the first time in history that there have been widespread crises of clerical discipline in matters of sexuality. Novatus, a priest in North Africa in the third century, abused his father and brutally assaulted his pregnant wife, causing her to miscarry. Novatus was not only guilty of abusing his family members but obviously of violating clerical continence. He left the Church of his own accord, having been accused of a great many other crimes as well.[109] In late antiquity, Bishop Simplician of Milan, for example, condemned deacons in northern Italy for fathering children after ordination,[110] while in the fifth century, Pope Innocent sent a letter condemning priests who violated the laws of continence and fathered children.[111] In the eleventh century, as we have seen, there were reports of widespread abuse in Liège.

Nor is this the first time that celibacy itself has been under scrutiny. In the fourth century, Jovinian suggested that celibacy and/or virginity were not nearly as important for salvation as baptism. Those who led married lives and those who led celibate lives received salvation equally through baptism.[112] In the fifth century, St. Jerome wrote passionately against the actions of Vigilantius, a priest in southern Gaul. Vigilantius pushed for the exclusive ordination of married clergy. He also wanted to allow younger clergy in the lower orders to marry after ordination. According to Jerome, many clergy in southern Gaul had children with their wives, continuing the use of their marriage after ordination.[113]

Throughout its history the Church has had crises of clerical discipline followed by intense scrutiny of its discipline of celibacy. It has always weathered the storm. In the midst of widespread complaints about clerical morality in the nineteenth century, M. Ernest Renan remarked,

> The fact is that what is commonly said about the morality of the clergy is, so far as my experience goes, absolutely devoid of foundation. I spent thirteen years of my life under the charge of priests, and I never saw the shadow of a scandal; I have known no priests but good priests. The confessional may possibly be productive of evil in some countries, but I saw no trace of it in my life as an ecclesiastic.[114]

Renan reminds us that where there are bad priests to be found, there are also as many or more good priests. The current crisis, as tragic as it is, is only one of many crises of sexual discipline in Church history. Its particularly heinous nature does not, however, necessarily say anything about celibacy. Abolishing celibacy will not remove the pain and suffering endured by the victims of sexual abuse. If, as Jenkins makes clear, married Protestant clergy are equally capable of sexual abuse, relieving priests of their obligation to be celibate will not prevent future cases of sexual abuse. It might, however, deprive the faithful of an important and prayerful testimony to the outpouring of grace among us.

Witnesses for the Kingdom

While some suggest that celibate priests are no longer effective in a world that is so radically different from that of early Christianity, a conservative critic, Dietrich von Hildebrand, has written that the modernist movement has missed the point. While modernists say times have changed, humanity, he says, has not changed.[115] Perhaps, as Schillebeeckx argues, it is precisely because of changing times that modern humans need more than ever "a speaking sign of transcendent grace." Those who freely choose celibacy choose to give up some of the deepest of human desires in order to serve God. From this point of view, celibacy "reveals the heart of religious life-values, namely, that only in self-transcendence does the grace of the kingdom of God come to us. ... [It] is a continuous summons which makes the heart of the kingdom of God ... visible in human history."[116]

While Schillebeeckx sees redeeming grace in the discipline of celibacy, when embraced inwardly and not merely mandated by outward laws, he is also open to the possibility of change. In the wake of the new questions raised by Vatican II, continued discussion is not only possible but also necessary. It may be that the Church will continue to reaffirm the apostolic discipline of clerical continence and the law of celibacy. We cannot know the future, but we would do well to contemplate what it means to live even now in the already-present-but-not-yet-realized kingdom of heaven. Even in the midst of one of the worst sexual scandals in Church history, we can and should be grateful for the continued charism of virginity, willingly embraced by those who would beget "spiritual children" through their lived marriage of the human soul and God. To turn our backs on the possibility that some among us may willingly embrace celibacy would be to turn our backs on Jesus, who reminded us that there will always be witnesses who, for the love of God, will be unable to do anything other than to leave the world behind. It may yet be that at some point the Church will modify its law of celibacy, but it will never be that the Church will find no place in her spiritual life for those who would, through this special way, witness to the living presence of Jesus. The presence of those who, by grace, persevere in the celibate life invites all of us to contemplate the question, "What will I give up to follow Jesus?"

Notes

1. Alfred McBride, "Optional Celibacy: A Key to Pastoral Renewal," in George H. Frein, ed., *Celibacy: The Necessary Option* (New York: Herder and Herder, 1968), 30.
2. 1 Timothy 3:2, 12. Though the authorship of this text is often disputed, it is customary to attribute it to Paul. See also 2 Timothy 2:24 and Titus 1:6.
3. Origen, *Hom in Num 22,4* in *Die griechischen christlichen Schriftsteller der ersten Jahrhunderte* (*GCS*) Origen 7, 208, 8–14.
4. Hippolytus, *Refutation omnium haeresium*, 9, 12, 21f, in *GCS* Hippolytus, 3, 249, 18–250.1.
5. See Justin Martyr, 1 *Apologia* 14, 2; Origen *Contra Celsum* 1, 26, in *GCS* Origen 1, 78, 17–28). Even the Montanist Tertullian allowed for second marriages if the first occurred and ended through the death of the spouse before one's baptism. Tertullian, *De monogamia*, 11, 9–12, in *Corpus Christianorum Series Latina* 2, 1245, 58–1426, 97. Hereafter abbreviated as CCL.
6. *Constitutiones apostolorum* 8, 47, 17, in *Sources Chrétiennes* (SC) 336, 278, 60–92.

[7] Jerome, *Comm in Tit* 1:5f, in J.P. Migne, ed., *Patrologia Latina* 26, 598A–599A. Despite the questions Jerome had on the bigamy issue, he accepted the church's teachings on this issue. Theodore of Mapsuestia also questioned the prohibition of bigamy on the same basis. See *Comm. in 1 Tim* 3:2, in H. B. Swete, ed., *Theodori Episcopi Mopsuesteni in Epistolas B. Pauli Commentarii, Latin Version with Greek Fragments 2* (Cambridge: Cambridge University Press, 1882), 99, 13–106, 24.

[8] Pope Paul VI recognized this fact in his encyclical, *Sacerdotalis Caelibatus* 5 (1967).

[9] It should be noted that both Clement of Alexandria and Tertullian did not interpret Paul to imply that a married couple should *not* practice abstinence. According to them, Paul only advised regular intercourse in order to produce children during the period the couple would be raising a family. See Clement of Alexandria, *Stromata* 3, 18, 107, 5–108, in *GCS* Clement of Alexandria 2[4], 246, 5–13; Tertullian, *Exhortatione castitatis* 10,2, in *CCL* 2, 1029, 13–1030, 18.

[10] Clement of Alexandria, *Stromata*, book 3. Clement's argument concerning the marriage of Paul was based on Philippians 4:3. The Encratic sects denied that marriage was a holy state and generally had a pronounced dislike of the body and sexuality. Clement goes even further to suggest that all of the apostles were married and that they had children. *Ibid.*, 3,6, 52, 5–53, 3, in *GCS* Clement of Alexandria, 2[4], 220, 15–24.

[11] Socrates, *Historic ecclesiastica*, I, II, in *PG* 67, 101b–4b. For an excellent discussion of the issues surrounding this story, see Stefan Heid, *Zölibat in der frühen Kirche: Die Anfänge einer Enthaltsamkeitspflicht für Kleriker in Ost und West* (Paderborn: Ferdinand Schöningh, 1997), translated as *Celibacy in the Early Church: The Beginnings of Obligatory Continence for Clerics in East and West* (San Francisco: Ignatius Press, 2000), 15–19. All references are to the English translation.

[12] The date of the Council in Trullo is sometimes given as 691 C.E., when the Emperor Justinian II first convened the Council. The Council is referred to as "in Trullo" rather than "of Trullo," because it was held in the same hall where the Sixth General Council had met in the Imperial Palace. The hall was domed, which is the meaning of the Latin word *trullus*. It is also often referred to as the *Quinisext,* meaning 56th, because the Byzantines viewed it as a continuation of the fifth and sixth general councils.

[13] See also the sixth-century *Codex* and *Novellae* of the Emperor Justinian. These laws upheld the prohibition against second marriages, especially after ordination, but did allow priests, deacons and subdeacons to cohabit with their wives and continue the use of their marriages, providing they had contracted no more than one marriage and only to virgins. Justinian also mandated that those with children were not eligible to become bishops. The reluctance with which some bishops obeyed this legislation is illustrated by the reaction of Synesius of Cyrene upon hearing that he was elected bishop of Ptolemais in North Africa. He protested that he wished to continue his relations with his wife and to eventually have more children, and so could not accept the post. The archbishop did not accept his argument and the ordination took place. See his *Epistulae* 105, in J. P Migne, ed., *Patrologia Graeca (PG)* 66, 1485 A. Canon 48 of the Second Council in Trullo mandated that Bishops separate from their wives and arrange for their care in convents. The western Church never recognized this council as ecumenical and so never abided by its precepts, though it respected Eastern practice as valid and their

divergent practices as legitimate for those areas governed by it.

[14] Already in the Middle Ages, Pope Gregory VII and Bernold of Constance had questioned this story. Valesius, who edited the works of Socrates for the *Patrologia Graeca* and was the first to report the story, suspected the story was a fraud. See *PG* 67, 100–102. Valesius also edited the works of Sozomen, who preserves the story of Paphnutius. See *PG* 67, 925f, note 74, for Valesius's criticism of the story in the Sozomen version. Friedhelm Winkelmann clearly exposed this story as myth in 1968 in his article, "Paphnutios, der Bekenner und Bischof. Probleme der koptischen Literatur," in *Wissenschaftliche Beiträge der Martin Luther-Universität Halle-Wittenberg*, 1968/1, 145–53. For a detailed account of the debate and an exhaustive list of references that support Winkelmann's analysis, see Heid, 18. See also Christian Cochini, *Origines apostoliques du célibat sacerdotal, Collection "Le Sycomore." Série "Horizon"* (Paris: Lethielleux, 1981), translated into English as *Apostolic Origins of Priestly Celibacy* (San Francisco: Ignatius Press, 1990), 197–200. It is worth noting that medieval canonists accepted the story as genuine. See *Concordia discordantium canonum (Decretum Gratiani)*, Distinctions 26–34 and 81–84, which deal with the question of clerical celibacy. The story is never mentioned in connection with the important Second Council in Trullo, further suggesting its spurious nature. In fact, eastern commentators do not even mention the story until the fourteenth-century account found in Matthaeus Blastares's *Syntagma Alphabeticum*, and this may have occurred then due to the influence of the western canonists. See also Alfons Maria Cardinal Stickler, *Der Klerikerzölibat: Seine Entwicklungsgeschichte und seine theologischen Grundlagen* (Abensberg: Karl Verlag, 1993), translated into English as *The Case for Clerical Celibacy: Its Historical Development and Theological Foundations* (San Francisco: Ignatius Press, 1995), 63–65. All references are to the English translation. See also Roman Cholij, *Clerical Celibacy in East and West* (Leominster: Fowler-Wright Books, 1988), 88–91.

[15] For an example of the continued acceptance of this story as genuine, see A. Kazhdan and A. Papadakis, "Celibacy," in *The Oxford Dictionary of Byzantium*, vol. I (1991), 395 ff. For a more complete list of references on this topic, see Heid, *Celibacy*, n. 6, p. 18.

[16] See John Chrysostom's ranking of celibates, widowers, and married men in *De non iterando coniugo* 2 (SC 138, 166, 75f). Gregory Nazianzen also chastised those who preferred that unmarried priests administer the Eucharist. See his *Oratio* 40, 26, in (SC 358, 256, 10–16). The Council of Gangres in 340 condemned this practice in Canon 4.

[17] *Constitutions apostolorum* 8, 47, 5, in *Sources Chrétiennes* 336, 276,17–19). Hereafter abbreviated as SC.

[18] *Constitutions apostolorum* 8, 47, 51, in *SC* 336, 294, 252–58.

[19] See Franz Xavier Funk, "Der Cölibat keine apostolische Anordnung," in *Tübinger theologische Quartalschrift* 61 (1879): 208–47; "Der Cölibat noch lange keine apostolische Anordnung," in *Tübinger theologische Quartalschrift* 62 (1880): 202–21; "Cölibat und Priesterehe im Christlichen Altertum," in *Kirchengenschichtliche Abhandlungen und Untersuchnungen* 1 (1897): 121–55; Henri Leclerq, "La Législation conciliaire relative au célibat ecclésiastique," Carl Josef v. Hefele, *Conciliengeschichte* vol. 2, part 2 (Paris, 1908), appendix 6, 1321–48; "Célibat," in *Dictionaire*

d'*Archéologie chrétienne et de liturgie* 2 (Paris, 1908): 2802–32. Roger Gryson, *Les Origines du célibat ecclésiastique* (Gembloux: Duculot, 1970).

[20] Quoted in Heid, *Celibacy*, 110. While many scholars read these decrees as mandating only clerical continence on the days of service at the altar, which also had a precedent in the east, Heid takes them as a general prohibition against clergy having sexual relations with their wives (or anyone else) at any time. According to the traditional view, Elvira introduced ritual continence on days of service at the altar, and only after the daily celebration of the Eucharist became the norm in the late fourth century, did the Church insistent on perpetual continence. Heid, however, disputes this interpretation, as the language of the decrees of Elvira, pointing out that the Latin phrase *omnis clericis positis in ministerio* means "to all those who have been appointed to office as clerics." Therefore, he argues clerics were required to practice continence at all times, whether they were serving the altar or not. See Heid, *Celibacy,* 110–14.

[21] Another gathering at Carthage in 401 C.E. once again confirmed these decrees. See also Pope Innocent I, *Dominus inter*, a fifth-century letter that confirms the law of continence and communicates the findings of a Roman synod to sixteen questions, in Hermann Theodor Bruns, ed., *Canones Apostolorum et Conciliorum saec.* IV–VII, 2 (Berlin, 1839), 2:274: Canon 3, 276–77. Innocent wrote three other letters affirming the same principles, found in *PL* 20, 465–77; 496–98; 605. See also Leo the Great's letter to Rusticus in 456 mandating continence without separation from the wife, in *PL* 54, 1199. For a good general discussion of these councils, see Cochini, 295–308; 355–79; 420–31. Even the Celtic church mandated continence in their Penitential Books. See Alfons Maria Stickler, "Tratti salienti nella storia del celibato," in *Sacra Doctrina* 60 (1970), 594, note 21. Stickler also discusses Celtic examples in "L'Évolution de la discipline du célibat dans l'Église en Occident de la fin de l'âe patristique au councile de Trente," in J. Coppens, ed., *Sacerdoce et célibat, Bibliotheca ephemeridum Theol. Lovanien* 28 (1971): 379–83.

[22] See Leo the Great's "Letter to Anastasius of Thessalonica" (446 C.E.), in *PL* 54, 666. This was further confirmed by Gregory the Great. See *Epistulae* 4, 36 in *PL* 77, 710 and Cochini, 371–82. The Councils of Limoges and Bourges in 1031 made it even more clear that no one would be ordained a subdeacon without vowing complete continence or leaving his wife. Can. 6, in Gian Domenico Mansi (continued by J.B. Martin and L. Petit), ed., *Sacrorum Conciliorum nova et amplissima collectio* (Florence, Venice, Paris and Leipzig, 1759–1927), v. 19, 503.

[23] See Heid, *Celibacy*, 184–87.

[24] For an excellent discussion of these episodes, see Heid, 240–62.

[25] Stickler, *Case for Celibacy*, 23.

[26] Pius XI, *Acta Apostolicae Sedis* 28 (Rome, 1936): 25.

[27] Stickler, *Case for Celibacy*, 17–20.

[28] Ibid., 69–81.

[29] Gustav Bickell was the first to find apostolic origins in the laws of clerical continence. See his "Der Cölibat eine apostolische Anordnung," in *Zeitschrift für katholische Theologie* 2 (1878): 26–64; "Der Cölibat dennoch eine apostolische Anordnung," in *Zeitschrift für katholische Theologie* 3 (1879): 792–99. See also Cochini; Cholij; Stickler, *Case for*

Celibacy; and Heid, *Celibacy.*

[30] Earlier commentators, such as Theodore of Mopsuestia and John Chrysostom, tended to argue that the passage prohibits pagan polygamous practices. Chrysostom also argued that Paul was not mandating that bishops be married but only forbidding polygamy. See Chrysostom, *Hom 10, 1 in 1 Tim* 3:1–4, in *PG* 62, 547. Theodoret of Cyrrhus also maintains the view that Paul was prohibiting polygamy but points out that continence is the main issue. See Theodoret of Cyrrhus, *Interpretatio in 1 Tim* 3:2, in *PG* 82, 804D–805B.

[31] See I Corinthians 7:2, 8, 39.

[32] For a fuller discussion of the orders of widows in the early Church, see Jo Ann Kay McNamara, *Sisters in Arms* (Cambridge: Harvard University Press, 1996), 10–60. Widows who took a vow of continence were considered virgins.

[33] Heid, *Celibacy*, 49.

[34] Gratian, *Glossa Ordinaria*, in the *Decretum*, distinction 26; Hostiensis, X, 1, 21, 3, adv. Alienum.

[35] Clement of Alexandria, *Stromata* 3,6, 53, 1–3, in *GCS* Clement Alexandria 2^4, 220, 16–24.

[36] Jerome, *Epistula ad Pammachium* 49, 21, 3, in *Corpus Scriptorum Ecclesiasticorum Latinorum* (Vienna, 1866), 54, 386, 20–287, 3. Hereafter abbreviated as CSEL.

[37] See Peter Brown, *The Body and Society: Men, Women, and Sexual Renunciation in Early Christianity* (New York: Columbia University Press, 1988), chapter 1.

[38] Clement of Alexandria, *Stromata*, 6,12,100.3 in *GCS* Clement of Alexandria 2^4., 482, 7–12.

[39] See Heid, *Celibacy*, 93–103.

[40] Origen, *Hom. in Lev 4, 6*, in *GCS* Origen 6, 324, 10–15.

[41] Origen, *Hom. in Lev 6, 6*, in *GCS* Origen 6, 370, 2.

[42] Origen, *Hom in Num* 23,3, in *GCS* Origen 7, 215, 11–16. For Heid, Origen's remarks here which Heid believes reflect widespread attitudes, cast grave doubt on the supposition that Elvira referred only to clerical continence while serving the altar. See Heid, 93–103.

[43] Origen, *Hom. in Lev 4, 6*, in *GCS* Origen 6, 368, 23–369.

[44] Pope Siricius, *Decretal Directa*, in *PL* 13:1131–47.

[45] Gregory the Great, *Dialogi*, bk. 4, C. II, in *PL* 77, 336.

[46] See Bruns, Canones, 19.

[47] C. 13 *CCL* 148 A, 108.

[48] See Jerome, *Adversus Jovinianum I*, 34, in *PL* 23^2, 268 D; see also Synesius, *Epitulae* 104, in *PG* 1485A.

[49] Origen, *Contra Celsum*, 3, 51, in *GCS* Origen 1, 248, 3–5. See also his *Hom in Luc* 17, 10. 2:33–38, in *Fontes Christiani Series* 4, 1, 204. 22–24. Cyprian of Carthage also argues the same point in *Epistulae* 66, in *CSEL* 3, 2, 727, 5–9.

[50] Siricius, *Epistula, 1, 9, 13 ad Himerium*, in *PL* 13, 1143A.

[51] *Codex Justinianus*, Novel 123, 13 (May 1, 546).

[52] Zeno, *Tractatus* 1, 1, 5, in *CCL* 22, 9, 40–47.

[53] *Didascalia apostolorum* 4 , in *Corpus Scriptorum Christianorum Orientalium, Scriptores*

Syri 176, 46, 2f.

[54] See also the Council of Elvira, canon 65 for the same prohibition.

[55] Heid, *Celibacy*, 313.

[56] There is some precedent for this claim in the fourteenth-century writings of Mattheus Blastares, who doubted the accuracy of the references to African texts in the documents of the Council in Trullo. See Stickler, *Case for Celibacy*, 69–81.

[57] *Constitutiones apostolorum* 8, 47, 26, in *SC* 336, 280, 83f.

[58] For an excellent discussion of this council and the issues relating to subdeacons, see Heid, *Celibacy*, 122–26. There are many conflicting interpretations of the canons of this council. Roger Gryson, for example, sees the declaration of intent by prospective deacons as proof that deacons could continue to marry after ordination; the Council of Neocaesarea only prohibited priests from marrying after ordination. See *Origines*, 86.

[59] Atto of Vercelli, *Epistulae* 9, in *PL* 134, 117–18.

[60] *Constutiones Imperatorum*, in *Monumenta Germaniae Historica*, v. 1, 70.

[61] See Gratian, *Decretum*, distinction 28.

[62] In the Latin, the word was *disiungi*. See Mansi, v. 21, 286.

[63] Canons of Lateran II, in H. J. Schroeder, ed., *Disciplinary Decrees of the General Councils: Text, Translation and Commentary* (St. Louis: B. Herder, 1937), 195–213; Latin text found in Mansi, volume 21, 526–33.

[64] Council of Trent, Session XXIII, canon 18. *Conciliorum Oecumenicorum Decreta*, 726–29. Hereafter abbreviated as COD.

[65] Pius XI, *Ad catholici sacerdoti fastidium*, in *AAS 28* (1936), 24 and 28. Second Vatican Council, *Decree on the Life and Ministry of Priests*, c. 3, n. 16.

[66] COD 504.

[67] *Fontes Christiani Series III*, vol. VII/1, 26, no. 74.

[68] R. De Martinis, *Jus Pontificium de Propaganda Fide* (Rome: 1888–98), III, 606, sect. 22.

[69] Mansi, XI, 957–58, article 10.

[70] *AAS* 22 (1930), 99–105.

[71] For an excellent discussion of issues surrounding the Roman Catholic treatment of other rites within Latin domains, see Petro B.T. Bilaniuk, "Celibacy and Eastern Tradition," in Frein, *Celibacy*, 52–62. A more recent example is the case of married Anglican priests who convert to Roman Catholicism. The papacy has permitted a few of these priests to serve as fully ordained Roman Catholic priests.

[72] Pope Paul VI, *Sacerdotalis Caelibatus*, 1967.

[73] For an excellent account of the various historical movements that petitioned for change, see John Lynch, "Critique of the Law of Celibacy in the Catholic Church from the Period of the Reform Councils," in William Bassett and Peter Huizing, *Celibacy in the Church* (New York: Herder and Herder, 1972), 57–75. See also Stickler, *Case for Celibacy*, 51–55.

[74] See Luke 9:23; 14:25–26; 18:22 and 29; Mark 8:34; 10:21; Matthew 16:24; 19:21. Note that while only Luke specifically mentions leaving wives behind, the references in the other synoptic gospels to leaving one's house behind effectively included this notion. For an excellent discussion of these issues, see Edward Schillebeeckx, O.P., *Clerical Celibacy Under Fire* (London: Sheed and Ward, 1968), 12–16.

[75] Schillebeeckx, *Clerical Celibacy*, 16; 126.

[76] Matthew 19:11. See also 1 Corinthians 77 for the Pauline view.

[77] For an excellent discussion of pagan celibates, see Elizabeth Abbott, *A History of Celibacy* (Cambridge, MA: Da Capo Press, 1999).

[78] Eusebius of Cesarea, *Demonstratio evang* I.9, in *GCS* xxiii, 43–44.

[79] See Gratian, *Decretum*, distinction 28, ed. Friedberg, I, 100; Roland Bandinelli (Pope Alexander III), *Summa*, in ed. F. Thaner, *Die Summa Magistrai Rolandi* (Innsbruck 1874), 117; Peter Lombard, IV *Sententiarum* , distinction 38, c. 2.

[80] Pope Paul VI, *Sacerdotalis Caelibatus* 10.

[81] Ibid., 5.

[82] Ibid., 5, 18.

[83] *Dogmatic Constitution on the Church*, c. 6, n. 44.

[84] Schillebeeckx, *Clerical Celibacy*, 85.

[85] *Presbyterorum Ordinis* 2,6,12; *Optatum Totius* 8, *Sacrosanctum Concilium* 7; for a discussion of these ideals, see Stickler, *Der Klerikerzölibat*, 87.

[86] *Lumen Gentium* 21; again, see Stickler, *Der Klerikerzölibat*, 87.

[87] *Lumen Gentium*, C. 5, n. 42.

[88] Quoted in Stickler, *Der Klerikerzölibat*, 102.

[89] See R. J. Runnik, "Theology of Celibacy," in Frein, *Celibacy*, 80–82.

[90] Petro B. T. Bilaniuk, "Celibacy in the Eastern Tradition," in Frein, *Celibacy*, 66–67.

[91] Runnik, "Theology," 76.

[92] Bilaniuk, "Celibacy," 68.

[93] See Schillebeeckx, *Clerical Celibacy*, 116–21.

[94] Jerome, "Letter to Eustochium" 20, in *CSEL* 54.

[95] McBride, "Optional Celibacy," 24.

[96] Joseph H. Fichter, "Sociology and Clerical Celibacy," in Frein, *Celibacy*, 104–7.

[97] For an excellent discussion of this issue, see Adrian Hastings, "Celibacy in Africa," in Bassett and Huizing, 151–56. Similar issues exist in India. See Sebastian Kappen, "Priestly Celibacy in India," in Bassett and Huizing, 143–50.

[98] Bilaniuk, "Celibacy," 64.

[99] James J. Gill, "Psychological Impact of the Change to Optional Celibacy," in Bassett and Huizing, 97.

[100] Jenkins, *Pedophiles*, 3.

[101] Andrew Greeley, "Bishops Paralyzed Over Heavily Gay Priesthood," in *The National Catholic Reporter*, November 10, 1989, quoted in Philip Jenkins, *Pedophiles and Priests*: *Anatomy of a Contemporary Crisis* (Oxford: Oxford University Press, 1996), 104.

[102] See Jenkins, *Pedophiles*, 80–83.

[103] Jenkins, *Pedophiles*, 3–5.

[104] Jenkins, *Pedophiles*, 78.

[105] Jenkins, *Pedophiles*, 66–68. A plethora of books have been published that are highly critical of the Church and of celibacy. See A. W. Richard Sipes, *Celibacy in Crisis: A Secret World Revisited* (New York: Brunner-Routledge, 2003). Sipes is a former priest who uses interviews victims to portray the spiritual failure of celibacy. See also his *Sex,*

Priests, and Power: Anatomy of a Crisis (New York: Brunner/Mazel Publisher, 1995), where he presents evidence that fifty percent of the clergy are sexually active and calls for an open discussion of sexuality in the Church. While Sipes recognizes celibacy as a gift of grace, he does suggest it is not meant to be followed at all times. Other writers, such as Jason Berry, argue for its abolition. See Jason Berry, *Lead Us Not into Temptation: Catholic Priests and the Sexual Abuse of Children* (Urbana: University of Illinois Press, 2000) and *Vows of Silence: The Abuse of Power in the Papacy of John Paul II* (New York: Free Press, 2004).

[106] See Jenkins, *The New Anti-Catholicism: The Last Acceptable Prejudice* (Oxford: Oxford University Press, 2003).

[107] Jenkins, *Pedophiles*, 11.

[108] Jenkins, *Pedophiles*, 50–52.

[109] This story is preserved in a letter of Cyprian to Pope Cornelius. *Epistulae* 52, 2f, in *CSEL* 3,2, 617, 18–619, 16.

[110] Synod of Turin, canon 8, in *CCL* 148, 58, 91–93. See also Roger Gryson, *Les Origines du célibat ecclésiastique* (Gembloux: Duculot, 1970) 175; and Heid, *Celibacy,* 248.

[111] Innocent, *Epistulae* 38, in *PL* 20, 605 BC. See also Heid, *Celibacy,* 248–49.

[112] Peter Brown, in fact, argues that Jovinian inspired Pope Siricius to continue to allow clerics to marry, while he mandated continence to appease those like St. Ambrose, who argued for strict ascetic ideals. See Peter Brown, *The Body and Society: Men, Women, and Sexual Renunciation in Early Christianity* (New York: Columbia University Press, 1988), 359–61. Stefan Heid, who seeks to find a uniform discipline of continence prior to written legislation at Elvira and other Councils, insists that Jovinian was aware of such a discipline, accepted it, and did not provoke a widespread controversy. See Heid, *Celibacy,* 245–56.

[113] See Heid, 267–80 for a discussion of these events. True to form, though, Heid denies Vigilantius advocated for the abolition of continence rules. For Jerome's arguments, see *Adverus Vigilantium* I, in *PL* 23², 255A. Certainly Jerome thought Vigilantius was attacking celibacy and continence, everything Jerome held dear in the monastic tradition.

[114] M. Ernest Renan, *Souvenirs 'Enfance et de Jeunesse*, 139.

[115] Dietrich von Hildebrand, *Zoelibat und Glaubenskrise* (Regensberg: Josef Habbel, 1971), trans. by John Crosby as *Celibacy and the Crisis of Faith* (Chicago: Seabury, 1971).

[116] Schillebeeckx, *Clerical Celibacy,* 107–08.

Bibliography

Abbott, Elizabeth. *A History of Celibacy.* Cambridge, MA: Da Capo Press, 1999.

Bassett, William, and Peter Huizing, ed. *Celibacy in the Church.* New York: Herder and Herder, 1972.

Berry, Jason. *Lead Us Not into Temptation: Catholic Priests and the Sexual Abuse of Children.* Urbana: University of Illinois Press, 2000.

———. *Vows of Silence : The Abuse of Power in the Papacy of John Paul II.* New York:

Free Press, 2004.

Bickell, Gustav. "Der Cölibat eine apostolische Anordnung." *Zeitschrift für katholische Theologie* 2 (1878), 26–64.

———. "Der Cölibat dennoch eine apostolische Anordnung." *Zeitschrift für katholische Theologie* 3 (1879): 792–99.

Bilaniuk, Petro B. T. "Celibacy in the Eastern Tradition." In *Celibacy: The Necessary Option*. Edited by George H. Frein. New York: Herder and Herder, 1968.

Brown, Peter. *The Body and Society: Men, Women, and Sexual Renunciation in Early Christianity*. New York: Columbia University Press, 1988.

Bruns, Hermann Theodor, ed. *Canones Apostolorum et Conciliorum saec*. IV–VII, 2, 1839.

Cholij, Roman. *Clerical Celibacy in East and West*. Leominster: Fowler-Wright Books, 1988.

Cochini, Christian. *Origines apostoliques du célibat sacerdotal, Collection "Le Sycomore." Série "Horizon."* Paris: Lethielleux, 1981. Translated into English as *Apostolic Origins of Priestly Celibacy*. San Francisco: Ignatius Press, 1990.

Coppens, J., ed. *Sacerdoce et célibat, Bibliotheca ephemeridum Theol. Lovanien* 28 (1971).

Fichter, Joseph H. "Sociology and Clerical Celibacy." In *Celibacy: The Necessary Option*. Edited by George H. Frein. New York: Herder and Herder, 1968.

Frein, George H., ed. *Celibacy: The Necessary Option*. New York: Herder and Herder, 1968.

Gill, James J. "Psychological Impact of the Change to Optional Celibacy." In *Celibacy in the Church*. Edited by William Bassett and Peter Huizing. New York: Herder and Herder, 1972.

Gryson, Roger. *Les Origines du célibat ecclésiastique*. Gembloux: Duculot, 1970.

Hastings, Adrian. "Celibacy in Africa." In *Celibacy in the Church*. Edited by William Bassett and Peter Huizing. New York: Herder and Herder, 1972.

Heid, Stefan. *Zölibat in der frühen Kirche: Die Anfänge einer Enthaltsamkeitspflicht für Kleriker in Ost und West*. Paderborn: Ferdinand Schöningh, 1997. Translated into English as *Celibacy in the Early Church: The Beginnings of Obligatory Continence for Clerics in East and West*. San Francisco: Ignatius Press, 2000.

Jenkins, Philip. *Pedophiles and Priests: Anatomy of a Contemporary Crisis*. Oxford: Oxford University Press, 1996.

———. *The New Anti-Catholicism: The Last Acceptable Prejudice*. Oxford: Oxford University Press, 2003.

Kappen, Sebastian. "Priestly Celibacy in India." In *Celibacy in the Church*. Edited by William Bassett and Peter Huizing. New York: Herder and Herder, 1972.

Kazhdan, A., and A. Papadakis. "Celibacy." In *The Oxford Dictionary of Byzantium* (New York and Oxford: Oxford University Press, 1991), 395.

Lynch, John. "Critique of the Law of Celibacy in the Catholic Church from the Period of the Reform Councils." In *Celibacy in the Church*. William Bassett, and Peter Huizing. New York: Herder and Herder, 1972.

McBride, Alfred. "Optional Celibacy: A Key to Pastoral Renewal." In *Celibacy: The Necessary Option*. ed. by George H. Frein. New York: Herder and Herder, 1968.

McNamara, Jo Ann Kay. *Sisters in Arms*. Cambridge, MA: Harvard University Press, 1996.

Runnick, R. J. "Theology of Celibacy." In *Celibacy: The Necessary Option*. Edited by

George H. Frein. New York: Herder and Herder, 1968.

Schillebeeckx, Edward. *Clerical Celibacy Under Fire.* London: Sheed and Ward, 1968.

Schroeder, H. J., ed. *Disciplinary Decrees of the General Councils: Text, Translation and Commentary.* St. Louis: B. Herder, 1937.

Sipes, A. W. Richard. *Celibacy in Crisis: A Secret World Revisited.* New York: Brunner-Routledge, 2003.

———. *Sex, Priests, and Power: Anatomy of a Crisis.* New York: Brunner/Mazel Publisher, 1995.

Stickler, Alfons Maria Cardinal. *Der Klerikerzölibat: Seine Entwicklungsgeschichte und seine theologischen Grundlagen.* Abensberg: Karl Verlag, 1993. Translated into English as *The Case for Clerical Celibacy: Its Historical Development and Theological Foundations.* San Francisco: Ignatius Press, 1995.

———. "Tratti salienti nella storia del celibato" *Sacra Doctrina* 60 (1970).

Swete, H. B., ed. *Theodori Episcopi Mopsuesteni in Epistolas B. Pauli Commentarii, Latin Version with Greek Fragments 2.* Cambridge: Cambridge University Press, 1882.

von Hildebrand, Dietrich. *Zoelibat und Glaubenskrise.* Regensburg, Josef Habbel, 1971. Translated into English by John Crosby as *Celibacy and the Crisis of Faith.* Chicago: Seabury, 1971.

Winkelmann, Friedhelm. "Paphnutios, der Bekenner und Bischof. Probleme der koptischen Literatur." In *Wissenschaftliche Beiträge der Martin Luther-Universität Halle-Wittenberg* (1968/1), 145–53.

8 Homosexuality in the Evolution of American Christianity

Lesley A. Northup

When in August 2003, the General Convention of the Episcopal Church ratified the election of the Rev. V. Gene Robinson, an openly gay man in a long-term committed relationship, as bishop of New Hampshire, it was widely pronounced, both internationally and internally, that everything had changed. Not only would the Church be torn asunder—an ongoing threat since the ordination of women in the 1970s—but Christianity as we know it, not to mention the foundations of American civilization, was predicted to suffer such grievous harm as to be irreparable. Those at the other extreme, applauding the decision, foresaw nothing less than a complete re-envisioning of Christianity. For them, justice had finally trumped ignorance, and two thousand years of traditional Christian history had been overthrown by new enlightenment.

For good or for ill, Robinson's election probably will not result in any of these extreme consequences. However, as a symbol of change, it was indeed powerful. Decades of debate, within and without American Christianity, over the morality of homosexuality and the status of homosexuals in the churches seemed to turn on the point of the vote. At the same church convention, a much more likely opportunity for overturning the old order slid through all the shouting, as the church also permitted, without officially sanctioning, religious ceremonies paralleling marriage for gay couples. That was followed in November 2003 by a Massachusetts Supreme Court ruling that same-sex couples cannot be excluded from the benefits of marriage, further heightening the rhetoric on both sides.

During the 1980s, few observers would have guessed that homosexuality would be the most consuming question in American churches by the turn of the millennium. Even fewer might have guessed that the hottest of the buttons being pushed in that debate would be same-sex unions. Civil rights in housing and employment for gays and lesbians; domestic partnerships revising health and death benefits; the demise of antiquated sodomy laws—all these seemed possible, if not likely, fields ripe for harvest. In religion, perhaps we could even foresee the eventual acknowledgment that many gay clergy would be regularly ordained without having to hide their sexuality. However, what prognosticator could have anticipated that the decade following the rise of the Religious Right would end with a serious drive to religiously sanction gay partnerships as equivalent to the ultimate "family value," marriage?

This proposition is under consideration not only in the Episcopal Church but also in other mainline denominations, as well as in liberal Judaism and a host of smaller sects ... not to mention in the courts. To be sure, marriage itself has changed, as high divorce rates and the increasing social acceptability of unmarried relationships have lessened the sanctity with which it once was viewed. Nonetheless, it seems a strange and rocky field on which to play out the evolution of the acceptability of homosexuality in American religious life.

The final score, depending on your viewpoint, will represent the triumph of either genuine Christian ideals or a creeping secular cancer. In any case, that the game is being played at all is the real news in a country whose cultural roots, from Puritan to Latino, have been firmly fixed in Judeo-Christian morality and conservative norms of family formation. Homosexuality, as a cultural reality, has come a long way.

A Ridiculously Brief History of Homosexuality and Religion in America

Early Jewish and Christian prohibitions against homosexual behavior occur primarily in reaction to the cultic sexual practices of other religions of the time. The settled, agrarian societies of the Middle East were principally concerned with mimetically ensuring the earth's fecundity, and their religions consequently celebrated sexuality. Their temple prostitutes and ritual intercourse were antithetical to the moral codes of the Hebrews, for whom they represented, among other things, a threat to an ordered and hereditary but nomadic society. For the preservation of the tribe, sex needed to be procreative—no seed could be wasted—and the resulting children required loyal male protection from predators, starvation, and a hostile environment. As the Jews moved into the lands of the Canaanites and others, the moral codes of the communities clashed, and the myth now encoded in the Hebrew Scriptures (the Christian "Old Testament") reflects a strong prohibition against non-procreative sex. When the land of Judah was later subsumed into the Roman empire, with its more liberal attitudes, these codes were reinforced as part of Jewish cultural distinctiveness.

Early followers of Jesus inherited this moral system and found it all the more necessary to be above reproach, given their tenuous position in the Roman world. The surrounding culture was already suspicious enough of a community that claimed to eat the body of its god and drink his blood. The apostle Paul's writings reflect the need to avoid practices inviting criticism. Heavily influenced by the Greek Stoic philosophers, he believed moreover that sex was a distraction from the contemplation of higher things, and his advocacy of celibacy reinforced a Christian disapproval of things bodily and led to the requirement, much later, of a celibate priesthood. Still, like other small groups before them, the early Christians had to produce and initiate children in order to flourish, so religious laws restricting them to procreative, monogamous sex were both socially adaptive and theologically orthodox.

Early Christian theologians fairly consistently rejected homosexual activity, but their emphasis fell on perversions such as pederasty and homosexually active heterosexuals. Their writings were both apologetic and anti-Hellenistic, so the motives of their condemnation may be mixed, if not thoroughly questionable. Officially, the Council of Elvira forbade communion to pederasts in 305–6, the first council action on homosexual practices. And in 314, the Council of Ancyra legislated a more sweeping range of punishments for sex among males.

In the fifth century, Augustine, a Christian convert with carnal experience of both sexes, articulated the policy on sex that would dominate Christian thought for two millennia, proposing *a la* Paul that it was acceptable only within marriage and only for procreation. Under this schema, homosexuality and adultery were equally sinful, although they could be expunged by a penance imposed by a confessor. In the Middle

Ages, books called penitentials, which listed sins and their appropriate penances, were in wide use and clarified the evils of homosexual behavior. However, it was not until the thirteenth century that a comprehensive theological opposition to same-sex acts was articulated; the systematic theology of Thomas Aquinas led to a recodification of Roman Catholic canon law and a subsequent elevation of homosexual behavior to the category of grievous sin, second only to bestiality among the many sins of "lust," because "sins against nature" are viewed as sins against God himself.

With the rise of the monasteries in the West, celibacy came into vogue, and priests—who often openly married or kept mistresses—were subject to more stringent discipline. A concomitant rise in homosexual behavior in same-sex institutions at least minimized the problem of lost church wealth and revenues caused by the earlier proliferation of clergy heirs. Over time, homosexuality began to be viewed by the rising merchant and artisan classes as principally an aristocratic and priestly vice. The fifteenth-century Venetian reformer and self-proclaimed visionary Savonarola, whose strident preaching led to people burning their clothing and jewelry in a "bonfire of the vanities," railed against homosexuality so fiercely that, upon his excommunication in 1497, one wag was heard to say, "Thank God, now we can sodomize again."[1]

Specific anti-sodomy laws prohibiting non-procreative sexual activity and specifically the "the detestable and abominable Vice of Buggery committed with mankind or beast"[2] were adopted in early sixteenth-century England under Henry VIII, when church and state became coterminous and the distinction between sin and crime was thus obviated. Although few were prosecuted under this law, its legacy in English common law came across with the European settlers to the New World, influencing the religious beliefs and consequent laws of early America. The heritage of Napoleonic French law, which had decriminalized sodomy, was brought by the Spanish to southern North America and Latin America. In contrast, the northern newcomers, already stiffened by continental Calvinism, found the open intimacy, nudity, sexuality, and apparent transvestism of Native Americans utterly reproachable and withdrew into their own rigid communities of morality.

Plymouth Colony had been founded by Puritans who left England because of persecution for their fundamentalist beliefs. Nonetheless, these same Puritans put their beliefs into secular law, demonstrating the same intolerance they had themselves faced in England. Plymouth's statute outlawed sodomy, based on the biblical proscription in the Book of Leviticus. The first written prohibition against sodomy, however, was enacted in Virginia in 1610, and nearly identical laws were adopted by Massachusetts Bay, Connecticut, New Hampshire, and even supposedly tolerant Rhode Island. This made sodomy a capital offense. At the time of the adoption of the Bill of Rights in 1791, twelve of the thirteen states had sodomy laws on the books (with wording at times drawn directly from the King James Bible) or had adopted anti-sodomy English common law.

As the settlements proliferated, the close-knit, religiously structured New England colonies were particularly attentive to sexual misconduct, monitoring the behavior of their members and enacting the death penalty for adultery, sodomy, and rape. Typically of his colony, John Winthrop, founder of the Massachusetts Bay Colony, said of executed homosexual William Plaine that his acts were "dreadful" and hindered "the generation of mankind."[3] By the end of the seventeenth century, at least five men had been executed for sodomy or punished with lashings and public confession.

In the glow of the Great Awakening of the mid-eighteenth century, particularly, charismatic preachers mined the Hebrew scriptures for allegorical tales of "sinners in the hands of an angry God," to use Jonathan Edwards' famous phrase. The dramatic destruction of Sodom and Gomorrah provided excellent rhetorical material, and the original sin of Sodom—inhospitality to strangers—was revisioned as homosexual behavior, a more horrifying and "preachable" sin. So effective was this homiletic line that the name of the city became forever associated with anal intercourse.[4]

Despite the more liberal Enlightenment philosophy that prevailed among the founders of the new American republic, public condemnation of homosexual acts remained high. Even Thomas Jefferson, that tireless defender of personal liberty, suggested only that the penalty for sodomy be lightened from execution to castration. After 1776, the death penalty for sodomy was dropped in most states, but many statutes were broadened to include such acts as oral sex and sex between women, and efforts continued to stamp out the vice. In 1780, for example, Pennsylvania made sure to include blacks as well as whites in its sodomy law. By 1850, even Hawaii, still far from being a state, was pressured by Christian missionaries into outlawing the practice.

Although the Establishment Clause of the First Amendment to the Constitution had erected the well-known and much-debated wall between the government and religious faith, many rulings regulating sexual behavior were couched in religious language and Christian moral imperatives. For example, an 1810 Maryland case indicted a sodomite who had been "seduced by the instigation of the Devil."[5] In 1897, an Illinois court described sodomy as a crime "not fit to be named among Christians."[6]

In the nineteenth century a variety of utopian religious communities adopted a wide range of approaches toward sex, yet despite their frequent openness to free sex and their breaching of other taboos, they all condemned homosexual acts. Nonetheless, intense friendships between members of the same gender, especially among women, resonated with the romantic views of the time, and the literature of the period is replete with expressions of deep longing and physical closeness—though little explicit sexual activity—in same-sex relationships.

Toward the end of the 1800s, changing social circumstances—the growth of the cities, increased individual mobility, and new patterns of work in the wake of the Industrial Revolution, among other things—resulted in changing social relationships. Medical literature began for the first time to refer to homosexuality as a distinct state of being. While doctors universally deplored same-sex preference as a form of illness, their work represented a quantum leap forward in its recognition that some people are constitutionally homosexual, rather than simply heterosexuals engaged in willful perversion of their own nature. Gradually, the language of disease replaced the language of sin as the idiom for discussion of homosexual persons.

Still, the medical literature was hardly enlightened. Rather than penance and lashing, the recommended new treatments for "deviant sexuality" included castration, hysterectomy, lobotomy, electroshock, hormone injections, and aversion therapy. "Degeneracy," a diagnosis that included not only homosexuality but also such conditions as idiocy, criminality, and poverty, was believed to be hereditary. The supposedly scientific study of homosexuality was permeated by expressions of outrage and disgust, rooted in a prevailing atmosphere of judgmentalism.

Around the turn of the twentieth century, the social purity movement gained momentum, spurred by Protestant ministers and church-trained women activists, attacking prostitution in particular in a campaign of moral reform. Not many were saved by the reformers, but the movement led to the establishment of organizations like the Women's Christian Temperance Union, the driving force behind Prohibition, as well as the White Cross crusade for male sexual self-restraint. While these efforts focused on heterosexual evils, the purity movement paralleled a concurrent drive to eradicate "obscene" literature and contributed to an anti-sexual climate in which Protestant mores dominated.

With the ascendancy of Freudian insights into human sexuality in the early 1900s, the belief that homosexuality was an acquired condition became prevalent. At the same time, the first evidence of a developing homosexual subculture emerged in the cities. In the Roaring Twenties, cross-dressing became nightclub fare; the Young Men's Christian Association ironically developed its enduring reputation as a cruising venue, and bars and clubs for homosexuals emerged. Despite its entertainment value, however, homosexuality remained very much an underground phenomenon, "the love that dare not speak its name."[7]

Throughout the first half of the century, the churches had been relatively silent on homosexuality. Such behavior was assumed to be beyond the pale, condemned by God and religion, and not something that polite Christians—or any other believers—spoke about. Gay love remained the "crime against nature,"[8] and there was little need for organized religion to deal with it directly, though the various campaigns for morality, such as that waged by the Catholic Legion of Decency, impugned the horrors of all forms of sexual impurity. Though it was a well-known fact among insiders that there were many homosexual clergymen in denominations that celebrated celibacy, especially Roman Catholicism and the Anglo-Catholic wing of the Episcopal Church, the public rarely made this connection. Discretion was a paramount value.

With the onset of World War II, large numbers of young people left home to live in same-sex environments, including the military, homes for working women, and wartime factories. Homosexuals, increasingly bolstered by the medical and psychological literature to understand themselves as having a distinct and fully imprinted lifestyle, built a thriving gay world of social establishments, insider jargon, distinctive grooming, and stinging humor. At the same time, the pioneering work of Alfred Kinsey on human sexuality confirmed that homosexuality was an orientation, not a set of behaviors, and that it was much more widespread than the common wisdom would have it.

With the persecution of homosexuals that attended the Cold War era, fueled largely by homosexual FBI head J. Edgar Hoover's paranoia about blackmail and culminating in President Dwight Eisenhower's executive order barring all gays from federal jobs in 1953, gays began to organize politically and socially. The Mattachine Society, the first sociopolitical homosexual organization, was formed in 1950, and in 1955, a lesbian group, the Daughters of Bilitis, was founded. On this tenuous foundation, the gay liberation movement started to build. By 1969, there were some fifty homophile organizations in the U.S., with a combined membership of a few thousand.

Still, no revision of civil codes or attitudes was forthcoming. The famously catalytic event occurred on the evening of June 27, 1969, when the New York City police raided the Stonewall Inn, a gay bar in Greenwich Village. Three nights of rioting ensued as patrons fought back. Almost overnight, a massive grass-roots gay liberation movement emerged. Taking to heart what they had learned from the civil rights movement earlier in the 1960s, gay activists proclaimed the advent of "gay pride" and began a campaign for social and legal acceptance that has charged every area of American religious discourse since.

The Stonewall riots marked the beginning of a widespread move to decriminalize homosexual behavior, remove state sodomy laws, and curtail police harassment. Over time, many cities passed or revised civil rights statutes to include sexual orientation as a protected category; Wisconsin and Massachusetts led the states in doing so. In 1973, the American Psychiatric Association eliminated homosexuality from its list of mental illnesses and adopted a resolution deploring anti-gay discrimination; two years later, the American Psychological Association followed suit. In 1974, the Civil Service Commission eliminated the 1953 ban on employing homosexuals in most federal jobs.

Reevaluating Homosexuality Theologically

Throughout the second half of the twentieth century, even before the advent of the gay rights movement, homosexuality began to receive attention in the writings of theologians and biblical scholars. Among the first issues they discussed were the applicable scriptural texts: the prohibition on homosexual behavior in Leviticus (which calls it an "abomination"); the paradigmatic male-female sexuality established in Genesis 1 and 2; and the variously interpreted tale of Sodom and Gomorrah. Christians also had to consider Pauline proscriptions against "giving up natural intercourse." Although in the gospels Jesus seems oblivious to the issue, certain passages in which he discusses marriage are often considered to be evidence of his opposition to non-marital sexual behavior (Mark 10:2–9; Matthew 19:3–9). Paul's concern with marriage seems to reinforce this position (1 Cor 6:12–20; 11:2–16).

So the first works to reexamine the Christian position focused largely on biblical texts. Perhaps the most influential early book of this period was Anglican Derrick Sherwin Bailey's 1955 *Homosexuality and the Western Christian Tradition*, the first scholarly work of substance to find the Christian tradition "erroneous" in its interpretation of the Sodom story and "defective" in its failure to distinguish "inversion as a condition due to biological, psychological, or genetic causes" from "perversion," or unnatural sexual behavior. He rightly noted the tradition's overemphasis on anal sex in understanding homosexuality and its near-total neglect of lesbianism.[9]

Bailey's groundbreaking book stood alone, the elephant in the living room about which hardly anyone would speak, for almost two decades. With the onset of the gay rights movement, however, theological exploration of homosexuality began in earnest. In 1966, Methodist minister Robert Treese presented "A Contemporary View of the Biblical Perspective," exploring biblical passages on homosexuality for the

Consultation on Theology and the Homosexual, a clerical organization that took a key role in early San Francisco gay activism. In the early 1970s respected British process theologian Norman Pittenger wrote a series of books, led by *Time for Consent*, proposing abandonment of the position that homosexuality is inherently sinful. His project was to articulate a Christian theology of sexuality: he suggested that to be human is to have a sexual nature and to be Christian is to be ontologically called toward relationship, modeled in the relationship of God with creation. He argued cogently for a Christian embrace of physically expressed love in all its diversity.

Throughout the 1970s, books and articles appeared pushing a new religious understanding of human sexuality in general and homosexuality in particular. These efforts did not go unanswered by more conservative voices, however. In 1975, the Vatican issued its *Declaration on Sexuality,* reaffirming the long-standing teaching that all homosexual acts were sinful and unnatural and reiterating that sex has its meaning and purpose only in marriage. Two years later, Summit Ministries president David A. Noebel, voicing the opinions of a probable majority of Americans, wrote, "Certainly the time has come to turn back such an ungodly tide for decency's sake, for morality's sake, for our children's sake, for our nation's sake and, most importantly, because the Lord would have us to love the good but hate the evil."[10]

The floodgates, however, had been opened. In 1976, Jesuit John McNeil published *The Church and the Homosexual*,[11] which went further than Bailey in developing a new exegesis of pertinent biblical passages, including the Pauline letters. McNeil reexamined the scriptural texts and appealed to the Catholic tradition as well as to newer psychological insights to posit that it is possible to have morally good homosexual relationships that are not offenses against the will of God. Coming as it did from a Roman Catholic priest, the book was extremely influential as well as controversial.[12]

In the latter part of the decade, books began to appear on related pastoral issues. Clinton R. Jones and others provided counseling handbooks for clergy and introductions to homosexuality for lay persons.[13] Gay spirituality also received attention in such early books as Silvia Pennington's *But Lord, They're Gay* [14] and Richard Woods's

Another Kind of Love: Homosexuality and Spirituality.[15] The literature suggesting an accepting and understanding pastoral approach was countered in 1976 by the formation of Exodus International, a fundamentalist Christian organization counseling gays to seek "freedom from homosexuality through the power of Jesus Christ."

Throughout the decade, the literature was prolific enough that by 1980, Edward Batchelor, Jr., was able to compile a substantial anthology of materials from leading religious thinkers in *Homosexuality and Ethics.*[16] Contributors included academicians, Roman Catholic and Protestant theologians and ethicists, psychologists, and religious leaders, including such luminaries as Karl Barth, Charles Curran, and Gregory Baum. At the same time, historian John Boswell attracted notice with his comprehensive and provocative in-depth study of same-sex love and religion, *Christianity, Social Tolerance and Homosexuality.* He followed this book with *Rediscovering Gay History: Archetypes of Gay Love in Christian History,* numerous high-impact articles and, finally, *Same-Sex Unions in Pre-Modern Europe.* Criticized from the right as an "advocacy scholar" and from the left as a Catholic apologist, Boswell nonetheless set the standard for a scholarly reclamation of historical data about the Church's treatment of homosexuals.

By the following year, the theology of sexuality had received sufficient attention that Fr. Richard P. McBrien's comprehensive opus, *Catholicism,* intended as a "bridge between the Church of yesterday and the Church of today," devoted seven full pages to homosexuality in its abridged study edition. McBrien reflected the newer biblical scholarship that identified same-gender sex in biblical times as pagan cultic practice and the sin of Sodom as a failure of hospitality. He also outlined three possible contemporary Catholic theological approaches to the issue: (1) that homosexual acts are always inherently sinful (the Thomist position); (2) that the morality of such acts depends on the circumstances and relationships involved (consistent with Baum's work), and (3) that homosexual behavior is "essentially imperfect"—not ideal but not, in the case of constitutional homosexuality, necessarily grievously sinful (Curran's compromise position).[17]

Traditional biblicism has also had to cope, at the same time, with modernist and postmodernist theological work that contextualizes God, the Bible, and human anthropology within an increasingly complex worldview. Process theologians, like Pittenger, posit that God is always changing along with the creation. Tillich and others rediscovered the symbolic nature of the biblical myth. Teilhard de Chardin reconstructed basic Christian doctrines from the perspective of science and attempted to reconstruct science from the perspective of faith. Liberation theology, demanding a "preferential option for the poor," and Moltmann's theology of hope shifted the emphasis of redemption from heaven to earth. More specifically, German pastor and homileticist Helmut Thielecke articulated an "optimal ethic approach," suggesting that sexually active homosexual relationships are a "lesser evil" in light of unavoidable human failing. These and other provocative theological viewpoints encouraged a fresh perspective on Christian anthropology, human behavior, the ontology of creation, sin, and salvation.[18]

In the 1980s a prophetic voice rose from among the ranks of the clergy, as John Shelby Spong, the Episcopal bishop of Newark, New Jersey, argued both in church councils and publicly for a more embracing Christian attitude toward gays and lesbians. His 1988 best-seller, *Living in Sin? A Bishop Rethinks Human Sexuality*, raised both hopes and hackles as he spoke forcefully against the traditional notion of homosexuality. Pulling together resources from psychology, literature, women's studies, biblical criticism, and theology, he challenged the churches to update both their thinking and their practice and has remained an explosive newsmaker even after his retirement in 1999.

As updated insights were offered in biblical studies and theology, advances in psychology and other social sciences reinforced the new hermeneutics. Before long, research in genetics drew connections between heredity and homosexual proclivities, spawning a studies emphasizing homosexuality as, at least in part, an innate trait. The definitive word from the biological sciences has still to be spoken, but subsequent scholarship has tended to view same-sex acts as the natural consequence of a psychosexual state of being, genetic or not, rather than a perversion or even a lifestyle choice.

Today the literature on homosexuality is dominated by scientific findings, as the genome has been mapped, and researchers are discovering the many ways in which identity is shaped by both nature and nurture. Ecclesiastical writings are largely in the form of extensive study and position papers issued by committees delegated to produce documents that can serve as foundations for policy. In this postmodern climate, the next wave of research may focus on biography, as the stories of gay church leaders are increasingly told.

Social and Legal Developments

Naturally, while the shapers of religious thought were producing a half-century of innovative theology and biblical scholarship, civil events did not remain static. Throughout the twentieth century, to say that homosexuality, whether defined as behavior or orientation, was not accepted by the majority of the populace would have been an understatement. In 1957 even a position paper released by the otherwise stoically liberal American Civil Liberties Union supported anti-sodomy laws. Hundreds of state court rulings and legislative enactments attempted to put social mores into law. A review of these decisions depicts an almost comical struggle to exempt heterosexual practices from anti-sodomy laws, to define lesbian sex and penetration, and to establish the heinousness of fellatio, mutual masturbation, and cunnilingus.

Even though a landmark 1950 California State Supreme Court decision ruled that bars could not be discriminated against solely because they catered to gays or lesbians, the United States hardly led in the modern movement to reevaluate homosexuality. In 1954, the Moral Welfare Council of the Church of England created an official Committee on Homosexual Offenses and Prostitution which, despite its rather unpromising name, brought the topic into the open and stimulated new thinking. The committee's Wolfenden Report, issued in 1964, challenged traditional thinking on homosexuality and led to the repeal of British laws criminalizing it. Catching up, in 1962 the American Law Institute proposed a "Model Penal Code" recommending that homosexual acts between consenting adults should be decriminalized and that morals should be the concern of spiritual, not legal, authorities.

Despite these advances, by 1960, anti-sodomy laws were universal. Court decisions upholding these laws were largely predicated on moral grounds. In a typical example, in 1959 a California court revoked the license of a Turkish bath for allowing sex on the premises, asserting that morality is more important than any right to privacy. The U.S. Supreme Court tacitly ratified such laws by refusing to hear cases challenging them. Nonetheless, change arrived by degrees; by 1977 twenty-seven states had repealed their anti-sodomy statutes as arguments for recognizing gay rights gained acceptance.

The Universal Code of Military Justice (UCMJ), which became effective in 1951, included a anti-sodomy provision for all members of the military. The military regularly discharged service members who were homosexual, or suspected of being so, often in large-scale purges that depended on internal blackmail to force gays and lesbians to identify others. By the eighties, these witchhunts even had a military acronym—HOMOVACS, short for homosexual evacuations. In that period alone, 3,663 investigations produced 5,951 discharges of suspected gays.[19]

In 1977, Dade County, Florida, became the latest in a series of localities to add sexuality as a protected category in its anti-discrimination ordinance. Former beauty queen and singer Anita Bryant felt called to combat this development, and launched a campaign called "Save Our Children," based on the premise that homosexuals are anxious to "recruit" children to swell their ranks. The efforts of the born-again Christian were rewarded when the ordinance was repealed.[20] The campaign attracted national attention, mobilizing both conservative Christians and the growing gay rights movement. Incidentally, however, the vitriol and potent emotionalism of the campaign also destroyed Bryant's career and marriage.

Bryant's campaign fanned into flame widespread public fear of approving homosexuality and contributed to the burgeoning Religious Right movement, which had politicized and learned how to exercise power. Religiously driven political action coalitions such as the Conservative Caucus—and later the Christian Coalition—recognized that there was political gold in sexual issues, from women's liberation to "family values." Televangelists took the lead, as the Rev. Jerry Falwell talked of a "moral majority" that embraced fundamentalists of all stripes, and the Rev. Pat Robertson turned his "700 Club" into a forum for an eventual presidential run. Falwell happily used anti-gay rhetoric in his fundraising, once asking inflammatorily, "Do you approve of known practicing homosexuals teaching in public schools?"[21] With the Reagan presidency throughout the '80s, the Religious Right was on the ascendant, and specific anti-gay legislation was adopted by Kentucky and Arkansas, the latter with the approval of the state Attorney General, Bill Clinton.[22] In 1986 a Chicago gay rights ordinance was defeated when the local Catholic hierarchy intervened to fight against it.

On April 28, 1980, President Carter invited representatives from twenty-one lesbian and gay religious groups to the White House to meet with his religious liaison, a major public recognition of the growing influence of the gay rights movement within the churches. With the election of Bill Clinton to the presidency in 1992, the gay rights movement (which helped elect him) anticipated major advances. But Clinton's attempt to open military service to gays and lesbians self-destructed, leading to the disastrous "Don't ask, don't tell" policy that resulted in more discharges for homosexuality than ever before. Gamely, the president proclaimed June "Gay and Lesbian Pride Month" in 1999, a small but visible acknowledgment.

But the legal situation for gays remained dismal. In 1982, Michael Hardwick and his lover were discovered having oral sex in Hardwick's home by police who had been let in by an unwitting houseguest. They were arrested under Georgia's sodomy statute. Although the charges were later dropped, Hardwick pursued the case as a challenge to the statute. Four years later, the U.S. Supreme Court ruled five to four in *Bowers v. Hardwick* that the state of Georgia's anti-sodomy statute was constitutional. The majority opinion affirmed:

> The Constitution does not confer a fundamental right upon homosexuals to engage in sodomy ... the proposition that any kind of private sexual conduct between consenting adults is constitutionally insulated from state proscription is unsupportable. ... To claim that a right to engage in such conduct is "deeply rooted in this Nation's history and tradition" or "implicit in the concept of ordered liberty" is, at best, facetious.[23]

Chief Justice Warren Burger, concurring with the decision, noted that condemnation of sodomy "is firmly rooted in Judeao-Christian moral and ethical standards."[24]

The *Bowers* decision stood until June of 2003, when the Supreme Court rather surprisingly agreed to hear *Lawrence, et al. v. Texas*. The circumstances in *Lawrence* were very similar to those in the Hardwick case, and the Texas Supreme Court had ruled the anti-sodomy statute constitutional. In overturning that decision, the Justices even more surprisingly ruled 6–3 that the Texas law violated the equal protection provision of the Fourteenth Amendment. While the lower court had relied on *Bowers v. Hardwick,* Justice Kennedy, writing for the majority, reflected a new judicial attitude: *"Bowers* was not correct when it was decided, and it is not correct today. It ought not to remain binding precedent. *Bowers v. Hardwick* should be and now is overruled." The Court thus reaffirmed both the right to privacy and the application of the Fourteenth Amendment to gays and lesbians. Moreover, it specifically rejected arguments on moral grounds. Justice Scalia, in his dissent, echoed the real concern of many conservatives: "This effectively decrees the end of all morals legislation."

Needless to say, the fallout among religious leaders and commentators was immediate and vocal. Bishop Wilton D. Gregory, president of the United States Conference of Catholic Bishops, reasserted in a June 27, 2003, press release that "the Catholic Church teaches, in agreement with other faith traditions and with what were once the norms generally accepted by society, that sexual activity belongs to the marital relationship between one man and one woman." Similarly, the organization Concerned Women for America, which had filed an *amicus* brief supporting the state in the case, claimed in a June 26, 2003, press release that "the Supreme Court … issued a radical ruling knocking down 3000 years of Judeo-Christian-based law." The American Society for the Defense of Tradition, Family, and Property also issued a June 26, 2003, press release that deplored "the monumental implications of this decision and the harsh burden it places on all Americans who strive to abide by the Ten Commandments." However, many religious groups had backed Lawrence's bid to strike down the law. Some fifty religious organizations and leaders signed on to a brief for the plaintiffs, including the United Church of Christ, Hadassah, the Unitarians, and the Presiding Bishop of the Episcopal Church, as well as the gay-friendly organizations of many communions.

On the day after the decision, a Gallup Poll indicated that about 6 out of 10 American adults thought that homosexual relations between consenting adults should be legal. This represented a significant change over the results of a similar survey in 1988, when a clear majority felt they should be illegal. The 2003 results showed that those most likely to continue to believe that homosexual relations should be outlawed included people who attend church regularly.

The last two decades of the century were, sadly, also characterized by the increasingly public anti-gay activities of the Rev. Fred Phelps and members of his Westboro, Kansas, Primitive Baptist Church. As the church cheerfully advertises on its Web page, www.GodHatesFags.com,

> WBC engages in daily peaceful sidewalk demonstrations opposing the homosexual lifestyle of soul-damning, nation-destroying filth. We display large, colorful signs containing Bible words and sentiments, including: God Hates Fags, Fags Hate God, AIDS Cures Fags, Thank God For AIDS, Fags Burn In Hell, God Is Not Mocked, Fags Are Nature Freaks, God Gave Fags Up, No Special Laws for Fags, Fags Doom Nations, etc.

Phelps has tried to buy pieces of courthouse property around the country with plans to erect "memorials" to a well-known gay-bashing victim reading, "Matthew Shepard, entered hell Oct. 12, 1998, at age 21, in defiance of God's solemn warning." While Phelps's tactics have not been publicly endorsed by other conservative religious groups, those who have spoken out against him are pathetically few.

In 2000, the Supreme Court voted 5 to 4 to overturn a unanimous New Jersey Supreme Court ruling against the Boy Scouts of America brought by a gay scoutmaster. The Scouts argued that the organization had Christian foundations and claimed their First Amendment right to freedom of religion in rejecting gay scouts. Among those filing *amicus* briefs for the Scouts were the Christian Legal Society, Campus Crusade for Christ International, Intervarsity Christian Fellowship/USA, the U.S. Catholic Conference, the General Commission on United Methodist Men, the Church of Jesus Christ of Latter-Day Saints, and the Lutheran Church-Missouri Synod. Arrayed on behalf of Dale were the deans of twelve seminaries and rabbinical schools, and the General Board of Church and Society of the United Methodist Church.

Homosexuality and the Churches

Against the backdrop of these social developments, churches found themselves facing key questions about sexuality. The importance of religion in the lives of gay people was an open question; several sociological studies of the 1960s and 1970s found that gay men tended to reject organized religion, while others found no difference in religious feeling between gay and straight men, and one established a very high correlation between homosexuals and religious commitment. That a large number of gays were involved with the churches and concerned about their status within them, however, could not be denied.

One of the earliest Christian organizations to adopt a stance of gay advocacy was founded in San Francisco in 1962. The Consultation on the Church and the Homosexual (later the Council on Religion and the Homosexual) resulted from the efforts of United Methodist minister Ted McIlvenna and sixteen other clerics to "to promote continuing dialogue between the Church and the homosexual." Episcopal bishops James Pike and, later, Kim Myers supported the Consultation, and representatives of the Methodists, Lutherans, UCC, Baptists, Roman Catholics, and Presbyterians participated in national symposia the organization sponsored.

In 1965, the CRH published "A Brief of Injustices: An Indictment of Our Society in Its Treatment of the Homosexual," cataloguing the intimidation, prejudice, discrimination, and harassment of gays and lesbians—a highly publicized document that drew national attention not only to the plight of homosexuals but to the efforts of those within the religious establishment to alleviate it. A crucial first step toward improving relations between the Christian churches and the homophile community, CRH nonetheless, as one commentator noted, "made much greater strides in the political/legal arena and in society at large, than in the churches it represented."[25]

In 1964, the Friends Home Committee published *Towards a Quaker View of Sex,* emphasizing that "it is the nature and quality of a relationship that matters: one must not judge it by its outward appearance but by its inner worth."[26] In 1966, the National Council of Churches met for the first time with gay activists. There, in 1967, the Episcopal

Diocese of California adopted a resolution calling for the end of anti-sodomy laws and police harassment and the institution of seminary education on human sexuality.

In 1968, a year before Stonewall, the Reverend Troy Perry founded Metropolitan Community Church (MCC) of Los Angeles, a religious organization specifically oriented toward the spiritual needs of homosexuals. Congregations catering to gays, such as New York's liturgically oriented and rather campy Church of the Apostles, had appeared already in the cities, but they were mostly short-lived. MCC, broad-based and well organized, quickly became almost mainstream, taking the classical creeds as its charter, espousing traditional Protestant principles, and carefully avoiding flamboyance. [27] By 1974, the church claimed some fifteen thousand members.[28] By the end of the century, it had become a denomination of over three hundred worldwide churches comprised not only of gays and lesbians, but of numbers of heterosexual Christians and children and parents of gays drawn to its inclusive worship and community.[29]

In 1973, gay activists disrupted the meeting of the Governing Board of the National Council of Churches, whose members include most of the large mainline denominations, to air their grievances against the attitudes of the churches. In consequence, the Board sponsored a consultation on "The Church and the Gay Community," the first successful meeting of church and gay leaders.[30] The result was a National Task Force on Gay People in the Church and an initial attempt at dialogue in the more liberal mainline churches.

By 1974, the mood of the country in general had begun to swing towards what was then called increased "toleration" of homosexuals. In that year, the Roman Catholic National Federation of Priests Councils adopted a resolution on the "Civil Rights of Homosexual Persons" typifying the new liberality. Considering the source, it was remarkable:

> BE IT RESOLVED that the NFPC hereby declares its opposition to all civil laws which make consensual homosexual acts between adults a crime and thus urges their repeal; and BE IT FURTHER RESOLVED that NFPC also expresses its opposition to homosexuality as such being the basis of discrimination against homosexuals in employment, governmental services, housing and child rearing involving natural or adoptive parents.

Of the various traditions, the United Church of Christ clearly led the pack in recognizing and affirming homosexual persons. In 1975, the General Synod passed a resolution in support of full civil liberties to persons of all "affectional or sexual preferences," and two years later, it "deplored the use of scripture to generate hatred and the violation of civil rights of gay and bisexual persons."

Also in 1975, the National Council of Churches passed a declaration affirming that everyone is entitled to equal treatment under the law, and urging members to work for civil rights for "all persons without regard to their affectional or sexual preference." A year later, the Episcopal Church passed a resolution saying, "Homosexual persons are children of God who have a full and equal claim with all other persons upon the love, acceptance, and pastoral concern and care of the Church." In 1977, however, the House of Bishops issued a statement describing homosexuality as unbiblical. Two years later, the church's General Convention passed a milder resolution that it was "inappropriate" to ordain anyone sexually active outside of marriage; this was rejected in writing by over three dozen bishops.

When in 1978 several congregations in what was then the United Presbyterian Church in the USA adopted policies explicitly welcoming lesbian and gay members and guaranteeing their full participation, including ordination, the More Light Church movement was born. This spawned similar movements in the United Methodist Church (Reconciling Congregations), the United Church of Christ (Open and Affirming Congregations), and the Evangelical Lutheran Church (Reconciled in Christ Congregations). Later, the idea spread to the Christian Church (Disciples of Christ), the American Baptist Churches, the Brethren and Mennonite churches, and the Unitarian Universalist Association, all of which now have identifiable networks of gay-friendly congregations. Other groups have arisen in opposition to this movement. Transforming Congregations, spanning several mainline denominations, includes congregations committed to developing programs to "transform" homosexuals into heterosexuals, or at least into celibates.

Gay-Oriented Church Organizations

In 1969, Fr. Pat Nidorf, OSA, of San Diego, founded Dignity for gay Roman Catholics, the first such church-based organization. His aim at the time was to offer support and acceptance to Catholic homosexuals, but the group soon took on a life of its own. It quickly grew as a gathering place for men and women who felt excluded by the church and by 1973 had twelve chapters.[31] A year after the establishment of Dignity, the Unitarian Universalist Association (UUA) General Assembly adopted a resolution calling for an end to discrimination against homosexuals, and shortly after, the UUA Gay Caucus was formed to speak from within the church on the issue. In 1972, the United Church of Christ Coalition joined these early pioneers, arguing at the church's General Synod that discussion of matters of gay and lesbian concern should include openly gay and lesbian persons.

Two years later, Integrity, an Episcopal group, and Presbyterians for Lesbian & Gay Concerns were formed, as was Friends for Lesbian, Gay, Bisexual, Transgender, and Queer Concerns. Other organizations soon followed. These included, to name but a few, the United Methodist Gay Caucus (1975), later renamed Affirmation; the Brethren/Mennonite Council for Lesbian and Gay Concerns and Seventh Day Adventist Kinship[32] (1977); Affirmation, a Mormon group (1978); EMERGENCE International, for Christian Scientists (1985); the Gay, Lesbian, and Affirming Disciples Alliance (1987); the Association of Welcoming and Affirming Baptists (1993); and AWARE (As We Are) in the Christian Reformed Church (1994).

Most, if not all, of these groups support lesbians, gay men, bisexual and transgender persons, other sexual minorities, and—significantly— friends, family members, and supporters. Their broad constituencies have helped them successfully pursue both pastoral and advocacy roles within their churches and to assume increasing influence in church deliberations. Soulforce, an interfaith group established in 1999 by activist minister Mel White, has become highly visible in its goal to end the religious persecution of any kind against sexual minorities. Its ecumenical base and media savvy may mark it as a model for future activism for gay and lesbian religious concerns.

As usual, the formation of these groups has not gone unanswered by those on the other side. In 1986, the Vatican issued yet another letter calling gay people "intrinsically disordered" and stating that homosexuality could never be reconciled with church doctrine.[33] Conservative groups have also proliferated as 1980s and 1990s traditionalists took a page from the organizing tactics of the liberal movements of the 1960s and 1970s. Most anti-gay activity is generated by national interest groups like the American Family Council or Concerned Women for America, supported by Exodus International and other groups pushing prayer and self-discipline to "cure" homosexuals. They have been countered by such national agencies as the Interfaith Working Group, which focuses specifically on sexuality issues, and by broad-interest rights organizations like People for the American Way and the Interfaith Alliance.

The Ordination Issue

The most explosive of the issues facing the churches was whether homosexuals should be ordained as priests and ministers. In ages past, homosexual activity by clergy was severely punished. In 1640 England, for example, John Atherton, an Anglican bishop, was hanged for sodomy, and a woodcut of the hanging was distributed to the public. In the Netherlands minister Andreas Klink was only banished for life for having committed—and defended—sodomy. This liberal spirit appears to have caught on in France, where the last execution for sodomy occurred in 1783, when a friar was broken on the wheel.

The United States also had its share of fallen clergy. A Mormon bishop, of all things—Thomas Taylor—was removed from his job in Salt Lake City in 1886 because of his same-sex escapades. Episcopal priest Alfred Mortimer was forced to resign and leave the country in 1912 for the same behavior. [34] The evidence—corroborated in many a work of fiction as well as history—is that homosexual men of the cloth have long been part of the profession. It is equally clear, however, that clergy have traditionally kept their sexual behavior as private as possible.

With the development of the gay rights movement and the general liberalization of attitudes toward sex that characterized the 1960s, clerical sexuality began to be openly addressed. A few hardy souls whose careers were already established or over came out of the closet and discussed their lives as gay priests and even bishops. However, the idea of officially accepting openly gay ordinands for the ministry was fresh, hot, and divisive.

The first salvo was fired across the bow of American Christianity in 1972, when William Johnson was ordained a minister in the United Church of Christ. Observers, both inside and outside the UCC, speculated that the denomination would be orphaned by its ecumenical partners, but the anticipated day of doom never arrived. Ordination of active homosexuals was formally accepted by the denomination in 1980.

In 1975 Paul Moore, Jr., bishop of the Episcopal Diocese of New York, ordained Ellen Barrett, an open lesbian, as a deacon. Opposition to that initial ordination was muted, but when women were approved for full holy orders in 1976, Moore ordained Barrett to the priesthood to a firestorm of national protest. She was only the second openly gay person to be ordained in any Christian denomination outside the Metropolitan Community Church. In 1979 the Episcopal Church's General Convention passed a resolution that ordination of homosexuals was "not appropriate." In protest, twenty bishops signed a statement calling the church's position on gays "a cruel denial of the sexual being of homosexual persons" and a "condemnatory judgment" that made them second-class citizens in the church.[35]

When Edmond Browning was elected Presiding Bishop of the Episcopal Church in 1985, he made it clear that he did not support the church's official position, and the issue continued to simmer. In 1989 Bishop John Spong ordained Robert Williams, an openly gay man, to the priesthood. The following year, the outspoken bishop approved the ordination of another open and active homosexual in his diocese, Barry Stopfel, who was ordained by Spong's assistant, Bishop Walter Righter. Four years later, a group of ten Episcopal bishops charged Righter with heresy, but the case came to a dramatic close when a church tribunal declared that "there is no discipline of the Church prohibiting the ordination of a non-celibate person living in a committed relationship with a person of the same sex, violation of which would constitute a violation of [Righter's] ordination vows."[36]

According to Integrity, the church's gay advocacy group, at least fifty known practicing homosexuals were ordained by 1991. In that year an Episcopal Church commission ended a three-year study by recommending that bishops be individually allowed to ordain openly homosexual seminarians to the priesthood. By 1993, a survey of nearly twenty thousand Episcopalians showed that some seventy percent believed "faithful Christians can be sexually active gays and lesbians,"[37] but the following year, a number of bishops issued a pastoral letter suggesting a moratorium on such ordinations. In response, seventy bishops signed a statement authored by Spong that affirmed gay priests and the acceptance of homosexual persons in the church. When Robinson was elected bishop, the final barrier to full incorporation of gays was breached.

A similar roller-coaster path has characterized the Presbyterian Church in the USA. In 1975, openly gay Bill Silver applied for ordination. Since the issue was not specifically addressed in the denomination's Book of Order, which deals with ordained ministry, the church decided to establish a task force in 1976 to study the question. Two years later, the task force concluded that homosexuality, per se, was not a bar to ordination, but the church's General Assembly voted otherwise, concluding that homosexuality "is not God's wish for humanity" and that, therefore, "unrepentant homosexual practice does not accord with the requirements for ordination." The Assembly specifically denied ordination to "self-affirming, practicing homosexual persons," identifying the two factors that would dominate the discussion of homosexuality within Christianity into the next millennium—celibacy and openness.

The Presbyterians' adventure into acceptance resumed shortly after. In 1974, the Reverend Jean Spahr had been ordained in the Presbyterian Church (USA) before she realized that she was a lesbian. In 1991, after she had become more self-aware, Spahr was chosen by the Downtown United Presbyterian Church in Rochester, New York, to become co-pastor. Some Presbyterians in the area formally challenged the call. Although the hiring was upheld twice by the local presbytery and the area synod, the Permanent Judicial Commission of the church eventually vetoed it, basing its decision on the 1978 policy. Rev. Spahr was allowed to remain a minister in good standing only because she had been ordained prior to that study.

This incident, among others, led to the creation of That All May Freely Serve, a Presbyterian organization supporting gay ordinations. The organization has continued to push for changes in the 1978 statement, which remains in force. In 1997 the denomination narrowly passed the controversial "Amendment B," aimed at active homosexuals, which insisted on chastity and repentance for gay clergy. The following year, a more liberally worded amendment, calling only for fidelity in all relationships, was passed by the General Assembly but rejected by the presbyteries. Another attempt was made in 1999 to reject the language of Amendment B, but though the committee appointed to make a recommendation that supported its deletion, another close vote in the Assembly retained it and led to the appointment of another study commission instead. In 2001 and again in 2002, the presbyteries turned down more inclusive amendments. Nonetheless, despite the church's official policy, a number of churches have openly defied the ban on gay clergy by presenting or hiring open candidates.

In a series of trials—or decisions not to go to trial—the United Methodists have opted in some locales not to oppose openly gay clergy, though the church's Book of Discipline includes a 1984 provision prohibiting only sexually active gays and lesbians who openly reveal their sexual orientation from serving as ministers. In 1987, Rose Mary Denman disclosed to her bishop that she was a lesbian. Charges were filed against her, and she was found guilty of violating the Book's limitation. In 2001, however, when minister Mark Williams came out, an investigating committee voted unanimously not to bring charges, and Karen Dammann's subsequent case likewise never went to trial. In the face of this uncertainty, the 2002 General Conference reaffirmed the position that sexually active gays and lesbians cannot be ordained.

In another generally liberal denomination, the Church of Christ (Disciples), the question is complicated by the church's system of congregational autonomy and regional authority over ordination. Although open gays were ordained in various regions of the church as early as 1981, broad variation reigns among them. In 1992, the Northeastern Regional Assembly adopted a resolution refusing ordination to any person who "openly communicates a homosexual lifestyle," while at the same time the Pacific Southwest Regional Assembly soundly defeated a move to bar gay ordinations.

The question of the suitability of gay persons for ordained ministry continues to be a hot topic in many Christian denominations. One visible symbol of the problem is the Shower of Stoles project, which began when a Presbyterian minister resigned her ordination in 1995 and asked for gay persons who had been denied ordination or required to stay in the closet to send her a liturgical stole; there are now over nine hundred stoles, representing homosexuals banned or discriminated against in at least twenty-three different churches. Today, close to thirty large, established churches around the world in the Anglican, Disciples, Lutheran, Old Catholic, Reformed, and UCC traditions, ordain homosexual clergy,[38] and an uncounted number of smaller and/or newer organizations also do so. In the United States, the Friends and many New Thought churches, such as Unity and Religious Science, welcome gay leaders. Even the Reorganized Church of Latter-Day Saints, the most liberal branch of Mormonism, has quietly ordained gays to lay ministries.

At the end of 2003, however, the issue was still being debated—and causing rifts—in many large communions. When Robinson was consecrated in the summer of 2003, the principal counter-argument was not that he was gay; in many ways, the question of whether gay people could be ordained was already settled by the incontrovertible evidence that they long had been. Robinson's chief disqualifications in the eyes of detractors, as the Presbyterian decision of 1978 had presaged, were his refusal to pretend to celibacy and his public indiscretion. These issues will continue to define the debate about the ordination of gay persons throughout the first decade of the twenty-first century.

Clergy Sexual Abuse

One troubling subset of the question of clergy sexuality has skewed public perceptions with recent revelations of large numbers of pedophiles in the Roman Catholic priesthood. Breathless news reports and massive personal injury awards to now-adult victims have promoted the idea that the problem results because the clerical ranks are largely homosexual. Even the Vatican has pushed this line of reasoning, blaming gay priests for the church's bad press. In January 2003, its Congregation for Worship published still another letter stating that ordaining homosexuals "is absolutely inadvisable and imprudent, and from a pastoral point of view, very risky" and suggesting a zero-tolerance policy, despite the increasing shortage of priests.[39]

Of course, as studies and statistics consistently demonstrate, child abuse is not solely, or even primarily, a feature of homosexual behavior. And the Roman Catholic clergy problem cannot be accurately considered a gay problem. Former priest and psychologist Richard Sipe, now the premier expert on sexual behavior among priests, has extensively analyzed the question. His findings show:

> At any one time ... half of the priest population is involved in some form of non-celibate activity. ... Twenty-five percent (25%) of priests are involved in heterosexual relationships, associations, experimentation or patterns of behavior. Thirteen percent (13%) of priests are involved with homosexual relationships, experimentation, or patterns of behavior. Six percent of priests (6%) involve themselves sexually with minors—twice the number (4%) with adolescents than with pre-pubescent children (2%).[40]

Sipe's research concludes that clergy abuse of minors results from several causes: behaviors passed on from older to younger priests; the emotional arrest inherent in clerical training that leaves young priests at an adolescent stage of development; the powerful personal attractions raised by counseling and confessional situations; the failure of the power structure to intervene in a timely way; and the presence of men who "consciously or unconsciously seek an environment to help control their sexual impulses," finding instead "colleagues who aid them in expressing themselves sexually and who are quick and eager to rationalize sexual activity, even with minors." He lays the blame for the current crisis on "bishops and religious superiors [who] strive to avoid decisive and responsible action because of fear of scandal and in spite of the known risk of harm to the welfare of minors and others who are at risk."

Even when abuse is correctly understood as a psychological rather than a sexual problem, and one that afflicts both heterosexual and homosexual clergy, it cannot be denied that large numbers of Catholic priests are gay—although Sipes's figures prove that homosexual behavior in the priesthood is roughly proportionate to that in the general population.

Same-Sex Unions

Another arena of major change was opened in 1996, when a Hawaii trial court ruled that banning same-sex marriages violated the equal protection clause of the state's constitution. The U.S. Congress immediately enacted the Defense of Marriage Act, prohibiting federal recognition of gay marriages and denying gays federal benefits accruing to surviving spouses. It also allowed states to refuse to recognize such marriages performed elsewhere. By late 2003, thirty-seven states had individually passed similar bills.

In 1998, Hawaii amended its constitution to allow the legislature to restrict marriage to a man and a woman, although a 1997 law recognizes "reciprocal beneficiaries," assuring gay partners of certain rights previously limited to heterosexual spouses in heterosexual marriages. California gave same-sex domestic partners similar rights. In 1999, the Vermont Supreme Court ruled that the state must give homosexual couples all the benefits afforded to married couples, including adoption and parental rights. The court ruled that nothing in the state constitution explicitly defined marriage as between a man and a woman. Vermont consequently offers a civil union license that affords gay couples the legal benefits of marriage under different terminology.

In 2002, the Supreme Court of Ontario ruled that same-sex unions must be registered along with heterosexual marriages, which led Canada to amend its marriage act to include gay unions (following Belgium, the Netherlands, France, and Germany). Gay couples from the United States are legally able to marry across the border, though the marriages may not be recognized when they return to the States.

On November 18, 2003, the Supreme Court of Massachusetts ruled 4–3 in *Goodridge et al. v. Department of Public Health* that same-sex couples have a right to civil marriages under the nation's oldest state constitution, saying that "the right to marry means little if it does not include the right to marry the person of one's choice." Massachusetts Chief Justice Margaret H. Marshall, in her opinion, defined "civil marriage to mean the voluntary union of two persons as spouses, to the exclusion of all others." The decision went further than those in Hawaii and Vermont in requiring that the term "marriage" be applied equally to all interested couples. Although the ruling, like those in other states, does not require religious weddings for same-sex couples, its broad definition of marriage brought an outcry from traditionalist religious groups.

A wide range of Christian advocacy organizations, conservative churches, Roman Catholic bishops, and ad hoc coalitions banded together to try to prevent Massachusetts from offering civil marriage licenses and to promote a national constitutional amendment banning same-sex unions. The Rev. Jerry Falwell, the Southern Baptist Convention, and the U.S. Conference of Catholic Bishops announced their support for such an amendment, as have Focus on the Family's James Dobson and the Traditional Values Coalition.

Although the current Defense of Marriage Act disqualifies same-sex unions for purposes of taxes and health and retirement benefits, the idea of a constitutional amendment has united religious supporters who consider it the only way to circumvent the courts. One version, introduced as House Joint Resolution 56 in 2003, reads: "Marriage in the United States shall consist only of the union of a man and a woman. Neither this constitution or the constitution of any state, nor state or federal law, shall be construed to require that marital status or the legal incidents thereof be conferred upon unmarried couples or groups." The first sentence is intended to ban gay marriage and the second to stop courts from finding a constitutional right to same-sex unions. The fate of the movement toward such an amendment will continue, no doubt, to be tied to national and state elections, and to the efforts of conservatives to reach agreement on whether to try to stop only gay "marriage" or to aim at eliminating all types of same-sex unions.[41]

Perhaps of all the major denominations, the United Methodists have suffered most over the question. The church's 1996 General Conference voted to add to the Book of Discipline's "Social Principles" section a statement saying, "Ceremonies that celebrate homosexual unions shall not be conducted by our ministers and shall not be conducted in our churches." In 1998, however, the Reverend Jimmy Creech was brought before a church court for marrying two women. Creech was acquitted when the jury fell one vote short of finding him guilty. However, in 1999, Creech again performed a marriage ceremony, and was again charged. This time he was unanimously found guilty and defrocked. The Reverend Gregory Dell was tried in 1999 for the same offense and was convicted and suspended. In that same year, however, a group of sixty-eight ministers, led by the Reverend Donald Fado, participated in a same-sex wedding in Sacramento, and an additional sixty-seven sent letters of support. Confronted with the logistical nightmare of trying so many clergy, church leaders declined to prosecute. In 1981, the first same-sex marriage in the Society of Friends occurred in Seattle, Washington, called a "celebration of commitment." In 1984, the Unitarian Universalists followed suit. The first Quaker ceremony for a same-sex couple to be called a marriage occurred in 1987 in New York City.

The Episcopal Church's House of Bishops had asserted in 1977 that the church should confine marriage exclusively to heterosexuals. In the summer of 2003, though, the General Convention "recognize[d] that local faith communities are operating within the bounds of our common life as they explore and experience liturgies celebrating and blessing same-sex unions," in effect endorsing the performance of such ceremonies without going so far as to call them "marriages." In saying further that "we expect such relationships will be characterized by fidelity, monogamy, mutual affection and respect, careful, honest communication, and the holy love which enables those in such relationships to see in each other the image of God," it even set up the conditions under which such unions could be embraced by the church, while formally rejecting the development of specific liturgies for such occasions.[42]

The Churches Today

Throughout the last decade of the twentieth century, the major Protestant denominations were mired in discussions and studies that produced lengthy documents outlining relevant (and often irrelevant) historical, biblical, and theological considerations of the issue.[43] While these studies provided valuable resources, they also served the alternative purpose of buying time before tough decisions were required. In a typical instance, the Episcopal Church called for dialogue in the mid-1980s, and though little was done, its General Convention called for three more years of discussion in 1991. In 2003, after Robinson's consecration and the tacit acceptance of same-sex marriages, the church is still forming commissions and conducting studies. As recent church history has consistently demonstrated, this strategy has well served the proponents of liberalization, forestalling *de jure* votes while *de facto* change flourishes.

By the end of the century every major ecumenical Protestant organization had at least supported the decriminalization of sodomy and opposed discrimination against homosexuals,[44] confirming the widespread change reflected in a 1992 Gallup survey that found 78 percent of American Catholics were in favor of gay/lesbian civil rights, and 46 percent agreed that "sexual relations between gay or lesbian persons in a committed relationship could be morally acceptable." Still, few churches yet embraced either gay ordination or same-sex unions.

Many enlightened proposals for change have failed in close denominational votes. For example, in 1987, a Presbyterian sexuality committee found no reason to bar lesbian and gay Presbyterians from ordained offices and recommended that gays and lesbians be accepted as full participants in the life of the church, that ordination be open to all regardless of sexual orientation, and that celibacy not be a requirement for ordination. The report did not survive the 1991 General Assembly. Similarly, a 1992 Methodist committee agreed that biblical references to homosexuality must be read in the context of ancient culture and that in our present-day culture, committed homosexual relationships can and should be affirmed. However, the recommendations of this committee, included in the infamous "Appendix G" to the Book of Discipline, were not adopted, and in 2002 a much more conservative position, affirming that homosexual behavior is incompatible with Christian teaching, was adopted by delegates to the General Conference. Discussions at this point suggest that a major church split may be the only possible resolution.

In 2003, many major denominations still consider homosexuality anathema. These include most Baptists and Pentecostals, conservative churches in the Reformed tradition (e.g., the Christian Reformed Church and the Presbyterian Church in America), and non-mainstream churches like the Seventh-Day Adventists and Jehovah's Witnesses. Among those that claim to still be studying the issue are the Church of Christ (Disciples) and the Reformed Church in America. A number of churches ordain and marry gays and lesbians, though with varying degrees of official approval; these include the United Church of Christ, the Episcopal Church, the Friends, and the Quakers.

Perhaps the most interesting of these groupings are those churches that do not excommunicate or bar homosexuals but require celibacy. The Evangelical Lutheran Church in America, the Presbyterians (USA), the Mennonites, the United Methodists, and even the Roman Catholics and Latter-Day Saints fall in this category. The intriguing feature of this position is its inconclusiveness; clearly these denominations are torn between their traditional commitments to biblical literalness and to social inclusiveness, between the unchallengeable reality of gay persons in their ranks and a paralyzing inability to acknowledge it. The message to homosexuals in these churches is that unnatural chastity is preferable to sexual activity, that pretense is less shameful than honesty, and that an imagined vision of church unity trumps principle.

Further Considerations

It would hardly be an exaggeration to say that homosexuality has been the most divisive issue of American Christianity since the 1980s and that it almost certainly will continue to be so. What factors have conspired to keep it at the forefront of religious controversy and consciousness?

At the most elemental level, homosexuality is perhaps the last minority category that society has permission to hate and the group most easily tarred with the biblical brush. Centuries of negative religious teaching and consequent social prohibitions have surrounded the subject with an aura of evil that has led to simplistic fear and loathing. The emotional response it occasions is visceral and powerful, and leaders in both religion and politics can score easy points by appealing to that. Politically, the Religious Right's call for "family values"—the buzzword meant to disguise anti-gay attitudes—has deflected attention from real issues and hit a nerve that leaders continue to jangle at will.

The poverty of biblical interpretation that all too often characterizes American Protestantism reinforces this kind of thoughtless response. Amazingly, after a century of careful and revelatory biblical scholarship, most Christians remain stunningly ignorant of the content, meaning, and interpretive methods that apply to the book they depend upon so trustfully. Exemplary of this is their continued reliance on what is arguably one of the most inaccurate and misleading translations ever made of the text, the King James version. Likewise, clergy are often poorly educated in matters on which they speak with authority.

Moreover, Bible-oriented Christians, for the most part, fail to grasp the difference between homosexual orientation and homoerotic sexual activity, despite a century of scientific developments that have clarified that distinction. An inability to perceive the subtleties of human nature, behavior, and moral norms mitigates against development toward a Christian anthropology that acknowledges the complexity of the human condition and appropriately assigns value within it.

With the battles for civil rights for women, African Americans, Hispanics, and people with disabilities won—in the courts and the churches, at least, if not yet in the "hearts and minds" of all citizens—the time for gay rights has come. The gay community, less identifiable than many others but no longer so fearful of blackmail or exposure, is larger, better educated, and more religious than is generally assumed. Homosexual persons have for so long been integrally involved in the life of the churches—discreetly, and often uncomfortably—that they are no longer willing to be second-class Christians, especially as theology and ethics evolve to prove them otherwise.

As the controversy has heated up and consumed almost all the mainline denominations, neither the churches nor their gay members can be immune to change. It would be fair to ask how the gay issue and religion have influenced each other. Certainly, the situation of gay people in the United States has been greatly affected by religious attitudes, as this essay has outlined. Indeed, it could be posited that there would be no need for such a thing as gay rights without the negative impact of the teachings of the semitic religions. The lobbying of right-wing religious organizations continues to promote misunderstanding about homosexuality and to inflame passions against gay men and lesbians.

On the other hand, the fight for greater acceptance has been supported over the years by liberal churches, which have been particularly effective in opposing hate crimes, anti-sodomy laws, and outright discrimination. The latter effort has led inevitably up the ladder—or down the slippery slope, depending on one's point of view—to a recognition of the need for fairness in domestic partnership laws and benefits. Basic equality cannot be granted without existing norms being challenged, and even though the church always arrives thirty years late and out of breath (as one churchman famously noted), matters eventually move to their unavoidable conclusion. The logical progression has been to validation of same-sex unions socially and, inch by inch, religiously.

The churches have a huge investment in their centuries-old near-control of the institution of marriage and, by extension, of social structures and social order. As gay unions are increasingly allowed by the law, religious groups will come under more pressure to either sanction gay marriages or lose their position as the ultimate arbiters of civil as well as legal marital status. As the churches gradually recognize that monogamous gay unions closely model core religious ideals and bring these couples within the orbit of their organizations, the impact on gay culture as well as American society generally will surely be felt.

Another key effect of the issue on the churches has been its fostering of schismatic sects, both traditional and liberal, breaking off the mainstream bodies. Even more daunting is the prospect of major splits in some of the largest and oldest denominations, which can ill afford a further diminution of their ranks as the mainstream continues to bleed members. Theologically, the movement has manifestly led to a rethinking of classic positions, especially in ethics, moral theology, and Christian anthropology. As unorthodox as that may seem to some, history shows that theological thought must keep up with social thought if it is to speak to the lives of people in changing times. Newer insights will ultimately have a profound effect even on those traditions that now cling to older views, forcing them either to adapt or to become irrelevant.

One benefit that growing attention to the issue has wrought has been the incidental housecleaning of the culture of disguise, protection, and denial endemic in the Roman Catholic (and, to a lesser extent, the Episcopal) hierarchy with regard to clerical celibacy. It has been the public's ability to discuss and debate the issue that has opened the doors to *glasnost* in the priesthood and, quite likely, ongoing consideration of the eventual elimination of the celibacy requirement. Although Robinson's consecration evoked an immediate threat from the Vatican to ecumenical talks with Anglicans, Rome can hardly long point to the mote in someone else's eye while ignoring the log in its own.

Finally, the rise of both homophilic and homophobic religious advocacy groups is pushing a realignment of religion and politics. Same-sex unions were popular fodder during the 2004 presidential election, and PAC monies streamed from pro- and anti-gay interest groups to acceptable candidates. The controversy has given new life to the waning Religious Right but also has mobilized large numbers of gays and lesbians to create a formidable voting block.

The push for gay rights is not merely a pressing social issue but, for many homosexual Christians and their supporters, a crucial religious issue as well. With deep convictions on both sides and an apparent widespread acceptance in the West of sexuality as a matter of human rights, religious recognition of gay persons has passed the realm of "if" and entered the realm of "when."

Notes

[1] See George Painter, "The History of Sodomy Laws in the United States," at *www. sodomylaws.org/sensibilities/introduction.htm.*

[2] H. Montgomery Hyde, *The Love That Dare Not Speak Its Name: A Candid History of Homosexuality in Britain* (Boston: Little, Brown & Co., 1970), 5.

[3] John D'Emilio and Estelle Freedman, *Intimate Matters: A History of Sexuality in America* (New York: Harper & Row, 1988), 30.

[4] It is interesting to note that this act was assumed to be the totality of homosexual sexual behavior. This speaks to the incomplete and wholly different understanding of same-sex activity that prevailed until the modern study of human sexuality. Anal intercourse has been a form of subjugation and dominance. While it may also be an expression of mutual sexuality, it is hardly a uniquely homosexual behavior.

[5] D'Emilio and Freedman, *Intimate Matters*, 122.

[6] Ibid.

[7] A phrase coined by Oscar Wilde's lover, Lord Alfred Douglas, in a poem printed in the *Chameleon* in 1894.

[8] This timeless appellation was coined by Aquinas, though in Latin, of course (*peccatum contra naturaum*), and picked up by the English jurist William Blackstone in 1769.

[9] Derrick Sherwin Bailey, *Homosexuality and the Western Christian Tradition* (Hamden, CT: Archon Books, 1975), 172–73. This is the reprint of the original edition of the same name (London: Longmans, 1955).

[10] David A. Noebel, *The Homosexual Revolution* (Tulsa: American Christian College Press, 1970), 47

[11] An outgrowth of several articles published in 1970 and later.

[12] Others were also addressing scriptural issues at about the same time. See, for example, Protestant theologian Tom Horner's *Jonathan Loved David: Homosexuality in Biblical Times* (Philadelphia: Westminster, 1978).

[13] Clinton R. Jones's works include *Homosexuality and Counseling* (Philadelphia: Fortress, 1974) and *Understanding Gay Relatives and Friends* (New York: Seabury, 1978). See also Jack Babuscio, *We Speak for Ourselves: Experiences in Homosexual Counseling* (Philadelphia: Fortress, 1976).

[14] Silvia Pennington, *But Lord, They're Gay* (Hawthorne, CA: Lambda Christian Fellowship, 1978).

[15] Richard Woods, *Another Kind of Love: Homosexuality and Spirituality* (Chicago: Thomas More Press, 1977).

[16] Edward Batchelor, Jr., *Homosexuality and Ethics* (New York: Pilgrim Press, 1980).

[17] Richard P. McBrien, *Catholicism* (Minneapolis: Winston Press, 1981), 1027–33.

[18] For some interesting overviews on the progress of Protestant theology in this regard, see the various essays in Saul Olyan and Martha C. Nussbaum's edited volume, *Sexual Orientation and Human Rights in American Religious Discourse* (New York: Oxford University Press, 1998).

[19] Randy Shilts, *Conduct Unbecoming: Gays and Lesbians in the US Military* (New York: St. Martin's Press, 1993), 570.

[20] A new ordinance prohibiting sexual discrimination was passed in Miami-Dade County, but not until December 1, 1998.

[21] Quoted in D'Emilio and Freedman, *Intimate Matters,* 350.

[22] Kentucky's statute was declared unconstitutional by the state's Supreme Court in 1992 in *Commonwealth v. Wasson.*

[23] The Court's reluctance to hear cases on sodomy had not changed substantially. Initially, it voted against hearing the appeal, which would have left the Georgia court's decision against the statute standing. But conservative justices White and Rehnquist

were joined by liberals Brennan and Marshall—all four hoping for a once-for-all decision, though in opposite directions. These four were sufficient to put the case on the docket. For more about the interesting battle over docketing the case and other aspects of the legal situation, see *www.sodomylaws.org*, from which much of this information has been gleaned.

[24] Justice Lewis Powell, the swing vote in the decision, had earlier advocated invalidating all sodomy laws. However, in *Hardwick,* he voted with the majority. In October 1990, after his retirement, Powell told a group of New York University Law students, "I think I probably made a mistake in that one."

[25] Cf. Kathleen A. McAdams, "The San Francisco Council on Religion and the Homosexual" at *www.oasiscalifornia.org/sfcrh.html.*

[26] Cf. Friends Home Committee, *Towards a Quaker View of Sex, Compendium* 6.

[27] In 1972, the first Jewish synagogue for gays, the Metropolitan Community Temple, was founded in Los Angeles, quickly followed by one in New York and other major cities. Perhaps more surprisingly, in 1980, the Gay Pentecostal Alliance was created as a distinct church for gays, lesbians, supporters, and others.

[28] Sally Gearhart and William R. Johnson, *Loving Women, Loving Men: Gay Liberation and the Church* (San Francisco: Glide Publications, 1974), 64.

[29] MCC since its inception lobbied for—and was denied—admission into the National and World Councils of Churches. In later years, it has elected not to resubmit an application for NCC membership, pursuing instead membership within state and regional councils of churches, into many of which it has been accepted. It now only "participates in the programs" of the NCC and holds observer status in the WCC.

[30] Gearhart and Johnson, *Loving Women, Loving Men,* 86.

[31] It was over fifty-five in 2003.

[32] Subsequently sued by the highly litigious church for using the name "Seventh-Day Adventist."

[33] In 1999, Sister Jeannine Gramick, who with Fr. Robert Nugent for years had been conducting a pioneering ministry to homosexuals in the Washington, DC, area, was directed by the Vatican to abandon the organization, New Ways Ministry. Although she decided to remain within the church, her silencing prompted support from religious orders and other quarters of the church and emphasized the pastoral dimension of the question.

[34] Cf. *www.sodomylaws.com.*

[35] Cf. *Christian News*, September 23, 1985, 1.

[36] The full text of the decision is widely available but can be found online at *www. newark.rutgers.edu/~lcrew/summary.html.*

[37] Cf. *Calvary Contender*, November 15, 1993.

[38] Andy Lang, "Global Trend: World's Oldest Protestant Churches Now Ordain Gays and Lesbians,"*United Church News,* June 2002.

[39] John L. Allen, Jr., "Homosexuality a Risk Factor," *National Catholic Reporter*, 18 (April 2003).

[40] A. W. Richard Sipe, *Sexual Abuse of Minors by Roman Catholic Clergy* (Preliminary Expert Report II, 2002).

[41] See George Lakoff's arguments regarding the political dimensions of same-sex marriage in his book, *Don't Think of an Elephant* (White River Junction, VT: Chelsea Green Publishing, 2004), 46–51.

[42] See *Report of the 2003 General Convention of the Episcopal Church, U.S.A.* (New York: Church Publishing, 2004).

[43] As Max L. Stackhouse has said, in the last twenty-five years, "more church documents, statements, background papers, study books, and proposals have been written on human sexuality … than in any comparable period of church history." Cited in Olyan and Nussbaum, *Sexual Orientation and Human Rights,* 119.

[44] Olyan and Nussbaum, *Sexual Orientation and Human Rights,* 118.

Bibliography

Anderson, James B. "The Lesbian and Gay Liberation Movement in the Churches of the United States, 1969–1993," www.mlp.org/resources/history.html.

Babuscio, Jack. *We Speak for Ourselves: Experiences in Homosexual Counseling.* Philadelphia: Fortress, 1976.

Bailey, Derrick Sherwin. *Homosexuality and the Western Christian Tradition.* Hamden, CT: Archon Books, 1975; reprint of 1955 ed., London: Longmans, Green.

Batchelor, Edward, Jr. *Homosexuality and Ethics.* New York: Pilgrim Press, 1980.

Bell, Alan P., and Martin S. Weinberg. *Homosexualities: A Study of Diversity Among Men and Women.* New York: Simon and Schuster, 1978.

Council on Religion and the Homosexual, "A Compendium of Opinions of Churchmen and Church Organizations," 1967.

D'Emilio, John and Estelle Freedman. *Intimate Matters: A History of Sexuality in America.* New York: Harper & Row, 1988.

Gearhart, Sally and William R. Johnson, *Loving Women, Loving Men: Gay Liberation and the Church.* San Francisco: Glide Publications, 1974.

Glaser, Chris. "The Gay and Lesbian Religious Movement in America." *Frontiers.* September 10, 1993.

Horner, Tom. *Jonathan Loved David: Homosexuality in Biblical Times.* Philadelphia: Westminster, 1978.

Hyde, H. Montgomery, *The Love That Dare Not Speak Its Name: A Candid History of Homosexuality in Britain.* Boston: Little, Brown & Co., 1970.

Jones, Clinton R. *Homosexuality and Counseling.* Philadelphia: Fortress, 1974.

———. *Understanding Gay Relatives and Friends.* New York: Seabury, 1978.

Lakoff, George. *Don't Think of an Elephant.* White River Junction, VT: Chelsea Green Publishing, 2004.

McAdams, Kathleen A. "The San Francisco Council on Religion and the Homo-sexual." *www.oasiscalifornia.org/sfcrh.html.*

McBrien, Richard P. *Catholicism.* Minneapolis: Winston Press, 1981.

Noebel, David A. *The Homosexual Revolution.* Tulsa: American Christian College Press, 1970.

Olyan, Saul, and Martha C. Nussbaum, eds. *Sexual Orientation and Human Rights in American Religious Discourse.* New York: Oxford University Press, 1998.

Painter, George. "The History of Sodomy Laws in the United States." *www.sodomylaws. org.*

Shilts, Randy. *Conduct Unbecoming: Gays and Lesbians in the US Military.* New York: St. Martin's Press, 1993.

Sipe, A. W. Richard. *Sexual Abuse of Minors by Roman Catholic Clergy.* Preliminary Expert Report II, 2002.

9 Mothers and Their Golden Sons: Exploring a Theology of Narcissism

Philip Culbertson

> Girls will be boys and boys will be girls:
> It's a mixed up muddled up shook up world (except for Lola).
>
> The Kinks

> In so vulgar an age as this we all need masks.
>
> Oscar Wilde

> One is not born, but rather becomes, a woman…this creature,
> intermediate between male and eunuch, which is described as feminine.
>
> Simone de Beauvoir, *The Second Sex*

I am sixty years old, have known I am gay most of my life, and have never told my mother. She must know. She must know, as well, that she does not want to know.[1] I am sure that I am the lesser for never having told her. My inability to share one of the foundational parts of my identity has deprived us both of opportunities for deeper intimacy, blocked by secrets and a modicum of deceit. When I am with her, I am never quite fully present, because part of me is walled-off from her. This essay is dedicated to her: It may be as close as I ever come to outing myself—in her "virtual presence."

This essay is a meditative exploration of five mothers. They are "constructed" mothers, in that most had no opportunity to speak for themselves (the exception is Lady Wilde, a minor author of repute). All that you will know of my mother is what I tell you. In that sense, I am constructing her before your eyes. Most of what we know of these other mothers is what someone else—sometimes their sons; sometimes their sons' biographers—have told us, have constructed.[2] Hence, all these women are "usable fictions," *textless texts*[3] into whom someone else's narrative and meanings are read. The five mothers in this essay have little in common: One of them, in fact, is not even a biological woman.

But all have had a significant impact on their sons, teaching them who they are expected to be, using these sons for their own needs, and subtly languaging homophobia and homosexual identity through the psychodynamics of this most consuming and destructive relationship: A narcissistic mother and her golden son.

Setting the Historical Stage for Our Mothers

Oscar Wilde was born in 1854; Sigmund Freud only two years later, in 1856.[4] This makes them almost exact contemporaries, at least until Wilde's early death, at age 46, in 1900, just when Freud was beginning to reach the peak of his own writing. Both men were the favored sons of their mothers; both experienced the death of siblings when they were children; both married at age 30; both, though married, were emotionally attracted to men.

Though the words in Act 2 of David Hare's play, *The Judas Kiss*, were describing Lord Alfred Douglas, they could just as well have been used of Oscar Wilde himself: "It may be—I admit this also—that he is known *throughout Europe* as a gilded pillar of infamy. By rumor alone, he is a universal byword for sin and depravity."[5] For most people, Wilde is now fondly remembered as "a great, almost legendary victim ... the foremost homosexual in the English mind."[6] Meanwhile, by the mid-1920s Sigmund Freud had become a household name. "Only a select minority could be expected to do Freud's teachings justice. ... Yet his name, and his photograph showing a stern, carefully dressed elderly gentleman with penetrating eyes and the inevitable cigar, became known to millions."[7] Wilde lived primarily in London; Freud in Vienna. There is no evidence that the two ever met nor that they ever read each other's work. However, given the stories above, and the sensationalist international newspaper coverage of the trial of Oscar Wilde—"the universal byword for sin and depravity"—it is extremely likely that Freud knew of Wilde's escapades and judicial defense. Certainly both were internationally significant in the critical two decades of 1890 to 1910, when both heterosexuality and homosexuality, as we presently use those terms, were being first defined as categories of identity.

Oscar Wilde's infamous trial took place in 1895. Two years later, the word *homosexuality* entered the English language.[8] In 1900, Freud published his first theoretical conceptualization of the Oedipal Complex, that ultimate psychoanalytical construction of heterosexuality as normative.[9] Indeed, according to the *Oxford English Dictionary*, the word *heterosexuality* first enters the English language one year later, in 1901, possibly in reaction to the coining of *homosexuality*. Thus, the end of the Victorian era, when Wilde and Freud were both causing considerable international interest, marks the first English use of these now familiar terms, along with their "scientific" definitions. In this way, the strange idea that a "normal" man will never feel desire for another man was constructed, and the world of human identity and social intercourse was divided into bipolar and oppositional camps. This was, in the words of literary critic and queer theorist Eve Kosovsky Sedgwick, "a world mapping by which every given person, just as he or she was necessarily assignable to a male or a female gender, was now considered necessarily assignable as well to a homo- or a hetero-sexuality."[10] The amorphous and often undirected male gaze was now quantified, given a set of names, and thereby a form of social control was set in place from which we men have not yet recovered.[11] With Wilde's trial and Freud's theories of human psychosocial development, heterosexism—the privileging of the experience of white heterosexual males as the measure of "normal," and the defining of all other experiences as ab- or sub-normal—was set firmly in place, including within the profession of psychoanalysis.

That the terms homosexual and heterosexual did not exist until 1897 and 1901 raises the interesting question of how same-sex experiences and feelings were languaged prior to that. In his book *Who Was That Man?* Neil Bartlett traces the creation of homosexual language in the same period of 1890 to 1910 in London.[12] When psychoanalysts first became fascinated with what we today call homosexuals, they termed them "Uranians," as though they were heavenly creatures from the planet Uranus.[13] In the *Oxford English Dictionary,* entries entitled *effeminate, invert,* and *pervert* make no reference to homosexuality. Only the entries for *sodomy* and *bugger* address homosexuality, but then these are words generally used about gay men, not by gay men.[14] *Drag* meant any fancy dress costume; *gay* referred to any man *or woman* who worked as a prostitute; *poof* was an elaborate female head-dress; *rough trade* was the livelihood of a working-class person.[15] There was no easy way to language homosexuality because the term had not been invented yet, and in fact, in the Wilde trial, many of the respectable middle-class jurors refused to believe that a man could commit such acts. That is why his trials were so scandalous: they attempted to name "the love that dares not speak its name." In fact, in the trial transcripts, much of what Wilde was accused of was referred to only by the cloudiest of euphemisms. How does one language an attraction for which there is no vocabulary? As Bartlett points out, "Wilde's private homosexual life was an elaborate drama of deception, lies and, most of all, inspired invention. He could not, even in 1895, after concealment had failed, reveal his true nature. There was no real Oscar Wilde, if by real we mean homosexual."[16] Men like Wilde were simply theater ... a walking fiction. As he himself said, "One should either be a work of art, or wear a work of art."[17]

Homosexuality could not speak its name, nor did many wish to speak their own names in relation to homosexual behavior. In Blidah, Algeria, in January 1895 Andre Gide was in the hall of a hotel, about to leave. His glance fell on the slate that announced the names of new guests: "Suddenly my heart gave a leap; the two last names ... were those of Oscar Wilde and Lord Alfred Douglas." Acting on his first impulse, Gide "erased" his own name from the slate and left for the station. It may, he later reflected, have been a feeling of *mauvais honte* or of embarrassment; Wilde was becoming notorious and his company compromising. In a letter a few days later to his mother, Gide described Wilde as a terrifying man, a "most dangerous product of modern civilization" who had already depraved Douglas "right down to the marrow."[18]

Gide, in his anxiety, turned to his mother. Surely she would understand him, comfort him, as a toddler runs to his mother for security when he is frightened. It would have been from her that he had his first indications of how to behave in intimate relationships. Through a history of internalized cues and rewards, mothers teach us what is right or wrong about sex, what must be open and what hidden. Our mothers (and by synecdoche, our fathers) teach us to trust who we are and yet be safe in a world where only heterosexuality is "normal." In that sense we learn to "language" our earliest senses of sexuality—usually metaphorically. Narcissistic mothers teach their children that they are "special," and if special, permitted to be different. At the same time, they offer little instruction in how to negotiate that difference or what to do with parental expectations of who we will become. Golden sons learn how to "perform" their sexuality, in its dance of openness and hiddenness, inside the cocoon of maternal adoration. "Specialness" makes it difficult to break the parental bond, for it is the source of our own narcissistic fantasies of self. "Coming out" can threaten our intimate relationship with narcissistic mothers because "gay" is not what they wanted for us.

Dutch psychoanalyst Hendrika Halberstadt-Freud describes the relationship between narcissistic mothers and golden sons as "a symmetrical symbiosis … a parasitic relation built on a mutual illusion."[19] Each is dependent upon the other to maintain this illusion.

> If she needs the child in order not to feel desperate and lonely and unloved herself, she will tend to treat him as part of her self, as an extension of her body, and as a depository of her mind's contents, not as a separate human being but as a plaything, a fetish. She cannot afford to allow him to be different and separate from her, and thus she will foster his false belief that he is able to satisfy all her needs, is more important than her husband, and totally indispensable for her emotional well-being.[20]

Halberstadt-Freud goes on to say:

> This situation finds its counterpart in the child's unconscious fantasy: "When I signify I want my independence, my mother hates me." "I had better remain a small, dependent needy child." "She likes me only when I need her, she gives her love on the condition that I show I cannot live without her support." "I have to show I agree to everything she wants or thinks; having a mind of my own is a mortal danger." Individuation is of course impossible under these circumstances.

As we shall see, the golden sons in this article all struggled with individuating because of this "symmetrical symbiosis." Their "way out" as adults was to establish homoerotic—platonic or sexualized—relationships with men who, unlike the Oedipal father, would not threaten to steal them away.

Oscar Wilde and His Mother

A story from Beverley Nichols' twentieth-century autobiography, *Father Figure*,[21] will illustrate the particular comic, educative, and terrorizing potential that the "unspeakable" had realized by the first decades of the twentieth century. Nichols' middle-class parents had a higher-class male friend who rouged, acted effeminate, and would to a knowing observer have seemed from first glance to be telegraphing his homosexuality. The elder Nicholses, reactionary but unworldly, saw none of this. They were simply delighted that their friend took such a keen interest in their young son. One night, though, Beverley's father came into the boy's room drunk and found him with a copy of [Wilde's] *Dorian Gray*—a present from the friend. The father nearly choked. He hurled the book at his son. He spat on it over and over, frothing at the mouth. Finally he began ripping the book to shreds—with his teeth.

> Beverley was terrified and puzzled: why was his father so angry? The father couldn't believe he didn't know, but finally the boy's obvious puzzlement overcame him. "What did Wilde do?" The father couldn't utter the words that would explain it. Instead, he stole into the bedroom again at daybreak, and left a slip of paper on which he had written down, he said, the man's crime. As his father left, Beverley, now delirious with anticipation, tiptoed across the room to where the paper lay. On it was written: ILLUM CRIMEN HORRIBLE QUOD NON NOMINANDUM EST (This is the horrible crime whose name may not be mentioned).[22]

Who first wouldn't speak this "name"? Oscar's mother was Jane Francesca Agnes Elgee, aka "Speranza," Lady Wilde. Wilde's biographer Melissa Knox describes her as "adoring, gifted, somewhat bizarre, and very self-centered."[23] Knox comments: "She seems to have called herself Speranza as a defense against depression. Apparently devoid of hope, she liked to pretend she embodied it."[24] A revolutionary in the Young Ireland movement, she fancied herself a nationalist poet, though unfortunately saddled with the wrong gender and the obligations of motherhood. She solved this dilemma by attempting to merge emotionally with her children. She was determined that Oscar would grow up to be what, as a woman and mother, she could not be: a hero-martyr to the Irish cause. Narcissistically, "she needed her sons to remain a part of her; any attempt by either boy to strike out on his own would have been regarded as a cruel abandonment."[25] Given the struggle that any golden boy suffers in differentiating from his narcissistic mother, it is no wonder that Oscar later wrote: "A mother's love is very touching, of course, but it is often selfish. I mean, there is a good deal of selfishness in it."[26]

Speranza had apparently hoped for a girl when she was pregnant with Oscar. Certainly, she dressed him in female clothes—"like a little Hindoo idol," she wrote—long past the age when little boys were customarily dolled up in feminine attire. Speranza herself was a flamboyant dresser, often startling members of the public by her outrageous attire. Henry Furniss later described her as "a walking burlesque of motherhood."[27] Ultimately, throughout their lives, both Oscar and his mother exhibited the sort of attention-seeking behavior— simultaneously arrogant and un-self-aware—that often characterizes narcissists. Defensively he later wrote, "In so vulgar an age as this we all need masks."[28] This is how she languaged him: to mask, to hide, including from himself. How else could he maintain his part of the mother-son dyad?

Apparently, Wilde had his first homosexual experience in 1886, when he was already a father.[29] (Interestingly, Freud established his deepest homoerotic friendship in 1887, with Wilhelm Fleiss, when he too was already a father.) Throughout his successive affairs, Wilde remained loyal to his mother, whom he referred to as Lady Wilde. There is not one word of mockery or disloyalty; rather, he seems to enjoy referring to her in all her grandeur.[30] His mother played her part. Even at the height of his notorious trial, she stood by him, encouraging him not to flee London, believing all the while in his innocence. Having endured her son's disgrace, Lady Wilde died in 1896, when Oscar was 42 years old. By then, Wilde had been tried and convicted of "indecent acts" and was already imprisoned in Reading Gaol. The death of his beloved mother was one of the several factors which contributed to the deep depression he suffered that year, which ultimately produced his greatest work, *De Profundis*.

Sigmund Freud and His Mother

Jacob Freud, an "impecunious Jewish wool merchant,"[31] married his first wife, Sally Kanner, in 1832, when he was sixteen years old. After bearing him two sons, Emmanuel and Philipp, she died. Jacob remarried, in 1851 or 1852, to a woman named Rebecca, about whom we know very little, including why their marriage terminated almost immediately.[32] There were apparently no children from this union. In 1855, at the age of 40, he married a third time, to Amalia Nathansohn (1835–1930). She was 20 years old, younger than both Jacob's sons, and by all accounts, she was a stunner. His father's third and his mother's first child, Sigismund (later, Sigmund), was born a year later.

Amalia doted on her first-born. She referred to him as "my golden Sigi," and for the rest of his life he held pride of place among his siblings. However, his reign of omnipotence was short-lived. Soon Amalia was pregnant again, and a nanny was hired to mind young Sigmund. Her name was Resi Wittek, a devout Catholic woman from Freiberg.[33] The new child, Julius, died in his infancy, though not before Amalia was pregnant with her third child. Paul Vitz writes,

> If we put it all together, it becomes clear that Freud must have found his mother, Amalia, relatively unavailable to him from the time he was a little under a year old until he was close to three years old. After all, his mother was busy with two pregnancies and two births, and had a sick child who died during this time, while Sigmund was put in the charge of his nanny. There is no evidence that there was anyone else available to help the mother out. Freud's father Jakob worked elsewhere in the town and often traveled in the surrounding area buying wool.[34]

In rapid-fire succession, Amalia delivered five more daughters (Anna, Rose, Marie, Adolfine, and Pauline) and a baby brother, all by the time Sigmund was ten years old. Young Sigmund effectively had two mothers: Amalia and Resi. It is not clear which was his "primary" mother, for he admits to loving them both, though it was with Amalia that he experienced his first sexual arousal.

At the age of two and a half, he told his close friend Wilhelm Fleiss, his "libido toward *matrem* had awakened" on an overnight railway journey from Leipzig to Vienna, a trip on which he had the "opportunity of seeing her *nudam*." Biographer Peter Gay explains:

> At times Freud made telling mistakes in remembering his childhood past, and here is one: he was actually nearly four, not just over two, on the occasion of the glimpse of his naked mother—he was bigger, stronger, more capable of voyeurism and explicit desire than he consciously allowed himself to be in retrieving the memory of seeing *matrem nudam*. It is no less telling that even at forty-one, already the most unconventional of explorers in the forbidden realms of sexuality, Freud could not bring himself to describe this exciting incident without lapsing into safe, distancing Latin.[35]

During his mid-life intensive self-analysis, Freud recognized the sexual nature of this arousal, but this was not the only source of confusion about who Amalia was to him. To his childish eyes, his older brother Philipp would have made a more fitting husband to his slim and beautiful mother than did his elderly father. Young Sigmund was confused: a baby had come out of his mother's body somehow, yet the wrong "father" seemed responsible for it. To make things even worse, Philipp had the nanny arrested for petty theft. Suddenly, she was gone. As Peter Gay points out, the boy was too young to grasp all the connections but not too young to suffer. "That Catholic nursemaid, old and unprepossessing as she was, had meant much to Freud, almost as much as his lovely mother. Like some figures who were to engross his fantasy life later—Leonardo, Moses, to say nothing of Oedipus—the young Freud enjoyed the loving ministrations of two mothers."[36]

Freud never saw his nanny again, but his mother eventually stepped back into the vacant maternal space. She pampered and protected her "golden son." In later life, Freud visited his mother every Sunday, without fail, for a meal, though he somatized his anxiety over mother-contact by having attacks of indigestion before each visit. Gay remarks:

> It is telling that the only emotional tie Freud ever sentimentalized was the mother's love for her son. While every lasting intimate relationship, he wrote in 1921, whether in marriage, friendship, or the family, conceals a sediment of hostile feelings, there is perhaps "one single exception," the "relation of mother to son which, founded on narcissism, is undisturbed by later rivalry." He characterized this maternal affection for the son as "the most perfect, easily the most ambivalence-free of all human relationships." This sounds far more like a wish than a sober inference from clinical material.[37]

Yet when Amalia died in 1930, at age 95, Freud chose not to attend her funeral. This hardly sounds like an ambivalence-free relationship. He pleaded that he was not very well and that he did not like ceremonies. Yet he also expressed a sense of relief at her death. He wrote to his colleague Ernest Jones: "I feel only two things: the growth in personal freedom I have acquired, since it was always an abhorrent thought that she would learn of my death, and secondly the satisfaction that she has at last the deliverance to which she had acquired the right in so long a life."[38] Freud himself died almost exactly nine years later. Freud protected his mother. Appignanesi and Forrester remark,

> The secrecy that surrounds Freud's relationship to his mother was akin to the secrecy that surrounded his sexual life with his wife. Intimately self-revealing as he was when he needed to persuade his readers of the truths he had discovered in himself and others, Freud was also extremely self-concealing and private; and in no area of his inner life was he more discreet and self-protective than in that tabernacle of his childhood, his mother.[39]

Freud's idealization of his mother expressed itself directly in his attempt to preserve for her sake her idealized image of him: the best possible son for the best possible mother.[40] A narcissistic twining.

Whose language was Freud's theory of sexuality and normalcy? Perhaps it was his mother's, a voluptuous and fecund young woman, surrounded by his charming older half-brothers. Perhaps it was his nanny's, because he remembered how much she taught him about traditional conservative religion, including Heaven and Hell. Yet homoeroticism was not unknown to the Freud family or to Freud himself. Later in life, Freud's niece, Mitzi's daughter, dressed as a man and called herself Tom. Freud's beloved youngest daughter and chief disciple, Anna Freud, lived in a lesbian relationship with Dorothy Burlingham, youngest daughter of the American glass millionaire, Louis Comfort Tiffany.[41]

Freud's "Male Love Affairs"

In 1873, at the University of Vienna, 19-year-old Freud met Eduard Silberstein, with whom he quickly struck up a deeply emotional friendship. The relationship lasted for ten years, and was "as close as [Freud] came to love during this period of his life."[42] The patterns of male-male attachment for Freud were established in this relationship and repeated again and again in his life, most notably with Wilhelm Fleiss, Carl Jung, and Sandor Ferenzi. The emotional intensity of this relationship is revealed in Freud's letters to Silberstein. Struggling to make sense of this intimacy, Freud wrote: "Come to Vienna, where I await you with longing...I dragged your letter about again because I was loath to be separated from it for another whole day."[43] Throughout these years of correspondence, Freud revealed the same characteristics as with other male intimates: fear of loss and the urgent longing for contact on demand.

Wilhelm Fleiss was born in 1858, the same year that Freud's younger brother Julius died at age seven months; Freud thus identified Fleiss with his younger brother.[44] Fleiss was a Berlin doctor whom Freud first met in 1887, a year after Freud's marriage to Martha Bernays. Fleiss encouraged Freud's specialization in psychology. He is widely remembered as an early researcher in biorhythms. Students of Freudian psychology remember him more vividly as the surgeon who performed nose surgery on Emma Eckstein, whose subsequent hemorrhaging led Freud to his theory that nose bleeds are the male version of menstruation. A number of scholars have commented on the intensely homoerotic nature of the three-year exchange of letters between Fleiss and Freud.[45] In fact, Breger argues that "Fleiss was the great love of Freud's adult life."[46] In his book *Unheroic Conduct,* Daniel Boyarin "fantasizes" that Freud panicked in the midst of their homoerotic correspondence.[47] Freud terminated his correspondence with Fleiss in 1900, the same year as Wilde's death, the same year as Freud's first published explanation of the Oedipal Complex, the year that—had there been a United Nations— would surely have been designated "The Year of the Heterosexual." Ironically, the passionate correspondence ended with an argument over bisexuality, even though Freud had described his own relationship with Fleiss as the natural product of an "unruly homosexual libido."

Boyarin describes this break on the part of Freud as a kind of "homosexual panic."[48] The term "homosexual panic," per se, doesn't seem to appear anywhere in Freud's writing, though he does speak of homosexuality as a kind of panicked warding off of certain wish phantasies.[49] Thus the term "homosexual panic" does not itself seem to be a Freudian invention, though the mechanism may be, in the guise of a paranoic reaction to a homosexual object-choice. Certainly, international society seemed to panic in response to the Wilde trials. In *The Judas Kiss*, Wilde reports to Bosie what he has heard about the after-effects of his trial in England:

> The Café Royal is still full. Men sit taking care not to cross their legs. The wink is outlawed as an acceptable form of social intercourse. Gentlemen seeking advancement in society cover their arses with three layers of tailored material. Frankly, I should be carried shoulder-high by the cutters down Saville Row, for now a whole generation of respectable people must conceal their nether parts behind high-priced, redundant fabric. My arrest, thank God, has had some commercial benefits.[50]

Wilde, Freud, and Homosexual Panic

I have thus far not been able to locate the first occurrence of the term "homosexual panic" in English. Nor does the term appear in the DSM-IV.[51] It certainly was not coined by Eve Kosofsky Sedgwick, as Joseph Nugent claims. According to Kathleen Kelleher, the phrase was coined in 1920, as part of a legal defense.[52] But what does it mean exactly? Kelleher hypothesizes: "The notion of 'homosexual panic' seems to be based on the Freudian theory that buried motivations and fears can be triggered by events or thoughts, and lead to aberrant behavior." In other words, Freudian thought, however derivative, connects homosexual panic with fear, often in the form of paranoia. However, if we track the term through the American and international legal literature, we discover that the definition of "homosexual panic" has become very confused. Sometimes in law it seems to be defined as fear; at other times it seems to be defined as anger. For example, the legal defense of "homosexual panic" is known in Australian and other Commonwealth law as the "Homosexual Advance Defense,"[53] usually framed as an angry, retaliatory, sometimes calculated, and occasionally fatal attack on homosexuals. As further example, the Homosexual Panic Defense was employed by the attorneys for the defense in the Matthew Shepherd murder trial. However, they used it to "justify" a premeditated murder of a young man, not a spontaneous and instantaneous reaction of fear.[54]

I propose the following narrowing of definition between homophobia and homosexual panic as a fear reaction. George Weinberg is generally credited with coining the term "homophobia" in his 1972 book, *Society and the Healthy Homosexual*. He defined homophobia as "the dread of being in close quarters with homosexuals—and in the case of homosexuals themselves, self-loathing."[55] The first half of Weinberg's definition, then, defines homophobia as a projection, a projected fear, from someone toward a homosexual person. The nature of this projected homophobia is made clearer by Gregory Herek, who argues for the synonym of "sexual prejudice, defined simply as negative attitudes toward an individual because of her or his sexual orientation."[56] I think this projected negativity is quite different from homosexual panic. Homophobia may indeed produce anger, but homosexual panic produces fear. Homophobia is a projection from one person to another. As I will claim in my case study, homosexual panic is an internal reaction which defends against engaging certain parts of one's own homosexual identity. Joseph Nugent of the University of California writes as follows:

> The installation of homosexual panic gave society leverage over all male bonding. The dissemination of homosexual panic can thus be seen for what it is: a form of social control. The panic Sedgwick describes is not the panic felt in the presence of one identified as queer, though it is that too, but the anxiety of everyone who feels, however fleetingly, homosexual desire, or even that whole set of desires and practices damned by association with queerness: a lisp, a limp wrist, eating quiche perhaps. The forced suppression of those desires, the fear that one just may be queer—the fear of what were, until the invention of normative heterosexuality, acceptable desires, though not necessarily desires that could be acted upon—is the cause of this anxiety. This anxiety directed outward is homophobia. Internalized it is homosexual panic.[57]

I would claim that homosexual panic produces in oneself the reactions of emotional shut-down, identity confusion, and mild dissociation.[58] These characteristics are ones of fear, thereby distinguishing a psychodynamic definition of homosexual panic from the common legal definition, which is based on anger. The distinction is subtle but critical.

Can gay men suffer from homosexual panic? According to Eve Sedgwick, "Homosexual panic is not only endemic to middle-class, Anglo-American men (presumably excluding some homosexuals), but a mainspring of their treatment of politics and power—not least, of course, in relation to women."[59] I'm not sure why Sedgwick excludes "some homosexuals." It seems to me that homosexual men often carry homosexual panic, as I will illustrate in my case study. Further—an idea I'm still playing with—there may well be a version of "heterosexual panic" in the gay male community. It's certainly a myth that all gay men desire to seduce a hunky straight man. Many gay men actually fear straight men: fear of being ridiculed by them, beaten up by them, outed by them, excluded by them. Perhaps both homosexual panic and heterosexual panic are variants of hysteria, a category which, as Boyarin points out (192–94), applies in Freudian thought to both men and women.[60]

Whether Freud held the newspaper coverage of Oscar Wilde's transgressive behavior in his conscious or his unconscious, I think it is fruitful to think of Freud's highly contradictory explorations of male and female homosexuality (as he termed them) as being influenced in some form by his own homosexual panic. Then I began to shop around in my head for what it might be in our contemporary life in Auckland that might induce homosexual panic in the public. Would it be the dominatrix float at the annual Gay Pride parade? Is it the buffed mostly naked Hero Marching Boys in that same parade? However, I rejected those two possibilities as inducing homosexual panic (except in New Zealand's conservative Christian political party) and instead settled on the over-the-top "professional" drag queens.

Life's a Drag: A Case Study

Freud said that when someone walks into the room, the first thing we register, however unconsciously, is "Is this person a male or a female?" Once we have resolved that question, we then know which of our various reaction-repertoires should kick in. Do I use my "reacting to males" repertoire, or my "reacting to females" repertoire? That reminds me of the sort of reaction I see when a straight man accidentally walks into a gay bar in Auckland. He freezes; he looks confused; he gets increasingly uncomfortable, and then he leaves discreetly. I have the same problem walking into straight pick-up bars on a Saturday night. The problem is our own; we don't know which repertoire to operate out of: our reacting-to-men, or our reacting-to-women repertoire. When we walk into a bar and encounter a drag queen, I think it is safe to assume that we will always have some sort of a reaction to a man in flamboyant female dress. In fact, I think it might sometimes cause us to panic.

Panic was one of the deep affective responses I had to deal with when I made my first venture into the world of drag. Invited to a Murder Mystery Dinner Party, I was assigned to come as a Parisian dress designer, in the mode of the great Coco Chanel. I approached my two favorite local drag queens—Bumpa and Onya Nees—and asked for their help in making this "performance identity" one not to be forgotten.[61] As I went through the preparations for this initial appearance in women's clothing, I often encountered my own panic, surely an internalization of the homophobic culture in which I was raised. I panicked about which wig I would borrow from Onya: one made me look like Agnes Moorehead, another like Cher before she had so many facelifts, another like Dolly Parton doing drugs. I finally settled for a blond bob that made me look like Dagmar. I panicked over the dressmaker's skill: Could she really turn my John-Denver-esque looks into something that would pass as Coco Chanel? Would I pop a fingernail? Lose an eyelash? Fall off of my 7-inch platform heels? Eventually the evening went without a hitch, so much so that my host didn't even recognize me until about twenty minutes after my arrival.

Bumpa and Onya, more "feminine" than most women, flirty performance artists known for their exceptionally fine lip-synching, invited me to join them in performing at "Surrender Dorothy," a popular Auckland drag bar. A drag queen must always be given her name by an "older" drag queen (and lest Onya or Bumpa read this, I will confess that both are at least twenty years younger than I). And that's how, for a year, 2001–02, I became Ophelia Sphincta, she who within a few months came first-runner-up for the Best New Up-and-Coming at "The Golden Stilettos," Auckland's annual drag "Oscars."

Roles emerged among the three of us. As Ophelia's persona unfolded, she became known as a tallish Joan Rivers, with a rapier-sharp tongue. Onya was my sister, and Bumpa our mother. We were roles without chronological ages. Like all drag queens, Bumpa is a narcissist, and she became the mother who absorbed, challenged, nurtured, and criticized her new child. We acted out the "symmetrical symbiosis" that Halberstadt-Freud describes. Bumpa seemed to think: "If he shows he loves me, that means I am a good mother." Ophelia seemed to think: "I have to show I agree to everything she wants or thinks; having a mind of my own is a mortal danger." However, underneath that symbiotic mother-daughter relationship, I was working through some of the most foundational aspects of my early identity as a golden boy.

Having a Mother, Being a Mother

One foundational principle of Freudian theory is that we "internalize" our mothers—we take our memory of them inside our sense of self, where that memory lives on and continues to prompt responses in us. Object Relations Theory takes internalization one step further, arguing that we internalize a whole variety of mothers—snapshots, if you will, of our mother when we were relating to her at a particular moment, through the eyes of a particular emotional configuration. Thus both Freudian and Object Relations theories claim that we "have" our mothers, in that they live on inside of us, coloring our interpretations of and responses to significant events in our lives.

Object Relations theorist Jessica Benjamin takes the argument another step further. "In my view, the unaccepted mourning for what one will never *be*—especially the boy's inability to face the loss entailed in not being the mother, even to acknowledge envy of the feminine—has particularly negative repercussions, often more profound and culturally pervasive, if less obvious, than the classically recognized oedipal frustration of not having a mother."[62] To Benjamin's way of thinking, "having" our mother is not enough, for having means that we can always lose what we have, setting in place an element of anxiety and anticipatory mourning that is intrapsychically difficult to bear. Internally we attempt to resolve that anxious tension by "being" our mother, instead of "merely" having her.[63] Herein lies, I believe, one unconscious motivation for appearing in drag. In drag, we, however briefly, become our mothers, or at least some of that mother which resides in our sense of self.

The Monday after my first appearance in drag, in my therapy appointment, I found myself ruminating on long fingernails, and what they meant to me. I discovered that when I was preening on the previous Saturday, I had been flicking the backs of my nails to clean them, and suddenly realized that it was my mother's gestures, buried somewhere in my unconscious, that I was imitating. My therapist encouraged me to follow that train of thought about fingernails, and I then remembered that I had painted my nails in just the same way my mother had: I spread a sheet of kitchen toweling on a table, and painted my nails with my hands carefully positioned as flat. Then I remembered a point in the evening when I had scratched a friend's back with my nails, drawing up a memory of moments of intimacy I enjoyed sitting on my mother's lap with her scratching my back in the same way. And I then realized that I had chosen a nail polish color that was identical with the color my mother always wore: long nails painted fire engine red, the same color that my mother has worn ever since I've known her. When I looked back at the photographs, I think I was upset because my hands looked like a man's hands, not my mother's.

My parents were married in 1940. When my mother was a beautiful young bride, one of the things she longed for most was nylon stockings, in extremely short supply during World War II. In fact, when I was a very small child, I remember her darning her stockings because they were too expensive to throw away and buy new ones. For the rest of her life, she treated stockings as though they were worth a king's ransom. To put them on, she would first don gloves so as not to snag them with her long red fingernails, and then she would roll the stocking leg down to the foot and carefully slip her foot inside. Then slowly, slowly she would roll them up, until the tops reached the snaps on her garter belt. And as I thought about it, I realized that Ophelia put on her stockings in the same way, even though by now they were panty hose: first the gloves, then roll the legs down carefully, insert the right foot, roll back up slowly. I was my mother in her boudoir, beautifying herself for public admiration.

Today, I have a photo of my mother, taken when she was 16 years old. Her hair is cut in the fashionable waves of the early 1930s, and she is pencil thin. She is standing before a mirror, in an ankle-length dress of some gauzy printed material, the lacy v-neck of the dress held demurely closed with a small broach. Her back is to the camera, and one sees her face only as reflected in the mirror. She gazes at herself, turned slightly to the left. In the mirror, oddly, only the right half of her face is reflected; the left half has whited out with the photographer's flash. Her reflected right eye gleams like a marble, the left eye is barely visible in the whiteout. For many years, the photo reminded me of Wilde's famous novel, *The Picture of Dorian Gray,* a person trapped in a reflected beauty that would never age. More recently, as my thoughts toward my mother have grown fonder as she nears the end of her life, I think a quote from Anaïs Nin is more apt:

> As June walked toward me from the darkness of the garden into the light of the door, I saw for the first time the most beautiful woman on earth. A startlingly white face, burning dark eyes, a face so alive I felt it would consume itself before my eyes. Years ago I tried to imagine a true beauty: I created in my mind an image of just such a woman. I had never seen her until last night. Yet I knew long ago the phosphorescent color of her skin, her huntress profile, the evenness of her teeth. She is bizarre, fantastic, nervous, like someone in a high fever. Her beauty drowned me. As I sat before her, I felt I would do anything she asked of me.[64]

This too was my experience, the first time I saw Ophelia in a full-length mirror: a true beauty—bizarre, fantastic, nervous—with a radiance that drowned me. I would do anything she asked of me.

My mother had three older sisters, for whom she was the beloved baby sister. But the three were so close in age that they ran in the same social circle, while my mother was too young to participate. Mom spoke often of "my sisters," her awe and affection tinged with the resentment of being excluded, even years afterwards. Me, I have no sisters, or had no sisters, until I met Onya and Bumpa. For a year we functioned like sisters, yet I asked myself, "Given that I am one of two brothers, and my father was an only child, how do I know to function like a sister?" Only later did I realize that I was being the sister my mother knew how to be, including the awe and affection—tinged with resentment at the places they were invited without me or when the applause they received overwhelmed mine.

If Benjamin's and my argument are correct, then drag is not simply about performativity, role, or even being transgressive. Drag becomes an identity issue, not only a performance. "Being" a woman, however temporary, functions intrapsychically to resolve the anticipated loss of one's own mother. Though we may at times lose what we have, we cannot ever lose what we are. "Being" provides a foundation for ego constancy that "having" can never enjoy.

Drag also has the capacity to reverse loss, or at least in Freudian terms, our mother's own loss. Robert Stoller personifies a conversation between a transvestite and his "perversion."[65]

> The transvestite states the question, "When I am like a female, dressed in her clothes and appearing to be like her, have I nonetheless escaped the danger? Am I still a male, or did the women succeed in ruining me?" And the perversion—with its exposed thighs, ladies' underwear, and coyly covered crotch—answers, "No. You are still intact. You are a male. No matter how many feminine clothes you put on, you did not lose that ultimate insignia of your maleness, your penis."

Of course, a drag queen is not a transvestite, but the principle crosses over: We become our mother "restored"—now with a penis where hers was missing.

The journey into drag has been healing for me, though it took months of reflection afterwards to understand that. "Being my mother" healed a brokenness that I had carried for many years, the woundedness of a boy who loved his mother desperately but was sent away into the world of men that mystified him, and left him bullied and unsure of his masculinity. My drag-year gave me what Bakhtin, Barthes, and Kristeva would called *jouissance*, the celebration that absolves and restores. Barthes observes, "The writer is someone who plays with his mother's body ... in order to glorify it, to embellish it, or in order to dismember it, to take it to the limit of what can be known about the body."[66] Carole-

Anne Tyler goes on to explain, "As a fetishist, the artist both worships and castrates the fetish object, identifies with it and disidentifies from it, attempting to produce and master difference—the difference from the mother the child requires in order to be a subject at all."[67] In finding my femininity, I found my masculinity. My foray into the world of drag had accomplished something that years in a therapist's office had not. By being my mother, her penis restored, I at last became a man.

Jesus and His Mother

One of the reasons that my coming-out-to-myself was so long delayed was my fear of the church. Like all narcissistic mothers, Mother Church threatens to withdraw her love from her children who misbehave or who explore individuation in a way that does not reflect her narcissistic phantasy back to her. I'm no Gene Robinson—I haven't his willingness to put my private life on display before an often-hostile institution—but the spectacle of a gay priest in drag is not one that everyone in the church is ready for.[68]

How do I dare put the mother of Jesus in the same company as Wilde's mother, Freud's mother, and my own mother? Perhaps we can begin with the most obvious parallels that hold these sons together. I, Oscar, Sigmund, and Jesus are all "golden sons," ones destined to be special, different, highly individuated over-achievers. Each of us have been misunderstood and occasionally vilified. We each found our earliest audience in our mothers, who believed in us before the greater public did. We each have struggled with issues of identity, all the while trying to stay in touch with what we thought our mothers wanted from us.

Was Mary the mother of Jesus a narcissist? Of course it is very difficult to do psychology out of either the biblical text or the pious Marian tradition of the church, since neither is intended as psychological resources. But the evidence is suggestive. Mary is portrayed as "the handmaiden of the Lord." To understand oneself as "chosen by God" for a special favor is easily a narcissistic position.

The Men's Movement says "We are wounded sons of wounded fathers."[69] However, these five mothers would suggest that we are also "wounded sons of wounded mothers." Narcissistic, wounded mothers produce narcissistic, wounded sons. If Jesus's claim to uniqueness can be read backwards in time, such a narcissistic position of uniqueness suggests that his mother too was a narcissist, wounded, a recently betrothed young woman, mysteriously pregnant in a culture that carefully regulated sex to keep it inside of marriage. Shall we blame her for her narcissistic tendencies? Some would claim that she is simply the victim of the patriarchal culture surrounding her. Perhaps we should understand her narcissism as a healthy defense rather than a pathology.

As I explored in my book *Caring for God's People*, each of us is deeply affected by the narratives told about us when we are *in utero* and are first-born. But how other than narcissistic can we understand the effect of having "wise men from afar" come to bow down before someone at his birth? How other than narcissistic can we understand Jesus's "messianic consciousness?" Claims to be "The Son of Man"—"The Human One" as some translations say—however else they are understood theologically, can also be understood as grandiose, and the typical outcome of being treated as a golden son. Conversely, Graham Ward has explored the idea that the role-names traditionally given to the members of the Trinity as not fixed definitions but "performatives."[70] If "Son" is a performative, then the Human One is forever trapped in a dangerous role vis-à-vis a wounded mother.

In this way, Jesus and Mary may serve as extensions of each other. The nature of a narcissistic relationship is addictive. To quote Freud again, while every lasting intimate relationship, whether in marriage, friendship, or the family, conceals a sediment of hostile feelings, there is perhaps "one single exception," the "relation of mother to son which, founded on narcissism, is undisturbed by later rivalry."[71] Perhaps he was ultimately able to individuate, to grow through some of his own narcissism to some healthier perception of himself as separate from the pressure of (m)other's needs to define him. This individuation might explain the shock spurning of his mother at John 2:4, or the out-and-out rejection of her at Mark 3:31–35.

I am not arguing in this essay that Jesus was gay, as some scholars have attempted to do.[72] However, like the others discussed above, Jesus was "languaged" to give priority of place to intimacy with other males.

In a previous book, I have discussed the issue of Jesus and male-male intimacy,[73] but there I overlooked an example which has only more recently come to my attention. In his exegesis of Matthew 8:5–13, Jesus's healing of the centurion's male companion, Gray Temple says:[74]

a. The Matthean passage reads quite differently than the Lukan parallel (7:1–10), for Luke "softens" the vocabulary at critical points.

b. The centurion's relationship with his male companion is a homosexual relationship, as indicated by Matthew's description of him as a παῖς, "street slang for a servant used as a catamite." St. Jerome, in translating the Vulgate, understood this well by using the parallel word *puer*, a word that had exactly the same sexual overtone in third-century Latin.

c. Jesus, as a resident of "pagan Galilee," would have been aware of the Roman tolerance for homoerotic behavior, as long as the two men were not of the same class.

d. Jesus's reference to foreigners coming into the Kingdom in advance and to the surprise of the Kingdom's proper Jewish heirs (Matthew 8:11–12) "appears to be a favorable acknowledgement of the Centurion's unconventional status in strict Jewish eyes."

Temple's exegesis of the Matthean passage supports my argument that Jesus understood male-male intimacy at a deep and generous level. However, in spite of the narcissism and male-male intimacy explored here, the message of a popular form of American Christianity is that there are only two people we can rely on for salvific love: Jesus and Mary.[75] In their country-and-western song, Confederate Railroad sings:

But Jesus and mama always loved me,
even when the devil took control;
Jesus and mama always loved me, this I know.[76]

The divine dyad of virgin mother and suffering son is the cocoon of mutual illusion, the symmetrical symbiosis. Both mother and son have been sanctified in a human sense but also sacralized and deified.[77] Salvific love, and its promise of salvific transformation, may occur in the relationship between mother and son, the love that an adult feels looking back on his or her parents and grandparents, or between lovers. Whatever its power, it is always found in relationship—including male-male relationships—and is always destabilized by narcissism.

Conclusion

Scottish theologian Marcella Althaus-Reid attempts to open up a space for a more inclusive and innovative way of doing theology by offering "a critique of what Heterosexual Theology has done with God by closeting the divine."[78] Are we to perpetuate the heterosexist heritage of theology by continuing to use a sexualized name, Father, or shall we do theology differently, speaking of God who is unsexed, the Human One, and the Spirit (who is traditionally intersex, claimed by both men and women as their own), she asks. The challenge which lies ahead of us is to learn to do theology that includes the most basic of human desires: for intimate relationships with others, whether those relationships are heterosexual, homosocial, or homoerotic.

Wilde's, Freud's, Ophelia's, Jesus's, and my mother were narcissistic. A narcissistic mother holds her golden son too tight, needing him to meet her needs, but she is unable to see his needs. She lives out her desire for him by not giving him space to individuate easily and by not "blessing his leaving," particularly in the Oedipal struggle.[79] Because he has no blessing, often his only other choice is to seek intimate friendships with his male peers, relationships that do not threaten the symmetrical symbiosis between mothers and their golden sons but which reflect the power of intimacy. These relationships, however broken, are the fertile ground of sexual theology.

Notes

[1] On "the unthought known," see Christopher Bollas, *The Shadow of the Object: Psychoanalysis of the Unthought Known* (New York: Columbia University Press, 1987).

[2] And what, then, can we trust? Wilde remarked, "Every great man nowadays has his disciples, and it is always Judas who writes the biography." See Melissa Knox, *Oscar Wilde: A Long and Lovely Suicide* (New Haven: Yale University Press, 1994).

[3] I learned this challenging term from Perry Dane, "The Oral Law and the Jurisprudence of a Textless Text," *S'vara* 2:3 (1991), 11–24.

[4] These dates make them contemporaries of most of my great-grandparents.

[5] David Hare, *The Judas Kiss* (New York: Grove, 1998), 85.

[6] Martin Fido, *Oscar Wilde: An Illustrated Biography* (New York: Peter Bedrick, 1985), 6.

[7] Peter Gay, *Freud: A Life for Our Time* (New York: Norton, 1988), 454.

[8] According to some, the term *homosexual* was coined by the Hungarian scientist, Carl Maria Benkert in 1869. See Simon Rosser, "A Scientific Understanding of Sexual Orientation with Implications for Pastoral Ministry," *Word & World* 14:3 (Summer, 1994), 248.

[9] In his *Unheroic Conduct: The Rise of Heterosexuality and the Invention of the Jewish Man* (Berkeley: University of California Press, 1997), Daniel Boyarin points out that Freud's first published use of the term Oedipal Complex did not occur until 1910, in a paper called "A Special Type of Choice of Object Made by Men."

[10] Eve Kosovsky Sedgwick, in Joseph Nugent, "Patrick Pearse and Homosexual Panic," downloaded from *www.aad.berkeley.edu/96journal/nugent.html.*

[11] On the male gaze and the construction of bodies, see Philip Culbertson, "Designing Men: Reading Male Bodies as Texts," in *The Spirituality of Men: Sixteen Christians Write about Their Faith,* ed. Philip Culbertson (Minneapolis: Fortress Press, 2002), 165–78.

[12] Neil Bartlett, *Who Was That Man? A Present for Mr. Oscar Wilde* (London: Serpent's Tail, 1988).

[13] Or so I thought, until several weeks after the first time I delivered this material, as part of a lecture series at the Auckland Family Counselling and Psychotherapy Centre. Then, ironically via one of my clients who is fascinated with alchemy, I was reminded of the identity of Uranus in Greek mythology. Much like the sky father Rangi in Maori mythology, Uranus, the sky god, made repeated efforts to kill his own children. Finally, he was bested by his son Cronus, who bit off his father's testicles and cast them into the sea. So perhaps "Uranians" was intended as a synonym for "eunuchs." Thus far I cannot find a better explanation for the term.

[14] Both the words *sodomy* and *bugger* originate within the Christian theological vocabulary. Sodomy is a reference to Genesis 19; bugger begins as a synonym for heretic, and gains its extra connotation of anal intercourse simply by inference: Heretics must do nasty things.

[15] Bartlett, *Who Was That Man?* 79–91.

[16] Ibid., 163.

[17] Ibid., 229.

[18] Jonathan Dollimore, *Sexual Dissidence: Augustine to Wilde, Freud to Foucault* (Oxford: Clarendon Press, 1991), 3–5. According to Colm Tóibín in *Love in a Dark Time: Gay Lives from Wilde to Almodovar* (Sydney: Picador, 2001), 37, Gide did not tell his mother the truth. Twenty-five years later, in *Si le grain ne meurt*, Gide admitted that rather than leaving, he had introduced himself to Wilde and Bosie, after which they went "trolling" for Arab boys.

[19] Hendrika Halberstadt-Freud, *Freud, Proust, Perversion and Love* (Berwyn, PA: Swets & Zeitlinger, 1991), 23

[20] Ibid., 24–25.

[21] Beverley Nichols, *Father Figure* (New York: Simon & Schuster, 1972), 92–99.

[22] Eve Kosofsky Sedgwick, *Between Men: English Literature and Male Homosocial Desire* (New York: Columbia University Press, 1985), 95.

[23] Knox, *Oscar Wilde,* xvi.

[24] Ibid., 5.

[25] Ibid., 7.

[26] Ibid.

[27] Tóibín, *Love in Dark Time,* 49.

[28] Knox, *Oscar Wilde,* 69, citing Rupert Hart-Davis, ed., *The Letters of Oscar Wilde,* 352.

[29] Ibid., 39, citing Richard Ellmann.

[30] Tóibín, *Love in a Dark Time,* 51.

[31] Gay, *Freud,* 4.

[32] Monica McGoldrick, Randy Gerson, and Sylvia Shellenberger, *Genograms: Assessment and Intervention,* 2nd ed. (New York: Norton, 1999), 128. Lisa Appignanesi and John Forrester, *Freud's Women: Family, Patients, Followers* (New York: Other Press, 2000), 15, suggest that she might have committed suicide because she could not give her husband the "required" boy-child.

[33] However, this is not entirely clear, for there were apparently two "nurses" in Freud's young life. The other was named Monika Zajic. See Appignanesi and Forrester, *Freud's Women,* 16.

[34] Paul Vitz, "Freud's Christian Unconscious," at *www.paulvitz.com/FreudsXtnUncon/006.html.*

[35] Gay, *Freud,* 11.

[36] Ibid., 7.

[37] Ibid., 505–6.

[38] Ibid., 573.

[39] Appignanesi and Forrester, *Freud's Women,* 13.

[40] Ibid., 15.

[41] McGoldrick et al., *Genograms,* 147.

[42] Louis Breger, *Freud: Darkness in the Midst of Vision* (New York: John Wiley, 2000), 46.

[43] Ibid., 44.

[44] McGoldrick et al., *Genograms,* 130.

[45] One of the first to point out the erotic nature of these letters was Erik Erikson, in "The Dream Specimen of Psychoanalysis," *Journal of the American Psychoanalytic Association* 2 (1954): 5–56.

[46] Breger, *Freud: Darkness,* 152, 332.

[47] Boyarin, *Unheroic Conduct,* 208.

[48] Ibid., 208–09.

[49] Sigmund Freud, "Psychoanalytic Notes on an Autobiographical Account of a Case of Paranoia (Dementia Paranoides) (1911)" (London: Hogarth Press, 1978), XII:3–82.

[50] Hare, *The Judas Kiss,* 97.

[51] *Diagnostic and Statistical Manual of Mental Disorders.* 4th ed. (Washington, D.C.: American Psychiatric Association, 2000).

[52] Kathleen Kelleher, "The Case Against the Notion of 'Homosexual Panic'" in *Affirmation: Gay and Lesbian Mormons*, November 8, 1999, at *www.affirmation. org/article173.htm.*

[53] David Plummer, *One of the Boys: Masculinity, Homophobia and Modern Manhood* (New York: Haworth, 1999), 21.

[54] In terms of its legal usage, two Canadian psychiatrists reviewed literature on the subject dating back to 1920 and concluded in the *Canadian Journal of Psychiatry* that the term "should be permanently assigned to the junkyard of obsolete psychiatric terminology." "Homosexual panic" is not a mental disorder, they said; rather, it is a culmination of our culture's homophobic attitudes.

[55] George Weinberg, *Society and the Healthy Homosexual* (New York: St. Martin's Press, 1972), 4.

[56] Gregory Herek, "Sexual Prejudice and Gender: Do Heterosexuals' Attitudes Toward Lesbians and Gay Men Differ?" *Journal of Social Issues* 56:2 (Summer 2000), 251–66; see also his "The Psychology of Sexual Prejudice," *Current Directions in Psychological Science* 9 (2000), 19–22.

[57] Nugent, "Patrick Pearse and Homosexual Panic"; see also Plummer, *One of the Boys,* 2, 4, 150.

[58] It seems to me that this would explain the psychodynamics of what Vivienne Cass calls "developmental foreclosure" in gay men and lesbian women. See her "Homosexual Identity Formation: A Theoretical Model," *Journal of Homosexuality* 4 (1979), 219–35.

[59] Sedgwick, *Between Men,* 201.

[60] Boyarin, *Unheroic Conduct,* 194. In his first model, Freud reconstructed (or invented) memories of child abuse not only for female patients but for boys as well—including his brother—as a means of accounting for his own male hysteria. Six out of the eighteen cases mentioned in the paper on which the seduction theory is based, "The Aetiology of Hysteria" (1896), are cases of boys, not girls. In one of the most famous of his letters to his friend Fleiss, Freud writes: "Unfortunately my own father was one of these perverts and is responsible for the hysteria of my brother (all of whose symptoms are identification) and those of several younger sisters." See Jeffrey Masson, *The Complete Letters of Sigmund Freud to Wilhelm Fleiss, 1887–1904* (Cambridge: Harvard University Press, 1985), 230–31; see also 264.

[61] On drag as a performance identity, see Stephen Thierman, "Drag's Subversive Potential: Performativity and the Possibility of Resistance," at *www. pensees.homestead.com/stephen.html.* See also Terry Goldie, "Dragging Out the Queen: Male Femaling and Male Feminism," and Steven Schacht, "Turnabout: Gay Drag Queens and the Masculine Embodiment of the Feminine," in *Revealing Male Bodies,* ed. Nancy Tuana, William Cowling, Maurice Hamington, Greg Johnson, and Terrance Macmullan (Bloomington: Indiana University Press, 2001), 125–45 and 155–70; and Steven Schacht, "Four Renditions of Doing Female Drag: Feminine Appearing Conceptual Variations on a Masculine Theme," *Gendered Sexualities* 6 (2002), 157–80.

[62] Jessica Benjamin, *Like Subjects, Love Objects: Essays on Recognition and Sexual Difference* (New Haven: Yale University Press, 1995), 66.

[63] See Knox, *Oscar Wilde,* 74: "Imitation, because it represents an attempt to identify with another personality, often has as its impetus a need to solve a conflict."

[64] Anaïs Nin, *The Diary of Anaïs Nin,* vol. 1 (New York: Swallow Press, 1966), 20.

[65] Robert Stoller, *Observing the Erotic Imagination* (New Haven: Yale University Press, 1985), 30.

[66] Roland Barthes, *The Pleasure of the Text,* translated by Richard Miller (New York: Hill and Wang, 1975), 14.

[67] Carole-Anne Tyler, *Female Impersonation* (New York: Routledge, 2003), 76.

[68] It's not only the church that scares me. So do my colleagues in my other profession, as a psychotherapist. The profession of psychotherapy has not always been tolerant of homosexuals, whether as clients or as therapists. While the DSM-II removed homosexuality as a diagnostic category in 1972, there are still instances within the past decade where gay men and lesbian women have been refused entrance into psychotherapy training programs on the basis of their sexual orientation, and some of the psychotherapeutic literature still perpetuates gross stereotypes about homosexuality, in some cases still describing it as a perversion. In general, many gays and lesbians consider psychotherapy to be a form of heterosexism—that which privileges the experience and worldview of white middle-class heterosexual males—and therefore believe that it is dangerous for gays and lesbians. And to affirm that perception, we have Freud, who couldn't decide whether homosexuality was a sort of "normal" gender inversion, or a more serious form of arrested development. Even worse, there is W. R. D. Fairburn, who believed that homosexuality is enough of a perversion that homosexuals should be rounded up and confined to special camps, sealed off from the general public.

[69] I believe the phrase comes from Samuel Osherson, *Finding Our Fathers: The Unfinished Business of Manhood* (New York: Free Press, 1986).

[70] Graham Ward, "Kenosis and Naming: Beyond Analogy and Towards Allegoria Amoris," in *Religion, Modernity and Postmodernity,* ed. Paul Heelas (Oxford: Blackwell, 1988).

[71] Gay, *Freud,* 505–6.

[72] Among those scholars who have attempted to argue that Jesus was gay, or at least acted homoerotically, see theologians Theodore Jennings, Morton Smith, and Rollan McCleary, and playwright Terrance McNally. For those who emphasize Jesus's transgressive sexuality, see Marcella Althaus-Reid and John Goss.

[73] "Friends, Associates and Lovers: Jesus, His Male Companions, and the Ancient Ideals of Friendship," in Philip Culbertson, *New Adam: The Future of Male Spirituality* (Minneapolis: Fortress Press, 1992), 91–106. See also Philip Culbertson, "Men and Christian Friendship," in *Men's Bodies, Men's Gods: Male Identities in a (Post-) Christian Culture,* ed. Björn Krondorfer (New York: New York University Press, 1996), 149–80. Eve Kosofsky Sedgwick describes the process whereby men attempt to establish some intimacy with each other, usually in a triangulated relationship with a woman who functions to disguise the gestures between the men, as

homosociality. The word is a neologism, obviously formed by analogy with *homosexual* and just as obviously meant to be distinguished from *homosexual.* See Sedgwick, *Between Men,* 1.

[74] Gray Temple, "The Biblical Case in Favor of Gene Robinson's Election, Confirmation, and Consecration," a speech delivered at Holy Innocents Episcopal Church, Atlanta GA, on September 11, 2003, at *www.stpat.net/pdf/hermeneutics.pdf.*

[75] Maxine Grossman, "Jesus, Mama, and the Constraints on Salvific Love in Contemporary Country Music," *Journal of the American Academy of Religion* 70:1, (March 2002), 83–115.

[76] "Jesus and Mama," words and music by Danny Mayo and James Dean Hicks, on the album *Confederate Railroad,* downloaded from *www.gospel.boltblue.net/other_ music/jesus_and_mama.htm,* on June 19, 2004.

[77] Grossman, 90, quoting Philip Vandermeer, "Religious Ideals, Musical Style, and Cultural Meaning in the Gospel Songs of Hank Williams," Ph.D. dissertation, University of Maryland School of Music, 1999.

[78] Marcella Althaus-Reid, *The Queer God* (London and New York: Routledge, 2003), 4.

[79] On the human inability to leave a relationship without being blessed to do so, see Herbert Anderson and Kenneth R. Mitchell, *Leaving Home* (Louisville: Westminster/John Knox Press, 1993).

Bibliography

Althaus-Reid, Marcella. *The Queer God.* London and New York: Routledge, 2003.

Anderson, Herbert, and Kenneth R. Mitchell. *Leaving Home.* Louisville: Westminster/John Knox Press, 1993.

Appignanesi, Lisa, and John Forrester. *Freud's Women: Family, Patients, Followers.* New York: Other Press, 2000.

Barthes, Roland. *The Pleasure of the Text.* Richard Miller, trans. New York: Hill and Wang, 1975.

Bartlett, Neil. *Who Was That Man? A Present for Mr. Oscar Wilde.* London: Serpent's Tail, 1988.

Benjamin, Jessica. *Like Subjects, Love Objects: Essays on Recognition and Sexual Difference.* New Haven: Yale University Press, 1995.

Bollas, Christopher. *The Shadow of the Object: Psychoanalysis of the Unthought Known.* New York: Columbia University Press, 1987.

Boyarin, Daniel. *Unheroic Conduct: The Rise of Heterosexuality and the Invention of the Jewish Man.* Berkeley: University of California Press, 1997.

Breger, Louis. *Freud: Darkness in the Midst of Vision.* New York: John Wiley, 2000.

Cass, Vivienne. "Homosexual Identity Formation: A Theoretical Model." *Journal of Homosexuality* 4 (1979), 219–35.

Culbertson, Philip. "Designing Men: Reading Male Bodies as Texts." In Philip Culbertson, ed. *The Spirituality of Men: Sixteen Christians Write about Their Faith.* Minneapolis: Fortress Press, 2002, 165–78.

————. "Men and Christian Friendship." In *Men's Bodies, Men's Gods: Male Identities in a (Post-) Christian Culture,* edited by Björn Krondorfer. New York: New York University Press, 1996.

————. *New Adam: The Future of Male Spirituality.* Minneapolis: Fortress Pres, 1992.

Dane, Perry. "The Oral Law and the Jurisprudence of a Textless Text." *S'vara* 2:3 (1991), 11–24.

Diagnostic and Statistical Manual of Mental Disorders. 4th ed. Washington, D.C.: American Psychiatric Association, 2000.

Dollimore, Jonathan. *Sexual Dissidence: Augustine to Wilde, Freud to Foucault.* Oxford: Clarendon Press, 1991.

Erikson, Erik. "The Dream Specimen of Psychoanalysis." *Journal of the American Psychoanalytic Association* 2 (1954): 5–56.

Fido, Martin. *Oscar Wilde: An Illustrated Biography.* New York: Peter Bedrick, 1985.

Freud, Sigmund. "Psychoanalytic Notes on an Autobiographical Account of a Case of Paranoia (Dementia Paranoides) (1911)." London: Hogarth Press, 1978, XII:3–82.

Gay, Peter. *Freud: A Life for Our Time.* New York: Norton, 1988.

Goldie, Terry. "Dragging Out the Queen: Male Femaling and Male Feminism." In *Revealing Male Bodies.* Edited by Nancy Tuana, William Cowling, Maurice Hamington, Greg Johnson, and Terrance Macmillan. Bloomington: Indiana University Press, 2001.

Grossman, Maxine. "Jesus, Mama, and the Constraints on Salvific Love in Contemporary Country Music." *Journal of the American Academy of Religion* 70:1 (March 2002), 83–115.

Halberstadt-Freud, Hendrika. *Freud, Proust, Perversion and Love.* Berwyn, PA: Swets & Zeitlinger, 1991.

Hare, David. *The Judas Kiss.* New York: Grove, 1998.

Herek, Gregory. "Sexual Prejudice and Gender: Do Heterosexuals' Attitudes Toward Lesbians and Gay Men Differ?" *Journal of Social Issues* 56:2 (Summer 2000), 251–66.

————. "The Psychology of Sexual Prejudice." *Current Directions in Psychological Science* 9 (2000), 19–22.

Kelleher, Kathleen. "The Case Against the Notion of 'Homosexual Panic.'" In *Affirmation: Gay and Lesbian Mormons.* November 8, 1999. *www.affirmation. org/article173.htm.*

Knox, Melissa. *Oscar Wilde: A Long and Lovely Suicide.* New Haven: Yale University Press, 1994.

Masson, Jeffrey. *The Complete Letters of Sigmund Freud to Wilhelm Fleiss, 1887–1904.* Cambridge: Harvard University Press, 1985.

Mayo, Danny, and James Dean Hicks. "Jesus and Mama." On *Confederate Railroad. www.gospel.boltblue.net/other_ music/jesus_and_mama.htm.* June 19, 2004.

McGoldrick, Monica, Randy Gerson, and Sylvia Shellenberger. *Genograms: Assessment and Intervention.* 2nd ed. New York: W. W. Norton, 1999.

Nichols, Beverley. *Father Figure.* New York: Simon & Schuster, 1972.

Nin, Anaïs. *The Diary of Anaïs Nin,* vol. 1. New York: Swallow Press, 1966.

Nugent, Jospeh. "Patrick Pearse and Homosexual Panic." *www.aad.berkeley.edu/96 journal/nugent.html.*

Osherson, Samuel. *Finding Our Fathers: The Unfinished Business of Manhood.* New York: Free Press, 1986.

Plummer, David. *One of the Boys: Masculinity, Homophobia and Modern Manhood.* New York: Haworth, 1999.

Rosser, Simon. "A Scientific Understanding of Sexual Orientation with Implications for Pastoral Ministry." *Word & World* 14:3 (Summer, 1994).

Schacht, Steven. "Four Renditions of Doing Female Drag: Feminine Appearing Conceptual Variations on a Masculine Theme." *Gendered Sexualities* 6 (2002), 157–80.

———. "Turnabout: Gay Drag Queens and the Masculine Embodiment of the Feminine." In *Revealing Male Bodies.* Edited by Nancy Tuana, William Cowling, Maurice Hamington, Greg Johnson, and Terrance Macmillan. Bloomington: Indiana University Press, 2001.

Sedgwick, Eve Kosofsky. *Between Men: English Literature and Male Homosocial Desire.* New York: Columbia University Press, 1985.

Stoller, Robert. *Observing the Erotic Imagination.* New Haven: Yale University Press, 1985.

Thierman, Stephen. "Drag's Subversive Potential: Performativity and the Possibility of Resistance." *www. pensees.homestead.com/stephen.html.*

Tóibín, Colm. *Love in a Dark Time: Gay Lives from Wilde to Almodovar.* Sydney: Picador, 2001.

Tuana, Nancy, William Cowling, Maurice Hamington, Greg Johnson, and Terrance Macmillan, eds. *Revealing Male Bodies.* Bloomington: Indiana University Press, 2001.

Tyler, Carole-Anne. *Female Impersonation.* New York: Routledge, 2003.

Vitz, Paul. "Freud's Christian Unconscious." *www.paulvitz.com/FreudsXtnUncon/006. html.*

Ward, Graham. "Kenosis and Naming: Beyond Analogy and Towards Allegoria Amoris," In Heelas, Paul, ed. *Religion, Modernity and Postmodernity.* Oxford: Blackwell, 1988.

Weinberg, George. *Society and the Healthy Homosexual.* New York: St. Martin's Press, 1972.

✧ Conclusion—I'm Okay; You're a Heretic: Sex as Power and Threat

C. K. Robertson

"I'll kill you!" I felt the adrenaline rise within me as he edged himself closer to my chair, the volume of his words matching the visible intensity of his emotions. A rapping on the door of my office and the voice of the church secretary asking if there was anything we needed assured me that I was not the only one to hear the harsh threat. This fact, along with the awareness that the man sitting in the chair across from me—so obviously enraged—was not actually intending to menace me personally, helped me unclench my own hands and relax a little ... but only a little. "I tell you I'll kill you!" There were those awful words again. Even as I attempted to voice an intelligible reply, I remembered that I had only myself to blame for my present sense of discomfort, inasmuch as I had offered church members the opportunity to vent their feelings about recent denominational decisions regarding a gay bishop-elect. The parishioner in front of me had taken me up on my offer to talk and was now reliving an encounter he had years before with a gay man who had propositioned him. The anger and the fear of that man's earlier encounter came flooding back on him as he shared his story there in my office.

In my role as a denominational consultant to parishes, I have visited many congregations throughout the country and each time have heard similar cries of anger and anguish, alongside sighs of relief from those who have in years past felt like second-class Christians because of their sexual orientation. The current debate is not likely to be resolved anytime soon, at least not in a way that can guarantee harmony within denominations and faith groups. Issues of sexuality rarely do. The issue today may be same-gender relationships, but at different points in time other aspects of sexuality have elicited similarly intense emotional responses from individuals and entire cultures. For those who desire and seek a significant degree of control and self-determination in life, sex may indeed be the ultimate wild card: an enemy to be fought, subdued, repressed, controlled. Inasmuch as the preceding two chapters have offered detailed examinations of the issue of homosexuality, this concluding section is not meant to repeat that work but instead draws upon the biblical story of Cain and Abel to explore the ways in which human sexuality on the whole has been, and often remains, a threatening force—especially for religious individuals and institutions that avoid chaos and value order.

There is nothing new in the power of human sexuality to intimidate or unsettle. In the ancient world, the second-century C.E. physician Galen offered a "vivid picture" of the dangers inherent in male ejaculation, the possibility of a "draining of vital spirit."[1] Indeed, today's popular joke of "dying happy" during the act of intercourse appears to echo Galen's warning that some sexually active persons in his time had perished "from an excess of pleasure."[2] To Galen and many like him, however, sex was no laughing matter. For a people who valued wholeness and health, sex appeared to be a dangerous commodity, something that could potentially weaken the participating individual. Even as the loss of blood could endanger the body, so the loss of semen—the literal stuff of life—could pose a threat to the stability of the body's operations. It is little wonder that sexual asceticism was applauded by many in the ancient world; such asceticism represented control of that which could weaken or even kill.

Control appears to be the operative word here, inasmuch as the ancient world offered humans little control over life, death, and their environment. The evolution of religion, some have said, represents intentional attempts to bring some form of control to an otherwise fearful and fragile existence. Where meaning could be found in the will of the gods or the divine order of the universe, there existed the very real possibility of a sense of well-being, hope, even some control.

In speaking about ancient religion, Alain Daniélou, noted Orientalist and author of several works on Indian faiths and deities, differentiates between two "opposed and contradictory forms," one tied to the natural world and the other to organized urban life.[3] The natural tradition, Daniélou says, understood all of creation as the tangible essence and expression of Divinity. Within this tradition, any long-term happiness that human beings could enjoy was the result of living in harmony with their environment and thereby embracing a naturalistic "intoxication of love and ecstasy" through which they could find true wisdom and experience the Divine.[4] With the genesis of the newly emergent cities, a very different religious understanding of the universe and humanity's place in it developed. As many ancient peoples abandoned the existence of a tribal hunter-gatherer in exchange for, first, structured agricultural and, ultimately, urban life, their spirituality reflected a desire for greater manipulation of, and dominion over, their environment. Daniélou has little praise and much contempt for these city-dwellers. As opposed to those who enjoyed "communion with nature and simplicity of heart," he decries the architects of urban religions as people who exploited their environment and fellow human beings, then rationalized their actions through appeals to "divinely-revealed" laws and beliefs.[5]

Whatever Daniélou's personal feelings, it is clear that from the start, the religions of the city opposed, and continually tried to eliminate, the religions of nature and the natural order. An interesting illustration of this hostility of the urban over the natural tradition may be found in the biblical account of Cain and Abel, the immediate progeny of Adam and Eve. The fourth chapter of Genesis introduces the brothers:

> Now Abel was a keeper of sheep, and Cain a tiller of the ground. In the course of time Cain brought to the LORD an offering of the fruit of the ground, and Abel for his part brought of the firstlings of his flock, their fat portions. And the LORD had regard for Abel and his offering, but for Cain and his offering he had no regard. So Cain was very angry, and his countenance fell. … Cain said to his brother Abel, "Let us go out to the field." And when they were in the field, Cain rose up against his brother Abel, and killed him. Then the LORD said to Cain, "Where is your brother Abel?" He said, "I do not know; am I my brother's keeper?" And the LORD said, "What have you done? Listen; your brother's blood is crying out to me from the ground! And now you are cursed from the ground, which has opened its mouth to receive your brother's blood from your hand. When you till the ground, it will no longer yield to you its strength; you will be a fugitive and a wanderer on the earth." … Then Cain went away from the presence of the LORD, and settled in the land of Nod, east of Eden. Cain knew his wife, and she conceived and bore Enoch; and he built a city, and named it Enoch after his son Enoch.

Several interesting features appear in this tale. First, it is worth noting the different vocations of the two sons: Abel was a herder of animals, a hunter-gatherer of sorts, while his brother Cain was "a tiller of the soil" and eventually, through the birth of his son, the first urban architect. Daniel Quinn, author of modern popular works such as *Ishmael* and *The Story of B,* speaks of the symbolic nature of the two professions in terms of two diametrically opposed tribal traditions in the ancient Near East: hunter-gatherers and what he refers to as "totalitarian agriculturalists."[6] Quinn asserts that the latter, represented by Cain, were members of a particular tribe that differed from other surrounding tribes in that its members demarcated land and practiced year-round crop rotation so that they could control their long-term food production and, thus, their future. This led to more advanced boundary-setting and the eventual creation of cities with armies to guard against external threats and police forces to guard against internal disruptions.

It may be argued that what lay at the heart of all development was fear ... fear of a lack of control. Rather than live in harmony with their human and non-human environment, such Cain-like tribesmen saw everything and everyone outside their own tribe as a potential threat: "So Cain was very angry and his countenance fell." Suspicion and envy led to a culture of violence, Quinn suggests, and the Genesis story of Cain and Abel simply reflects the murderous hatred of those who sought control toward outsiders and refused to look out for anyone but themselves: "Am I my brother's keeper?" Eventually, such "brothers" were assimilated when possible, or eliminated.[7] Citing fellow scholar Miréa Eliade, Daniélou argues, "The first murder is thus accomplished by a man who in some way is the incarnate symbol of ... urban society."[8] In the words of George Lucas's Muppet-sized sage, Yoda, "Fear leads to anger; anger leads to hate; hate leads to suffering." This suffering is not only the obvious oppression or annihilation of indigenous tribes by aggressive urbanites, but also the ongoing internal anxiety experienced by all "Cain's descendants." As Cain responds to God: "My punishment is greater than I can bear! Today you have driven me away from the soil, and I shall be hidden from your face; I shall be a fugitive and a wanderer on the earth, and anyone who meets me may kill me" (4:13–14).

All this brings us back to the issue of sexuality and its power to threaten. The ascent in power of "Cain's descendants" during the second millennium before the Common Era brought with it the formulation of urban religions with strict ceremonial and moral laws that clearly defined who was in … and who was out of the community. The Torah—the first five books that comprise the heart of the Hebrew Scriptures and contain over nine hundred commandments—is devoted largely to the creation and preservation of clear boundaries for God's "chosen people." Indeed, when the proclamation is made, "You shall be holy, as the LORD your God is holy," the word *holy* literally means "to be set apart." The ancient Hebrews thus defined and understood themselves as a people not in intrinsic terms as much as in comparative terms, i.e., to be *a part of* Israel meant being *apart from* other tribes and peoples. Inclusion in Israel was defined largely in exclusive terms: "Who are we? We are *not* you!"

Although the care and hospitality afforded to resident aliens in the Torah is fairly remarkable—one line is later quoted by Jesus as part of the greatest commandment: "You shall love your neighbor as yourself"—there remain clear defining boundaries about what and with whom you should eat, and with whom and in what way you could have sexual relations. Through what we may term a religiously based "exclusive inclusion," the composition of the tribe was controlled and its future seemingly assured. The ultimate end of such boundary-setting is seen in the biblical books of Joshua and Judges, with the concept of the *herem*. Not unlike its Arabic equivalent, the *jihad,* the *herem* involved the total destruction by Israel of an "enemy" camp or village, including not only its male combatants, but women and children, the elderly and sick, even any animals that lived there, all offered to God as a religious sacrifice. Although many modern believers exhibit appropriate revulsion at such tales, they fail to comprehend the danger posed by the non-combatants in the minds of the people of Israel. Through sexual relations and accompanying intermarriages, the threat to the "chosen people" was in some ways greater, albeit more subtle, than the swords and spears of the soldiers. Sex was thereby understood as dangerous, a two-edged sword that had to be controlled. We may rightly dismiss the results of fear—the *herem,* the *jihad,* Crusades, Inquisitions, witch hunts, pogroms, inter-religious wars—but we should not be blind to the power of the underlying fear. Franklin D. Roosevelt may have been correct that "we have nothing to fear but fear itself," but fear itself can be a powerful, destructive force, especially when supported by religious beliefs. The fear of contamination by "the other" has too often led to "the other's" annihilation. Thus, biblical texts such as "Whoever is not for us is against us" are cited far more often than the other gospel quotation, "Whoever is not against us is with us" (Luke 9:50), not to mention various passages about the inclusive call of God to all tribes and people in prophetic books such as Amos (9:7) and Jonah (4:11).

In an earlier book, *Conflict in Corinth: Redefining the System,* I drew upon business and systems theories to speak at length of the effects of fear and consequent conflict.[9] The foundational principle is that we, whether individuals or groups, do not experience ten thousand different contentious issues; rather, we experience ten thousand variations of a handful of the same old familiar issues. Insofar as we fail to resolve or even manage a problem when it surfaces, we can be assured that it will reappear again and again in different guises. Indeed, a predictable pattern commences the moment a potentially contentious issue arises. First, sides begin to form, as one person or group is "for X" and the other is "against X." If not resolved or managed, the next time that X appears, now looking a little different from X^2, positions will begin to harden between the sides as they become "pro-X" and "anti-X." When we reach the point of X^3, resources are committed to what is now a cause. With X^4, communications cease between the now warring parties, and with X^5, the conflict begins to spill outside the immediate participants. To anyone looking in from the outside, the emergent pattern is all too clear: With the passage of time and the failure to resolve or manage the conflict, the intensity of emotion and conviction that each party brings to the table dramatically increases. What is most intriguing, and most unnerving, is the next step in this pattern. By the time the involved parties get to the next level of conflict, their perceptions of reality become distorted. In other words, they cease to view one another as three-dimensional human beings with whom they disagree and instead see only "the enemy," a two-dimensional caricature at best and an inhuman, evil beast at worst. It is after this stage that the inevitable results of divorce, dissolution of a company, war between nations, or splits of religious groups occur. I say "inevitable" because once I am dealing with "the evil enemy" instead of a "brother," then I no longer have to be his keeper; indeed, my only responsibility is to protect myself from him! I, Cain, can then kill Abel.

As is hopefully evident from what has just been described, fear lies at the very heart of the process, from a more rational anxiety caused by disagreement with another over issue X to an irrational terror that "the other" is evil and will either contaminate or destroy me if I do not protect myself. As shown, the intensity of feeling and accompanying conviction increases as time goes on, but when X is something that already has intense feelings associated with it for an individual or group, then the parties speed through the process at a breakneck pace. Such has certainly been the case in religious circles with issues of human sexuality. Psychologists and sociologists can offer arguments regarding the internal and social preconditions for the fear/anxiety/threat of sex, but it is the reality of that fear with which we are contending and that takes precedence over all other issues at hand, even a religious group's own growth and future. In my own denomination, the Episcopal Church, we have seen both the so-called Decade of Evangelism in the 1990s and, more recently, the 20/20 proposal to double active membership by the year 2020 overshadowed by severe disagreements over same-gender sexuality, with the conflict spilling over into other parts of the Anglican Communion and different parties referring to one another in more two-dimensional than three-dimensional terms. There are no easy answers ahead either for my own denomination or for many other faith groups in America and throughout the world. To reverse the process of unresolved conflict described above is never easy, and once the parties have come to the point of "unreality," the way back is nigh-impossible. Any conflict manager will admit that after that stage the goal is simply to keep the bloodshed to a minimum. The fact that the bloodshed today is more often figurative rather than literal, wrought by verbal assaults rather than swords or spears, does not diminish the pain that is caused by the time the process of unmanaged conflict reaches its apex.

It can be noted that there is an apparent bit of naïveté about Abel in the biblical account, one that Daniélou, Quinn, and Eliade might say is representative of the naïveté of tribal people who embraced an intimate kind of communion with their fellows and their environment, a communion in which the sensual and the spiritual intertwined and shame was noticeably absent. Georg Feuerstein speaks of this as "sacred sexuality." Again, it is possible to hear echoes of the book of Genesis, more specifically of the story of Cain and Abel's parents, Adam and Eve, who displayed a complete lack of concern about their nakedness—"and they were naked and not ashamed" (2:25)—at least, until the arrival of the serpent and the promise that they would be "like God" (3:5). The temptation to become gods unto themselves, to control and be in control, reaches its zenith several chapters later in Genesis, with the building of a great city and its ziggurat, the famed Tower of Babel (11:4). It is probably not coincidental that the harmony of the Garden of Eden is eventually replaced by a giant phallic symbol, "the ideology of male supremacy … the modus operandi for urbanized humanity."[10]

The naiveté of Abel and his parents can be seen today in the statements of those who seek a greater appreciation of sacred sexuality and inclusive religion, who genuinely think there are real possibilities for dialogue and conversation with those who disagree with them. These modern Abels, however, often fail to understand the conflict process described above and, thus, fail to comprehend that conversation is impossible with Cains who see them only as "the enemy." What is to be the end of our current crisis regarding difficult questions of sexuality? There is no way to say with certainty, although we may predict with some confidence that sex will continue to evoke deep anxiety in religious-minded individuals and institutions of all types with heart-wrenching effects. Agreement appears impossible. The challenge facing all persons of faith is to decide whether or not convictions about sexuality are to be the litmus test for community. If this is the case, then it may be predicted that our passionate debates will persist with little progress.

Notes

[1] Cited in Carolyn Osiek and David L. Balch, *Families in the New Testament World* (Louisville: Westminster-John Knox Press, 1997), 107.

[2] Ibid.

[3] Alain Daniélou, *Gods of Love and Ecstasy* (Rochester, VT: Inner Traditions, 1992), 13.

[4] Ibid, 16.

[5] Ibid.

[6] As related in Daniel Quinn, *Ishmael* (New York: Bantam, 1995).

[7] Though he does not use the "Cain" biblical imagery, Georg Feuerstein, author of *Sacred Sexuality*, concurs with Quinn's and Daniélou's assessment of the ancient world. He speaks of the "aggressive pastoralists" who, in the time period described by the first

several chapters of the Book of Genesis, began to overwhelm their hunter-gatherer counterparts either by assimilation or outright destruction. See Feuerstein, *Sacred Sexuality* (Rochester, VT: Inner Traditions, 2003), 61.

[8] Ibid. Cf. Miréa Eliade, *Histoire des croyances et des idées religieuses* (Paris: Crois, 1976), 180–81.

[9] C. K. Robertson, *Conflict in Corinth: Redefining the System* (New York: Peter Lang, 2001). See especially chapters four and five.

[10] Ibid, 62.

Bibliography

Daniélou, Alain. *Gods of Love and Ecstasy.* Rochester, VT: Inner Traditions, 1992.

Eliade, Miréa. *Histoire des croyances et des idées religieuses.* Paris: Crois, 1976.

Feuerstein, Georg. *Sacred Sexuality.* Rochester, VT: Inner Traditions, 2003.

Osiek, Carolyn, and David L. Balch. *Families in the New Testament World.* Louisville: Westminster-John Knox Press, 1997.

Quinn, Daniel. *Ishmael.* New York: Bantam, 1995.

Robertson, C. K. *Conflict in Corinth: Redefining the System.* New York: Peter Lang, 2001.

✧ Contributors

Philip Culbertson is Professor of Pastoral Theology in the School of Theology of the University of Auckland, New Zealand. He is also a psychotherapist in private practice and teaches psychotherapy at two training institutes in Auckland. A native of the U.S. and an ordained Episcopal priest, Dr. Culbertson has lived and worked in Israel and Switzerland, and authored over 80 scholarly articles and books, including *The Spirituality of Men: Sixteen Christians Write about Their Faith.*

John W. Gamble has been a student of religions for the past forty years. He has been involved in meditation for the past three decades and has served on the board of Southern Dharma Retreat Center, a meditation center near Asheville, North Carolina, since 1989. He holds a Ph.D. from Georgia State University and is a clinical psychologist who has spent his professional career working in both public service and private practice.

Douglas MacLeod is completing doctoral studies at The State University at Albany, New York, specializing in English and Communications/Film Studies. Previously, he has taught at the College of Staten Island and the SUNY Albany Writing Center. MacLeod's current writing projects include an article on children and science fiction and a book review for *Film and History* magazine.

Douglas C. Mohrmann is Instructor of Religion at Cornerstone University, Grand Rapids, Michigan. With two master's degrees from Gordon-Conwell Theological Seminary and a Ph.D. from Durham University, Dr. Mohrmann is also Co-Director of the Center for the Study of Antiquities. He has published articles in areas as diverse as Pauline Studies, the Dead Sea Scrolls, and American Evangelicalism. Dr. Mohrmann lives in Michigan with his wife and four children.

Georgia A. Newman is a Flannery O'Connor scholar and has served formerly as both a college administrator at Polk Community College in Florida and a professor of southern literature at Georgia College & State University. She lives with her husband Jim Powell in Milledgeville, Georgia, and, with him, serves there as a lay leader at St. Stephen's Episcopal Church.

Lesley A. Northup has served as Associate Professor of Religious Studies and Associate Dean of the Honors College at Florida International University. Her research in American religion has included particular focus in the areas of religion and sexuality, women and religion, ritual studies, and mythography. Dr. Northup is the author of two books and numerous articles, the editor of two collections, and the editor of the reference work, *Religious Documents of North America Annual.*

B. J. Oropeza holds a Ph.D. from the University of Durham and is a professor at the C. P. Haggard School of Theology at Azusa Pacific University in California. An internationally acclaimed author, his many publications include *The Gospel according to Superheroes* (Peter Lang, 2004), *Paul and Apostasy, A Time to Laugh,* and *99 Answers to Questions about Angels, Demons, and Spiritual Warfare.* Dr. Oropeza has worked as a research editor for Victory Outreach International in La Puente, California, and as a research associate for the Christian Research Institute (CRI) in Rancho Santa Margarita, California.

David D. Peck holds a Ph.D. in the History of the Middle East and is an award-winning history professor at Brigham Young University-Idaho. His writings include a quarterly op-ed column on the Middle East, a series of articles on Islam intended especially for members of the Church of Jesus Christ of Latter-day Saints, and *A Nobler Estimate of Islam: Building Latter-day Bridges.* Dr. Peck lives in the small town of Rexburg, Idaho, with his wife Rachel and their four children.

C. K. Robertson is Canon to the Ordinary in the Diocese of Arizona, Honorary Canon of the Diocese of Dar es Salaam, Tanzania, and a

Fellow of the Episcopal Church Foundation. Formerly a professor of ethics and communications, he holds a Ph.D. from Durham University and serves on Advisory Boards for both The Protestant Hour/Day 1 and Film Clips, Inc. Dr. Robertson has written or edited several works, including the following books published by Peter Lang: *Conflict in Corinth: Redefining the System* (2001), *Religion as Entertainment* (2002), and *Religion and Alcohol: Sobering Thoughts* (2004). He lives in Phoenix with his wife Debbie and their children, David, Jonathan, and Abigail.

Deborah Vess is a professor of history and interdisciplinary studies at Georgia College & State University. An oblate of St. Benedict through Mount St. Scholastica Monastery in Atchison, Kansas, she has published articles in *The American Benedictine Review*, *Word and Spirit, Mystics Quarterly*, *The Modern Schoolman*, and *The Encyclopedia of Monasticism*. Dr. Vess, a mother of four, is a University System of Georgia Board of Regents Distinguished Professor of Teaching and Learning and, in 1999, was named a Pew Scholar with the Carnegie Foundation for the Advancement of Teaching in 1999.

✧ Index